Style Writs for the Sheriff Court

Fifth Edition

Style Writs for the Sheriff Court

Fifth Edition

Andrew Stevenson
Solicitor Advocate, Waddell & Mackintosh

Bloomsbury Professional
LONDON • DUBLIN • EDINBURGH • NEW YORK • NEW DELHI • SYDNEY

BLOOMSBURY PROFESSIONAL

Bloomsbury Publishing Plc
50 Bedford Square, London, WC1B 3DP, UK
1385 Broadway, New York, NY 10018, USA
29 Earlsfort Terrace, Dublin 2, Ireland

British Library Cataloguing-in-Publication Data

A catalogue record for this book is available from the British Library.

ISBN: PB: 978 1 52652 539 0
Epdf: 978 1 52652 540 6
Epub: 978 1 52652 542 0

Typeset by Evolution Design and Digital (Kent)
Printed and bound by CPI Group (UK) Ltd, Croydon, CR0 4YY

To find out more about our authors and books visit www.bloomsburyprofessional.com. Here you will find extracts, author information, details of forthcoming events and the option to sign up for our newsletters

Preface

The format and content of this book owe a great deal to Siggi Bennett's earlier editions, and many of the styles here have been adapted from those found in his work. Virtually all these tales are based on real cases that I have seen over the decades amongst tens of thousands of actions in Glasgow Sheriff Court. There are very few areas of human activity, some very outlandish, which do not find their way into pleadings in the civil courts. These styles are offered simply as examples which could be adapted to the infinite number of real scenarios that might be encountered.

Court procedure has diversified and become enormously specialised since I began appearing in 1989 (when the first edition of this book was first published). Before the Ordinary Cause Rules 1993 came into force all types of action, from child access cases to personal injury claims, all called in the Ordinary Court in volume and under largely the same procedure. Much of it was uncodified and left to the discretion and common practice of sheriffs. Those times have changed radically. Litigation has become ever-increasingly specialised and regulated. This applies not only to purely statutory procedures such as licensing appeals but also in relation to common law remedies such as multiplepoindings where the procedure to be followed is closely prescribed (some might say overprescribed) in the Ordinary Cause Rules.

It must be emphasised that the rules and the law itself evolve with bewildering rapidity and that they must be checked with extreme care to ensure that a writ is not founded on obsolete provisions or that additional rules and requirements have not come into existence. It is all too easy to fall foul of regulation, which always proliferates and never diminishes.

We are enjoined to plead only facts and not law. In my experience, this is increasingly difficult to justify, due to the need to provide clear, convenient and immediate notice to the sheriff clerk, the sheriff and one's client's opponent of the legal basis on which an action is based. Courts are busy places and it is advantageous to set out legal foundations explicitly and accessibly. As a matter of practice such statements cannot always be confined to the craves or pleas in law.

The prevailing wish amongst those who devise the rules of procedure is to have litigation front loaded, managed and with succinct pleadings. This is sensible. However, practitioners know that it is safer to err on the side of caution and to include the superfluous rather than to risk omitting the essential.

This book is aimed at practitioners and it tries to recognise that clients are more interested in practical remedies that in abstract rights. The purpose of litigation is to obtain a practical outcome and, in particular, a decree which is recognised and acted upon by third parties such as sheriff officers, the commissary clerk, banks and a multitude of others. Obtaining an unenforceable court order is a futile exercise and merely creates an unhappy client. These styles include company registration numbers, postcodes, Land Register title numbers and such identifying details – which are readily available online – to illustrate the need to make decrees effective.

I hope that the contents of this book provide some assistance to my fellow practitioners.

Andrew Gordon Stevenson
January 2023

With the exception of the Lord Advocate and Advocate General for Scotland all parties to these imaginary actions are fictitious.

My thanks go to Gayle for all her assistance and support.

Contents

Table of Ordinary Cause Rules

I PERSONAL INJURY ACTIONS

1. COSWORTH AND OTHERS v HUDSON

Damages — Fatal case — Damages (Scotland) Act 2011 — Road traffic accident — Negligence — Apportionment with third party — Intimation to connected person

a. Initial writ (OCR 36.B1, Form PI1)

SHERIFFDOM OF GLASGOW AND STRATHKELVIN AT GLASGOW

INITIAL WRIT

(Personal Injuries Action)

in the cause

ASTON COSWORTH, residing at 11 Vauxhall Street, Glasgow. G3 9HD suing both as an individual and as legal representative of MARTIN COSWORTH, residing with him

FIRST NAMED PURSUER

and

DIANE AUSTEN, residing at 27 Anglia Street, Glasgow G2 6AH

SECOND NAMED PURSUER

against

KIA HUDSON, residing at 113 Bently Street, Manchester M8 4YS

DEFENDER

The pursuers crave the court:

(1) to grant decree:

(a) for payment by the defender to the first pursuer as an individual of the sum of ONE HUNDRED AND FIFTY

THOUSAND POUNDS (£150,000) STERLING, with interest thereon at *8 per centum per annum* from 15 February 2021 or such other date and at such other rate as to the court shall seem appropriate until payment; and

(b) for payment by the defender to the first pursuer as legal representative of Martin Cosworth of the sum of SIXTY THOUSAND POUNDS (£60,000) STERLING with interest thereon at *8 per centum per annum* from 15 February 2021 or such other date and at such other rate as to the court shall seem appropriate until payment; and

(c) for payment by the defender to the second pursuer of the sum of THIRTY THOUSAND POUNDS (£30,000) STERLING with interest thereon at *8 per centum per annum* from 15 February 2021 or such other date and at such other rate as to the court shall seem appropriate until payment; and

(d) for the expenses of the action.

(2) In terms of OCR 36.3. to grant warrant for intimation to Maurice Ford, residing at 14 Albion Street, Glasgow G2 8TJ, as a connected person and in the event of his being sisted as an additional pursuer to allow the instance to be amended accordingly.

STATEMENT OF CLAIM

1. The parties are as designed. The first named pursuer was born on 21 November 1988. He is a factory manager. He is the widower of the late Morgan Cosworth, latterly residing with him at 11 Vauxhall Street, Glasgow. G3 9HD (hereinafter 'the deceased'). She was born on 12 May 1988. She died on 18 February 2021. Her National Insurance number was FD 278836 D.

2. The first named pursuer and the deceased had two children, namely the second named pursuer, born on 3 December 2005, and Martin Cosworth (hereinafter 'Martin'), born on 8 August 2018.

3. There is a connected person, namely Maurice Ford, residing at 14 Albion Street, Glasgow G2 8TJ. He is the father of the deceased.

4. The court has jurisdiction to hear this claim against the defender because the harmful event giving rise to the pursuers' loss, injury and damage occurred in Glasgow. This court has jurisdiction in terms of Section 20 of and Rule 2(c) of Schedule 8 to the Civil Jurisdiction and Judgments Act 1982.

5. The parties have complied with the Personal Injury Pre-Action Protocol in respect that settlement discussions took place but proved to be fruitless.

6. On or about 15 February 2021 the deceased was driving her motor vehicle along Great Western Road, Glasgow in an easterly direction. At a point about 100 yards from its junction with Crow Road, a motor vehicle being driven by the defender in the opposite direction suddenly and without warning crossed over onto the deceased's side of the road.

The defender thereby caused the vehicles to collide. As a result of the collision, the deceased died on 18 February 2021.

7. As a result of the death each pursuer has suffered loss, injury and damage. The first named pursuer claims damages under the following heads and with reference to the relevant provision of the Damages (Scotland) Act 2011:

(A) Section 4(3)(a); loss of support, and funeral expenses:
Throughout the marriage and until her death the deceased was self employed as a flower arranger. In the year to 5 April 2020 her net profit was £7,296. From 5 April 2020 to 18 February 2021 it was £5,649. The first pursuer incurred funeral expenses in the sum of about £5,115.

(B) Section 4(3)(b)(i); distress and anxiety in contemplation of deceased's suffering:
The first named pursuer remained at the deceased's bedside from the date of her admission to hospital until her death.

(C) Section 4(3)(b)(ii); grief and sorrow:
The first named pursuer and the deceased had married in 2013. They were happily married. Immediately prior to 15 February 2021 both the deceased and the first named pursuer were in good health. But for the deceased's death they would probably have continued cohabiting in a loving relationship until such death by natural causes. This is likely to have been in around 2068 when they reached the age of 80.

(D) Section 4(3)(b)(iii); loss of society and guidance: the deceased provided company, advice and help in everyday matters.

(E) Section 6; personal services:
The deceased carried out household tasks such as cleaning and cooking for the family. She had the primary role in the care of the children of the marriage. She would have continued to render personal services to the first pursuer for the remainder of their married life.

In the circumstances, the sum first sued for is a reasonable estimate of the loss, injury and damage sustained by the first pursuer.

8. Martin has suffered loss, injury and damage. The first pursuer claims damages on his behalf under the following heads:

(A) Section 4(3)(b)(ii); grief and sorrow:
He was greatly attached to the deceased and enjoyed her company as his main carer.

(B) Section 4(3)(b)(iii); loss of society and guidance. But for her death he would have benefited from her society as well as her guidance for at least 50 years.

(C) Section 6; personal services:
The deceased ran the household. She would have continued to render personal services to Martin for so long as he lived in the parental home. In the circumstances, the sum second

sued for is a reasonable estimate of the loss, injury and damage sustained by Martin.

9. The second pursuer has suffered loss, injury and damage. She claims damages under the following head:

Section 4(3((b)(iii); loss of society and guidance:

She was an engineering student at the date of death of the deceased. But for her death the second pursuer would have benefited from her society as well as her guidance for at least 50 years. In the circumstances, the sum third sued for is a reasonable estimate of the loss, injury and damage sustained by the second pursuer.

10. The claim is based on fault at common law. Damages are sought under and with reference to the said Act. Interest is sought from the date of the collision under the Interest on Damages (Scotland) Act 1958.

11. The pursuer received treatment from Mr Seamus O'Leary, Consultant Orthopaedic and Trauma Surgeon, King Solomon Infirmary, Glasgow.

IN RESPECT WHEREOF

Solicitor
Lincoln and Company
15 Talbot Avenue, Glasgow
Agent for the pursuers

b. Minute of sist of connected person

SHERIFFDOM OF GLASGOW AND STRATHKELVIN AT GLASGOW

GLA-A69-23
MINUTE OF SIST

Under Ordinary Cause Rule 36.6

for

MAURICE FORD, residing at 14 Albion Street, Glasgow,G2 8TJ

MINUTER

in the cause

ASTON COSWORTH, [*designation*]

FIRST NAMED PURSUER

and

DIANE AUSTEN, [*designation*]

SECOND NAMED PURSUER

against

KIA HUDSON, [*designation*]

DEFENDER

The minuter craves the court:

1. To grant the minuter leave to be sisted as an additional pursuer to the action; and
2. To grant the minuter leave to adopt the existing grounds of action and to amend the initial writ as follows:
   (i) by inserting in crave (1), before the word 'and;' and '(d)' the following: '(d) for payment by the defender to the third pursuer of the sum of FIFTY THOUSAND POUNDS (£50,000) STERLING with interest thereon at *8 per centum*

per annum from 15 February 2021 or such other date and at such other rate as to the court shall seem appropriate until payment;'

(ii) by re-numbering existing crave 1(d) as (1)(e) and deleting crave (2);

(iii) by deleting Condescendence 3 and substituting therefor the following: '3. The third named pursuer is Maurice Ford, residing at 14 Albion Street, Glasgow G2 8TJ. He is the father of the deceased. He is retired'; and

(iv) by inserting a new Condescendence; '10. The third named pursuer has suffered loss, injury and damage. The third named pursuer claims damages under the following head: Section 4(3)(b)(ii); He suffered much grief and sorrow. He is a widower and the deceased was his only child. She visited him weekly and would have continued to do so for the rest of his life. In the circumstances, the sum fourth sued for is a reasonable estimate of his loss, injury and damage.'

and renumbering the existing Condescendences 10 and 11 as 11 and 12.

IN RESPECT WHEREOF

Solicitor
Langan Bell
14 Green Street, Glasgow
Agent for the minuter

c. Defences (OCR 9.6.(2) subject to 36.E1(5))

SHERIFFDOM OF GLASGOW AND STRATHKELVIN AT GLASGOW

GLA-A69-23
DEFENCES

in the cause

ASTON COSWORTH, [*designation*]

FIRST NAMED PURSUER

and

DIANE AUSTEN, [*designation*]

SECOND NAMED PURSUER

and

MAURICE FORD, residing at 14 Albion Street, Glasgow G2 8TJ

THIRD NAMED PURSUER

against

KIA HUDSON, [*designation*]

DEFENDER

ANSWERS TO STATEMENT OF CLAIM

1. Believed to be true.
2. Believed to be true.
3. Believed to be true.
4. Admitted.

5. With reference to OCR 3A.2. the third named pursuer has not complied with the Protocol.

6. Admitted that on 15 February 2021 at the said locus the deceased was driving in an easterly direction when the defender's vehicle, being driven by him in the opposite direction crossed over onto the deceased's

side of the road and that there was a collision shortly after which the deceased died. *Quoad ultra* denied. The defender was caused so to cross by the actions of another driver, namely Harvey Hesketh, residing at 21 Triumph Street, Greenock GR3 6RD (hereinafter 'the third party'). Immediately before the collision, the third party was mounted on a motorcycle at the kerb of Great Western Road. Suddenly and without warning, he pulled out into the path of the defender's vehicle, caused the defender to take evasive action to avoid a collision, swerving and entering the deceased's side of the road.

7. The nature, extent and consequences of any loss, injury and damage sustained by the first named pursuer, Martin, the second and the third named pursuers are not known and not admitted. *Quoad ultra* denied. The sums first, second, third and fourth sued for are excessive.

8. Reference is made to Answer 7.

9. Reference is made to Answer 7

10. Reference is made to Answer 7.

11. The accident was caused by the fault of the third party. Separately, *esto* the accident was caused to any extent by fault on the part of the defender (which is denied), it also having been caused by the third party's fault, any liability to the pursuers in damages and expenses should be apportioned between the defender and third party in terms of the Law Reform (Miscellaneous Provisions) (Scotland) Act 1940, s 3(2).

12. Admitted.

IN RESPECT WHEREOF

Solicitor
Sienna McLaren and Co
76 Leyland Street, Glasgow
Agent for the defender

d. Motion for order for service of third party notice (OCR 20.1.) and for certification of a skilled person (Rule 5.3(1) of the Act of Sederunt (Taxation of Judicial Expenses Rules) 2019)

SHERIFFDOM OF GLASGOW AND STRATHKELVIN AT GLASGOW

GLA-A69-23

MOTION FOR THE DEFENDER

in the cause

ASTON COSWORTH, [*designation*]

FIRST NAMED PURSUER

and

DIANE AUSTEN, [*designation*]

SECOND NAMED PURSUER

and

MAURICE FORD, [*designation*]

THIRD NAMED PURSUER

against

KIA HUDSON, [*designation*]

DEFENDER

The defender moves the court:

(1) In terms of OCR 20.1.(1) to grant an order for service of a third party notice in Form O10 on Harvey Hesketh, residing at 21 Triumph Street, Greenock GR3 6RD.

(2) In terms of Rule 5.3(1) of the Act of Sederunt (Taxation of Judicial Expenses Rules) 2019 for certification as a skilled person of Ormand Norman, in respect that he has 24 years' experience as a traffic officer with Leith Police, he is now an advisor with O.N. Road Accident Consultants, and he possesses a decree in forensic accident reconstruction from the University of Wigtownshire; and in respect that his fee is unlikely to exceed £1200 plus VAT, a reasonable and proportionate cost in the context of a high value fatal accident case.

Enclosed; CV of Ormand Norman.

IN RESPECT WHEREOF

[*designation*]

Agent for the defender

e. Answers for third party (OCR 20.5. subject to 36.E1(16))

SHERIFFDOM OF GLASGOW AND STRATHKELVIN AT GLASGOW

GLA-A69-23

ANSWERS

for

HARVEY HESKETH, residing at 21 Triumph Street, Greenock GR3 6RD 21

Third Party in the action at the instance of

ASTON COSWORTH, [*designation*]

FIRST NAMED PURSUER

and

DIANE AUSTEN, [*designation*]

SECOND NAMED PURSUER

and

MAURICE FORD, [*designation*]

THIRD NAMED PURSUER

against

KIA HUDSON, [*designation*]

DEFENDER

ANSWERS TO STATEMENT OF CLAIM AND ANSWERS TO AVERMENTS FOR DEFENDER

1. Not known and not admitted.
2. Not known and not admitted.
3. Not known and not admitted.
4. Not known and not admitted.
5. Not known and not admitted.
6. The pursuers' averments are believed to be true. *Quoad ultra* denied except insofar as coinciding herewith. Prior to the collision the third party was parked by the side of the road. He decided to move off. He checked his wing mirror and looked over his shoulder. There was no traffic behind him. He pulled out and drove off. *Esto* the defender swerved her manoeuvre had nothing to do with any action on the part of the third party. The defender was driving at an excessive speed.
7. The nature, extent and consequences of any loss, injury and damage sustained by the first named pursuer, Martin, the second and the third named pursuers are not known and not admitted. The sums sued for are excessive.
8. Reference is made to Answer 7.
9. Reference is made to Answer 7
10. Reference is made to Answer 7.
11. Denied. The accident was caused by the fault of the defender. *Esto* it was caused to any extent by fault on the part of the third party (which is denied), it also having been caused by the fault of the defender, any liability to the pursuers in damages and expenses should be apportioned between the defender and third party in terms of the Law Reform (Miscellaneous Provisions) (Scotland) Act 1940, s 3(2).
12. Admitted.

IN RESPECT WHEREOF

[*designation*]
Agent for the third party

f. Minute of tender (Williamson tender)

SHERIFFDOM OF GLASGOW AND STRATHKELVIN AT GLASGOW

GLA-A69-23

MINUTE OF TENDER

for the Defender

in the cause

ASTON COSWORTH, [*designation*]

FIRST NAMED PURSUER

and

DIANE AUSTEN, [*designation*]

SECOND NAMED PURSUER

and

MAURICE FORD, [*designation*]

THIRD NAMED PURSUER

against

KIA HUDSON, [*designation*]

DEFENDER

and

HARVEY HESKETH, residing at 21 Triumph Street, Greenock GR3 6RD 21

THIRD PARTY

COOPER for the defender states that without prejudice to and under reservation of his whole rights and pleas and without admission of liability, the defender hereby tenders to the third party to make reparation along with the third party to the pursuers but only upon the basis that the defender and the third party shall contribute to the amount of any award of damages and expenses to which the pursuers may be found entitled in the proportions of 60 per cent to the defender and 40 per cent to the third party.

IN RESPECT WHEREOF

Solicitor
Buchan and Co
120 Bath Place, Glasgow
Agent for the defender

2. MONMOUTH v AVALON INSURANCE CO LTD

Payment — Damages — Personal injuries — Road traffic accident — Negligence — Direct action against driver's insurers

a. Initial writ (OCR 36.B1, Form PI1)

SHERIFFDOM OF LOTHIAN AND BORDERS AT EDINBURGH

INITIAL WRIT

(Personal Injuries Action)

in the cause

FIONA MONMOUTH; residing at 4 Lancelot Row, Edinburgh EH12 7BT

PURSUER

against

AVALON INSURANCE COMPANY LIMITED, a company registered under the Companies Acts, company registration number SC223456 and having a place of business at 3 Main Drive, Edinburgh EH3 HDF

DEFENDER

The pursuer craves the court:

(1) To grant decree for payment by the defender to the pursuer of the sum of SEVENTY THOUSAND POUNDS (£70,000) STERLING with interest thereon at 8 *per centum per annum* from 21 December 2018 or such other date and at such other rate as to the court shall seem appropriate until payment; and
(2) For expenses as taxed.

CONDESCENDENCE

1. The parties are as designed in the instance. The pursuer was born on 21 September 1970. Her National Insurance number is DT 274870 F. The

defender is the insurer of Gwendoline Andrews (hereinafter 'GA') for the purposes of section 143 of the Road Traffic Act 1988. The defender is sued in that capacity under the terms of The European Communities (Rights against Insurers) Regulations 2002.

2. The harmful event with which this action is concerned occurred on Lothian Road, Edinburgh. Accordingly, this court has jurisdiction in terms of Section 20 of and Rule 2(c) of Schedule 8 to the Civil Jurisdiction and Judgments Act 1982.

3. On or about 21 December 2018, at or about 1.30am, the pursuer was walking along Lothian Road, Edinburgh in a southerly direction. At a point near its junction with Spittal Street, she resolved to cross the road. The applicable speed limit for vehicular traffic there was 30mph. The pursuer looked both ways and commenced crossing the road from north to south. She had almost reached the other side when a vehicle drove into her. It was being driven by GA. It was travelling at around 40mph

4. As a result, the pursuer suffered injury. She sustained loss, injury and damage as hereinafter condescended upon. In connection with the collision GA was prosecuted. On or about 5 June 2019, following trial at Edinburgh Sheriff Court, GA was convicted of driving without due care or consideration under Section 3 of the Road Traffic Act 1988.

5. The pursuer required to give evidence at the trial. She suffered anxiety and distress as a result of said court proceedings. There was delay in her instructing solicitors to embark upon a claim for reparation. This action was raised to avoid the claim becoming time-barred by means of limitation under the Prescription and Limitation (Scotland) Act 1973. There was insufficient time to enable the pursuer to comply with the Personal Injury Pre-Action Protocol.

6. As a result of the said collision the pursuer has suffered loss, injury and damage. She claims damages under the following heads and with reference to the Administration of Justice Act 1982:

(A) **Solatium** The pursuer sustained fractures to her skull, right arm and right leg. She was taken by ambulance to Electress Sophia Hospital, Hanover Street, Edinburgh, where she was admitted to the intensive care unit. She experienced pain and discomfort.

(B) **Loss of earnings**. At the time of the collision the pursuer was employed as a fitter by Babbage Limited, a company with a place of business at 45 Malory Street, Edinburgh. She earned about £897 net per week. Details of earnings lost will be provided. In the circumstances, the sum sued for is a reasonable estimate of the pursuer's loss, injury and damage.

(C) **Services to injured person** (Section 8 of the Act). The pursuer's husband Geoffrey Monmouth rendered services to the pursuer by way of helping her to get in and out of bed, to wash, to use the toilet, get dressed and undressed and to move around the home and outside.

(D) **Services to relatives** (Section 9 of the Act). Until her accident the pursuer undertook DIY around the house, home decoration and gardening. She would spend around six hours a week on such activities. Due to her injuries she was unable to render such services to her family for around eight months.

7. The claim is based on fault at common law and damages at common law and under the 1982 Act. Interest is sought from the date of the collision in terms of the Interest on Damages (Scotland) Act 1958.

8. The pursuer received treatment from Mr Faisal Khan, Consultant Orthopaedic and Trauma Surgeon, Electress Sophia Hospital, Hanover Street, Edinburgh and from Dr Jemima Wolsley, Corstorphine Clinic, St John's Road, Edinburgh.

IN RESPECT WHEREOF

Solicitor
McQuillans
14 Union Drive,
Edinburgh
Agent for the pursuer

b. Defences (OCR 9.6.(2) subject to 36.E1(5))

SHERIFFDOM OF LOTHIAN AND BORDERS AT EDINBURGH

DEFENCES

EDI-A67-21

in the cause

FIONA MONMOUTH [*designation*]

PURSUER

against

AVALON INSURANCE COMPANY LIMITED, [*designation*]

DEFENDER

ANSWERS

1) The pursuer's designation is believed to be true.

2) Not known and not admitted.

3) Admitted that this court has jurisdiction.

4) Admitted that the pursuer was injured in a collision with a vehicle being driven by GA on or around 21 December 2018 on Lothian Road, Edinburgh and that she sustained injury as a result under explanation that the pursuer was greatly inebriated immediately prior to the collision. Her judgement was seriously impaired. In addition, she was looking at a mobile telephone whilst walking. As a result she failed to keep a proper lookout for vehicles on Lothian Road. She did not use a pedestrian crossing to cross the road. She walked into the road when it was both unnecessary and unsafe to do so. Admitted that GA was driving at excessive speed under explanation that the pursuer was contributorily negligent. Any damages ought to be reduced in terms of Section 1 of the Law Reform (Contributory Negligence) (Scotland) Act 1945.

5) Admitted that there has been non-compliance with the Personal Injury Pre-Action Protocol, under explanation that under service of these proceedings there had been only token communication by agents instructed by the pursuer. A claim was intimated only five days prior to service of the action. The proceedings ought to be sisted to enable settlement discussions to take place and for compliance with the Protocol. The defender shall move accordingly in terms of OCR 3A.3.(2)(a).

6) Not known and not admitted.
7) Not known and not admitted.
8) Not known and not admitted.

IN RESPECT WHEREOF

Solicitor
Taylor and Clough
74 Derby Street, Edinburgh
Agent for the defender

c. Motion for Pursuer

SHERIFFDOM OF LOTHIAN AND BORDERS AT EDINBURGH

EDI-A67-21

MOTION

for the pursuer
in the cause

FIONA MONMOUTH, [*designation*]

PURSUER

against

AVALON INSURANCE COMPANY LIMITED, [*designation*]

DEFENDER

Allan for the pursuer moves the court:

1. To recall the sist granted on 16 January 2023 and to re-enrol the cause for further procedure; and
2. With reference to OCR 29.6. to assign a preliminary proof on liability only; and
3. In respect that with reference to Section 11 of the Law Reform Miscellaneous Provisions (Scotland) Act 1968 it is presumed that the defender's insured drove without due care and consideration in relation to the collision condescended upon, to ordain the defender to lead at said proof.
4. In terms of OCR 28.10., in respect that he is unable to attend the proof due to age and infirmity, being 84 years old and immobile due to arthritis, to grant commission for the examination of Brigadier Alistair Courtney, 70, Stangmoor Street, Gibraltar GX11 7TD, witness for the pursuer, and to appoint Morris Wallace, solicitor advocate, 16 Black Watch Corner, North Berwick EH39 6RD as commissioner and to refrain from dispensing with interrogatories and to allow the commission to take place by remote means in respect that the evidence of the witness is in short compass, interrogatories would focus matters and the defender's agent has stated that cross-interrogatories are unnecessary and would not be lodged.

IN RESPECT WHEREOF

[*designation*]
Agent for the pursuer

d. Draft Interrogatories (OCR 28.11.)

SHERIFFDOM OF LOTHIAN AND BORDERS AT EDINBURGH

EDI-A67-21

INTERROGATORIES

Interrogatories to be administered to Brigadier Alistair Courtney, 70 Stangmoor Street Gibraltar GX11 7TD a witness to be sworn and examined on behalf of the pursuers before Morris Wallace, solicitor advocate, North Berwick, commissioner appointed by interlocutor dated 17 April 2023

in the cause

FIONA MONMOUTH, [*designation*]

PURSUER

against

AVALON INSURANCE COMPANY LIMITED, [*designation*]

DEFENDER

1) What is your full name?
2) What is your address?
3) What is your date of birth?
4) What is your occupation?
5) You are giving evidence in respect of a case in which Fiona Monmouth is suing Gwendoline Andrews' insurers. It is not disputed that on or about or about 21 December 2018 on Lothian Road, Edinburgh, near its junction with Spittal Street a car being driven by Gwendoline Andrews collided with Fiona Monmouth. Did you witness the collision?
6) What time was it?
7) Prior to the collision did you know either of these two people or did you have any connection whatsoever with either of them?
8) How did you come to be at that junction on that date and at that time?
9) Were you alone or with someone else?
10) How far were you from the collision?

11) How was the weather that night?
12) How busy was the area with traffic and pedestrians?
13) How clear was your view of the incident?
14) Without in any way giving any opinion as to who you think was responsible please tell us in your own words what you heard and saw happen.
15) What did you do immediately after the collision?
16) Other than the driver who else, if anyone, was in the car?
17) Did the driver say anything to you?
18) Did anyone else there say anything to you?
19) Were there any other people there, standing at or near the scene?
20) To your knowledge did anyone call the police or ambulance service?
21) When and how did you leave the scene?

It shall be competent to the commissioner to put any question or questions to the witness touching the matter in the cause, besides those points upon which he has been interrogated and to require the witness to make such additions and explanations as the commissioner shall think necessary; and to ask the witness whether he knows of any other matter or thing touching the matters and questions in the cause, besides what he had been interrogated upon and, if yes, to declare the same fully and at large as if he had been particularly interrogated thereupon.

e. Joint minute of settlement

SHERIFFDOM OF LOTHIAN AND BORDERS AT EDINBURGH

EDI-A67-21
JOINT MINUTE
OF SETTLEMENT

in the cause

FIONA MONMOUTH, [*designation*]

PURSUER

against

AVALON INSURANCE COMPANY LIMITED, [*designation*]

DEFENDER

LEWIS for the pursuers and CLARK for the defender state to the court that this action has been settled extra-judicially; and they hereby crave the court to assoilzie the defender from crave 1 of the initial writ and to find the defender liable to the pursuer in the expenses of the action as taxed.

IN RESPECT WHEREOF

[*designation*]
Agent for the pursuer

[*designation*]
Agent for the defender

f. Joint motion for decree in terms of joint minute of settlement

SHERIFFDOM OF LOTHIAN AND BORDERS AT EDINBURGH

EDI-A67-21
JOINT MOTION FOR THE PARTIES

in the cause

FIONA MONMOUTH, [*designation*]

PURSUER

against

AVALON INSURANCE COMPANY LIMITED, [*designation*]

DEFENDER

The parties jointly move the court to interpone authority to the joint minute of settlement, number 25 of process, and to grant decree in terms thereof.

Part of process lodged with the motion:

Joint minute of settlement

IN RESPECT WHEREOF

[*designation*]
Agent for the pursuer

[*designation*]
Agent for the defender

3. FOWLIS v NEW MONKLANDS COUNCIL

Payment — Damages — Personal injuries — Accident in tenement — Occupiers' liability — Breach of statutory duty

a. Initial writ (OCR 36.B1, Form PI1)

SHERIFFDOM OF SOUTH STRATHCLYDE, DUMFRIES AND GALLOWAY AT AIRDRIE

INITIAL WRIT

(Personal Injuries Action)

in the cause

HENRIETTA FOWLIS, residing at 14 Menin Road, Airdrie ML6 4ES (Assisted Person)

PURSUER

against

NEW MONKLANDS COUNCIL, a local authority established under the Local Government etc (Scotland)Act 1994 and having its headquarters at Scargill House, Main Street, Airdrie ML6 T84

DEFENDER

The pursuer craves the court to grant decree:

(a) for payment by the defender to the pursuer of the sum of THIRTY THOUSAND POUNDS (£30,000) STERLING with interest thereon at eight *per centum per annum* from 11 December 2022 or such other date and at such other rate as to the court shall seem appropriate until payment; and

(b) for expenses as taxed.

STATEMENT OF CLAIM

1. The parties are as designed in the instance. The pursuer was born on 3 September 1981. Her National Insurance number is GH 456734B She

is a receptionist. The defender is a local authority constituted in terms of the Local Government (Scotland) Act 1994.

2. The harmful event with which this action is concerned occurred at Violet Rise, Airdrie. Accordingly, this court has jurisdiction in terms of Section 20 of and Rule 2(c) of Schedule 8 to the Civil Jurisdiction and Judgments Act 1982.

3. On or about 11 December 2022, at or about 7.20pm, the pursuer was descending the common stairs of a tenement block (hereinafter 'the tenement') at Violet Rise, Airdrie. On that date the tenement was owned and occupied by the defender.

4. The flats within the tenement were leased to tenants who had right of access thereto by way of the common stairs. The defender retained responsibility for the maintenance and repair of the stairs, including their illumination. It was common practice for local authority and housing association landlords of such buildings to inspect the common stairs quarterly.

5. On the said date, the stair lights were inoperative. It was dark. The pursuer had to guide herself down the stairs by feeling the walls with her hands. She struggled to see where she was placing her feet. Whilst descending carefully she placed her foot on a slippery fluid or substance of a nature unknown to her. Her foot thereby lost its grip and slipped, whereupon she fell and sustained injury.

6. As a result of the accident the pursuer has suffered loss, injury and damage. She claims damages under the following heads:

(1) ***Solatium.*** The pursuer sustained in the accident an injury to her lower left leg, including an oblique fracture of the lower third of the tibia extending to the ankle joint and involving the posterior malleolus together with a spiral fracture of the fibula. She required surgical and other treatment at Vigilantibus General Hospital, Hare Square, Caldercruix. She also attended her General Practitioner, Dr Robert Knox, Burke Street Practice, Airdrie. She suffered pain and inconvenience as a result of her injury. Her left leg remains sore, especially in cold weather. Her mobility has been reduced. Her ability to enjoy her pre-accident hobby of line dancing has been reduced.

(2) **Loss of earnings.** At the time of the accident she was employed by Kalamazoo Pet Supplies, 3 Glen Street, Millersneuk. She earned around £548 net per week. Her injuries required her to be absent from work for about three months whilst recuperating. Details of earnings lost will be produced.

(3) **Necessary services** (Section 8 of the Administration of Justice Act 1982). The pursuer was rendered necessary services by her husband. For a period of about three months

he assisted her with personal care and carried out household tasks such as cooking, cleaning and shopping that she would otherwise have performed. He required to spend an average of about two hours each day thereto. The sum sued for is a reasonable estimate of the pursuer's said loss, injury and damage and reasonable remuneration for the said necessary services.

7. The claim is based on breach of the duties incumbent upon the defender in terms of the Occupiers' Liability (Scotland) Act 1960 and interest is sought from the date of the incident in terms of the Interest on Damages (Scotland) Act 1958.

8. The pursuer received treatment from Kim Huang, Orthopaedics, Caldercruix Hospital and from Dr Ethel Wragg, Plains Road Health Centre, Airdrie.

IN RESPECT WHEREOF

Solicitor
63 Zoffany Crescent, Airdrie
Agent for the pursuer

b. Joint minute of agreement of quantum

SHERIFFDOM OF SOUTH STRATHCLYDE, DUMFRIES AND GALLOWAY AT AIRDRIE

AIR-A211-23
JOINT MINUTE OF
AGREEMENT OF QUANTUM

for the parties

in the cause

HENRIETTA FOWLIS, [*designation*]

PURSUER

against

NEW MONKLANDS COUNCIL, [*designation*]

DEFENDER

LEWIS for the pursuer and HARRIS for the defender state that for the purposes of this action only the parties hereby agree that on full liability the loss, injury and damage sustained by the pursuer as a result of her accident on 11 December 2022 amounts to SIXTEEN THOUSAND POUNDS (£16,000) STERLING, inclusive of interest to the date of any decree to follow hereon.

IN RESPECT WHEREOF

[*designation*]
Solicitor for the pursuer

[*designation*]
Agent for the defender

4. TRADESCANT v MANDALAY GARDEN SUPPLIES LTD

Payment — Damages — ASSPIC — Accident at work — Manual handling operation — Negligence — Breach of statutory duty

a. Initial writ (OCR 36.B1, Form PI1)

SHERIFFDOM OF LOTHIAN AND BORDERS AT EDINBURGH IN THE ALL SCOTLAND SHERIFF PERSONAL INJURY COURT

INITIAL WRIT

in the cause

BRANDON TRADESCANT, residing at 18 Arboretum Road, Greenock GR2 6DS

PURSUER

against

MANDALAY GARDEN SUPPLIES LIMITED, a company registered under the Companies Acts company registration number SC223751 and having a place of business at South Shore Street, Greenock GR4 8SN

DEFENDER

The pursuer craves the court to grant decree:

(a) for payment by the defender to the pursuer of the sum of TWO HUNDRED THOUSAND POUNDS (£200,000) STERLING with interest thereon at *8 per centum per annum* from 15 September 2020 or from such other date and at such other rate as to the court shall seem appropriate until payment; and

(b) for expenses as taxed.

STATEMENT OF CLAIM

1. The parties are as designed in the instance. The pursuer was born on 2 November 1981. He is unemployed. His National Insurance

number is SH 867463 D. The defender is a company registered under the Companies Acts.

2. The defender is domiciled in Scotland. Accordingly, this court has jurisdiction under section 41 of the Courts Reform (Scotland) Act 2014.

3. On or about 15 September 2020, the pursuer was working in the course of his employment with the defender as a machine operator at South Shore Street, Greenock GR4 8SN.

4. The defender's duties included placing pine timber sheets upon the top surface of a guillotine machine for them to be cut. The sheets were stacked on a pallet on the floor in front of the machine to a height of about two feet. The surface of the machine was about four and a half feet from floor level.

5. The pursuer required to bend down and lift each sheet individually. He then had to twist round 180 degrees, whilst still bending, and place the sheet on the top of the machine. He was required to process 150 sheets per hour.

6. This placed considerable strain on his back.

7. The process of cutting the sheets could have been fully automated. The operation itself could have been mechanised by use of an electric or hydraulic hoist or powered vacuum lifter or rotating lift-table and roller conveyors or conveyor belt. The machine could have been repositioned with a plinth of suitable height adjacent thereto upon which the sheets could be stacked.

8. On the said date, in the course of one such manoeuvre, the pursuer felt severe pain at the base of his spine. He had sustained the injury hereinafter condescended upon.

9. As a result of the incident the pursuer has suffered loss, injury and damage. He claims damages under the following heads:

(1) ***Solatium***. The pursuer sustained in the accident a lumbar disc lesion. He attended his General Practitioner, Dr Stephen Gore, Inverkip Medical Centre PA16 5RS, who referred him to King Cymbeline Infirmary, Garvock, Inverclyde PA16 9FS for investigation and treatment. The pursuer suffered pain and inconvenience as a result of his injury. He required to be treated with physiotherapy and traction. He continues to suffer pain, affecting his back and both legs, as well as stiffness. His movements are restricted and he is obliged to wear a lumbo-sacral support. He is now unable to walk long distances. He can no longer engage in his pre-accident pursuits of metal detecting and husky dog sledging. It is unlikely that his back condition will improve materially in the future.

(2) **Loss of earnings**. Since the accident the pursuer has been unfit for work. He initially received full pay from the defenders. On or about 6 November 2020, however, his

employment was terminated owing to his injury. But for the accident he would have worked for the defenders until attaining the age of 65 years in 2046. He is now unlikely to work again in any capacity. He has accordingly lost and will continue to lose earnings at the rate applicable from time to time to machine operators employed by the defender, which rate has increased since the accident. The sum sued for is a reasonable estimate of the pursuer's said loss, injury and damage.

10. The claim is based on fault at common law and on breach of the duties incumbent upon the defender by virtue of the Health and Safety at Work Act 1974 and regulation 4 of the Manual Handling Operations Regulations 1992, regulation 4 of the Provision and Use of Work Equipment Regulations 1998 and regulations 5 and 11 of the Workplace (Health, Safety and Welfare) Regulations 1992. Interest is sought from the date of the incident in terms of the Interest on Damages (Scotland) Act 1958.

IN RESPECT WHEREOF

Solicitor
5 Charles Street, Greenock
Agent for the pursuer

b. Statement of valuation of claim (Form PI6); OCR 36. G1(1A)(d) as amended by Sheriffdom of Lothian and Borders P.N. No.1 of 2017.

SHERIFFDOM OF LOTHIAN AND BORDERS AT EDINBURGH IN THE ALL SCOTLAND SHERIFF PERSONAL INJURY COURT

PIC-PN 365-23

STATEMENT OF VALUATION OF CLAIM

for the pursuer

in the cause

BRANDON TRADESCANT, [*designation*]

PURSUER

against

MANDALAY GARDEN SUPPLIES LIMITED, [*designation*]

DEFENDER

Head of claim	*Components*	*Valuation*
Solatium	Past	£9,500
	Future	£9,500
Interest on past *solatium*	Percentage applied to past *solatium*: 4%	£380
Past wage loss	Date from which wage loss claimed: 6 November 2020	
	Date to which wage loss claimed: 16 March 2023	
	Rates of wage loss: (a) 6 November 2020 – 31 December 2021 60 weeks @ £532 net per week = £31,920	

	(b) 1 January 2022– 18 March 2023 63 weeks @ £538 net per week = £33,894	
	Total (a) + (b):	£65,814
Interest on past wage loss	Percentage applied to past wage loss: 4%	£2632.56
Future wage loss	Multiplicand: £27,976 (£538 × 52)	£139,880
	Multiplier: 5	
Total		£227,706.56

Supporting documents:

1. Report by Dr Stephen Gore, Inverkip Medical Centre Consultant Orthopaedic Surgeon, dated 2 January 2022.
2. Supplementary report by Dr Stephen Gore, dated 2 June 2022.
3. King Cymbeline Infirmary records.
4. GP records.
5. Letter from the defender to the pursuer's agents dated 2 February 2022, with earnings details.

c. Joint minute of admissions

SHERIFFDOM OF LOTHIAN AND BORDERS AT EDINBURGH IN THE ALL SCOTLAND SHERIFF PERSONAL INJURY COURT

PIC-PN 365 --23
JOINT MINUTE OF ADMISSIONS

for the parties

in the cause

BRANDON TRADESCANT, [*designation*]

PURSUER

against

MANDALAY GARDEN SUPPLIES LIMITED, [*designation*]

DEFENDER

SIMONE for the pursuer and FINKELSTEIN for the defender state that the parties have agreed that:

1. Productions numbered 5/21 and 5/22 are, respectively, the records relating to the pursuer of Inverkip Medical Centre and King Cymbeline Infirmary, Garvock; and

2. They accurately record the nature of the injury sustained by the pursuer on 15 September 2020 and the treatment received by him in relation thereto; and

3. Productions numbered 5/23 and 5/24 are, respectively, reports prepared by the persons by whom they bear to have been prepared and, insofar as their contents relate to an injury suffered by the pursuer as a result of the accident referred to on Record and its sequelae, are true and accurate reports.

4. That had the pursuer remained in the employment of the defenders his average net weekly earnings throughout the following periods would have been as follows:

(a) 6 November 2020 – 31 December 2021: £532.
(b) 1 January 2022 – 31 December 2023: £538.
(c) 1 January 2024 – 31 December 2025: £545.
(d) 1 January 2026 – 16 March 2028: £550.

IN RESPECT WHEREOF

[*designation*]
Solicitor for the pursuer

[*designation*]
Agent for the defender

d. Proposed Issue for jury trial (OCR 36B.2.(1))

SHERIFFDOM OF LOTHIAN AND BORDERS AT EDINBURGH IN THE ALL SCOTLAND SHERIFF PERSONAL INJURY COURT

PIC-PN 365 --23
ISSUES FOR JURY TRIAL

in the cause

BRANDON TRADESCANT, [*designation*]

PURSUER

against

MANDALAY GARDEN SUPPLIES LIMITED, [*designation*]

DEFENDER

Whether on or about 15 September 2020 at South Shore Street, Greenock during the course of his employment by the defender the pursuer was injured in his person through the fault of the defender, to his loss, injury and damage?

Damages claimed;	
Past solatium	£9,500
Future solatium	£9,500
Past wage loss	£65,814
Future wage loss	£139,880

Of which £20,000 represents compensation for earnings lost during the 5 years from 15 September 2020, £10,000 represents compensation for the cost of care incurred during that period and £5,000 represents compensation for loss of mobility during that period.

5. KIPLING v KATHMANDU (UK) LIMITED

Payment — Damages — Personal injuries — Accident at work — Workplace safety — Negligence — Breach of statutory duty — Contributory negligence — Time-bar

a. Defences (OCR 9.6.(2) subject to 36.E1(5))

SHERIFFDOM OF TAYSIDE, CENTRAL AND FIFE AT DUNDEE

DUN-A29-23
DEFENCES

in the cause

JAMES KIPLING, residing at 44 Whitehouse Grove, Dundee DD3 7TD (Assisted Person)

PURSUER

against

KATHMANDU (UK) LIMITED, a company registered under the Companies Acts company registration number SC948755 and having a place of business at Anstruther Park, Dundee DD2 9GS

DEFENDER

ANSWERS TO STATEMENT OF CLAIM

1. Believed to be true.
2. Admitted.
3. Admitted.
4. Admitted that on 8 July 2019 the pursuer was working in the course of his employment with the defender as a panel manufacturer at the defender's said place of business. Admitted that in order to operate the machine, the pursuer required to stand on a steel platform at a height of about five feet. *Quoad ultra* denied. Explained and averred that an incident similar to that averred was reported by the pursuer to the defenders as having occurred on 18 December 2018. No such incident occurred on that date.

5. The nature, extent and consequences of any loss, injury and damage sustained by the pursuer are not known and not admitted. *Quoad ultra* denied. Explained and averred that the sum sued for is excessive.

6. The said Regulations are referred to for their terms. *Quoad ultra* denied. Explained and averred that the defender fulfilled all duties incumbent upon the defender. Separately, *esto* the pursuer had an accident as averred by him, it being his responsibility to take reasonable care for his own safety, to look where he was going and to watch where he was placing his feet, he failed to do so and any accident was materially contributed to by his own fault. Further and in any event, *esto* the pursuer had an accident as averred by him, such occurred on 8 July 2019. The initial writ in the present action was served upon the defender on 10 July 2022. In these circumstances, the action is time barred.

IN RESPECT WHEREOF

Solicitor
1 Tank Avenue, Dundee
Agent for the defender

b. Motion by defender for expenses (OCR 31A.2.)

SHERIFFDOM OF TAYSIDE, CENTRAL AND FIFE AT DUNDEE

DUN-A29-23

MOTION FOR THE DEFENDER

in the cause

JAMES KIPLING, [*designation*]

PURSUER

against

KATHMANDU (UK) LIMITED, [*designation*]

DEFENDER

The defender moves the court to find the pursuer liable to the defender in the expenses of the cause as taxed, in respect that:

1) With reference to OCR 31A.2.(2)(a), having been allowed to bring this action by virtue of Section 19A of the Prescription and Limitation (Scotland) Act 1973, the pursuer chose to proceed to proof following which the court awarded him £30,000, the defender having on 16 November 2022 lodged and intimated a tender for the sum of £35,000 together with expenses as taxed and accordingly the pursuer failed to beat the said tender; and

2) For the purposes of Section 8(4)(b) of the Civil Litigation (Expenses and Group Proceedings)(Scotland) Act 2018 the pursuer behaved in a manner which is manifestly unreasonable in connection with the claim and the proceedings insofar as:

a) in extra-judicial correspondence between parties' agents the pursuer was offered a global settlement payment of £50,000 which payment he declined unreasonably given the value of the claim and that in so doing he compelled the defender to incur the expense of defending the action at proof; and

b) in respect that at no time did he lodge a Pursuer's Offer; and

c) he abused his position as an assisted person to pursue the action in circumstances where no privately funding litigant would have done so.

IN RESPECT WHEREOF

Desmond Nixon Law
28 Tay Bridge Road,
Dundee
Agent for the pursuer

c. Motion for modification of award of expenses; Section 18 of the Legal Aid (Scotland) Act 1986.

SHERIFFDOM OF TAYSIDE, CENTRAL AND FIFE AT DUNDEE

DUN-A29-23

MOTION FOR THE PURSUER

in the cause

JAMES KIPLING, [*designation*]

PURSUER

against

KATHMANDU (UK) LIMITED, [*designation*]

DEFENDER

The pursuer moves the court to modify to nil or to such other sum as to the court shall consider reasonable his liability in expenses, all in terms of Section 18 of the Legal Aid (Scotland) Act 1986 in respect that he is an assisted person and he is currently unemployed and impecunious, he possesses no capital and he is unable to pay the defender's expenses. Reference is made to the Schedule of the pursuer's income and expenditure and to the copy bank statements of May, June and July 2023 enclosed herewith.

IN RESPECT WHEREOF

[*designation*]

Agent for the pursuer

6. ADIMBOLA'S GUARDIAN v YORUBA LTD

Payment — Damages — Personal injuries — Accident at work — Work at height — Negligence — Breach of statutory duty — Injured person an Adult with Incapacity — Interim damages

a. Initial writ (OCR 36.B1, Form PI1)

SHERIFFDOM OF GLASGOW AND STRATHKELVIN AT GLASGOW

INITIAL WRIT

(Personal Injuries Action)

in the cause

TUNDE ADIMBOLA residing at 123 Chamber Street, Glasgow, guardian of Ebunoluwa Adimbola, residing at 15 Evergreen Road, Glasgow by virtue of a guardianship order granted by the Sheriff at Glasgow and Strathkelvin on 15 June 2022

PURSUER

against

YORUBA LIMITED, a company registered under the Companies Acts company registration number SC106422 and having a place of business at The Old Forge, 29 Andrew Road, Glasgow

DEFENDER

The pursuer craves the court to grant decree:

(a) for payment by the defender to the pursuer as guardian of Ebunoluwa Adimbola, of the sum of TWO MILLION POUNDS (£2,000,000) STERLING; with interest thereon at eight *per centum per annum* from 20 March 2021 or from such other date and at such other rate as to the court shall seem appropriate; and

(b) for expenses as taxed.

STATEMENT OF CLAIM

1. The parties are as designed in the instance. The pursuer is guardian of his brother, Ebunoluwa Adimbola (hereinafter referred to as 'EA'), who is an adult with incapacity. The pursuer was appointed guardian to EA by virtue of a guardianship order granted by the Sheriff at Glasgow and Strathkelvin on 15 June 2022. EA was born on 20 June 1977 and resides at 15 Evergreen Road, Glasgow. His National Insurance number is YT 365488 H. The defender is a company registered under the Companies Acts.

2. The harmful event with which this action is concerned occurred at Greenock Road, Glasgow. Accordingly, this court has jurisdiction in terms of Section 20 of and Rule 2(c) of Schedule 8 to the Civil Jurisdiction and Judgments Act 1982.

3. On or about 20 March 2021 EA was working in the course of his employment with the defender as a labourer. He had been sent with two colleagues to premises owned by Lagos Limited at 153 Greenock Road, Glasgow to remove corroded corrugated iron sheets from the roof of a warehouse there. The roof was approximately 40 metres from ground level.

4. None of the three workers was provided with any safety net, safety harness, hard hat or safety headwear. There were no roofing ladders or scaffolding or ropes from which they could work.

5. The sheets were secured by bolts to steel girders which comprised the roof of the structure. The nuts securing the bolts were rusted to the extent that they were sealed onto the bolts. In order to remove the sheets, EA and his colleagues required to cut off the heads of the bolts. This they did by kneeling on the sheets and applying bolt cutters to the bolt heads.

6. Whilst kneeling on one such sheet, EA proceeded to cut through a bolt head. As he did so, the sheet suddenly collapsed. EA fell through the resultant hole. He struck his head on the steel support beam underneath before falling to the ground. As a result, he sustained serious loss, injury and damage as hereinafter detailed.

7. The pursuer claims damages on his behalf under the following heads:

(1) ***Solatium***. EA sustained a severe head injury involving a skull fracture and brain contusion, resulting in left hemiplegia with dysphasia. He also suffered damage to his cervical vertebrae. He was admitted to Montcalm Infirmary, Quebec Street, Glasgow, with a score of nine on the Glasgow Coma Scale. He required a percutaneous tracheostomy whilst in intensive care before being transferred to the Department of Surgical Neurology. He was treated at the Infirmary by Consultants Mr John Zanzibar and Leopold Zhou. He subsequently attended his General Practitioner, Dr Alhazen,

Cairo Medical Practice, Allison Street, Glasgow G4 8FS. He suffered considerable pain and discomfort. He suffered and continues to suffer headaches, sleep and mood disturbance, severe memory and concentration impairment, loss of verbal function and depression. He has undergone a marked personality change. Having been affable and sociable before the accident, he has become disagreeable, irritable and demanding. He tires easily and is aware of and frustrated by his disabilities. He has developed post-traumatic epilepsy and has suffered from epileptic seizures. There is a 20% chance that these will persist indefinitely. He has weakness and loss of co-ordination in his dominant left arm and hand. His left leg is now splayed. He can walk only short distances and only with great difficulty. He is at increased risk of premature mental ageing. His condition is unlikely to improve.

(2) **Loss of earnings**. EA has suffered and will continue to suffer a loss of earnings and increases in earnings. As at 20 March 2021 he was earning about £300 net per week. Since then he has been wholly unfit for work due to his injuries. His employment has been terminated. But for the accident he would have worked on until the age of 67 years. He is now permanently incapable of any form of employment. Details of earnings lost will be provided.

(3) **Loss of pension rights**. By virtue of the termination of his employment, and his continuing incapacity for work, EA will suffer a diminution in benefits received at the age of 67 years, being the normal retirement age. Details of pension rights lost will be provided.

(4) **Personal services**. EA has been unable to render personal services to his elderly mother. He is no longer able to carry out household repairs, home decoration or gardening for her. Prior to 20 March 2021 he spent an average of two hours per week on such activities. But for the accident he would have continued to render such services. It is highly unlikely that he will be able to render such services in the future.

(5) **Outlays and expenses**. EA has reasonably incurred outlays and expenses and will continue to do so. He has required and will continue to require professional care. Since 20 March 2021 local authority care has been provided to him at a cost of about £220 for each four-week period. In the event of EA deriving an income from an award of damages in these proceedings, the cost of care will be at commercial rates. EA requires to purchase alternative accommodation. The house in which EA lives is unsuitable for him. The bedrooms are upstairs and he has difficulty in managing stairs, especially

when he is tired. The bathroom and toilet are downstairs, which causes inconvenience and disturbance at night. There are suitable properties available locally at a price of about £180,000. Removal, refurbishment and some alteration costs would require to be incurred. EA requires to employ a case manager to oversee his care and needs provision. Guardianship costs have been and will continue to be reasonably incurred in relation to EA. Details of outlays and expenses incurred and likely to be incurred will be provided. In all the circumstances, the sum sued for is a reasonable estimate of EA's said loss, injury and damage.

8. The claim is based on fault at common law and on breach of the duties incumbent upon the defender by virtue of the Health and Safety at Work Act 1974 and regulation 4(1) of the Personal Protective Equipment at Work Regulations 1992, regulation 26(2) of the Construction (Design and Management) Regulations 2002 and regulations 4(1) and (3), 6(3), 7 and 9(1) of the Work at Height Regulations 2005. Interest is sought from the date of the incident in terms of the Interest on Damages (Scotland) Act 1958.

IN RESPECT WHEREOF

Solicitor

1 Eyre Place, Glasgow

Agent for the pursuer

Document attached; Form PI2 (OCR 36.B1)

b. Motion for interim payment of damages (OCR 36.9.)

SHERIFFDOM OF GLASGOW AND STRATHKELVIN AT GLASGOW

GLA-A45-23

MOTION FOR THE PURSUER FOR INTERIM DAMAGES

in the cause

TUNDE ADIMBOLA, [*designation*]

PURSUER

against

YORUBA LIMITED, [*designation*]

DEFENDER

In terms of Ordinary Cause Rule 36.9 the pursuer moves the court to make an order against the defender for payment to the pursuer in the sum of TWO HUNDRED THOUSAND POUNDS (£200,000) STERLING or such other sum as the court thinks fit by way of an interim payment of damages, in respect that liability is admitted and the defender is insured in respect of the claim.

Document lodged with the motion:

Schedule of damages

IN RESPECT WHEREOF

[*designation*]

Agent for the pursuer

c. Minute of tender (recoverable benefits)

SHERIFFDOM OF GLASGOW AND STRATHKELVIN AT GLASGOW

GLA-A45-23

MINUTE OF TENDER

for the defender

S8 and Sch.2, Social Security (Recovery of Benefits) Act 1997

in the cause

TUNDE ADIMBOLA, [*designation*]

PURSUER

against

YORUBA LIMITED, [*designation*]

DEFENDER

BAXTER for the defender states to the court that without prejudice to and under reservation of its whole rights and pleas and without admission of liability the defender hereby tenders to the pursuer the sum of FOUR HUNDRED AND FIFTY THOUSAND POUNDS (£450,000) STERLING whereof SEVENTY THOUSAND POUNDS (£70,000) STERLING represents compensation for earnings lost during the relevant period, TWENTY FIVE THOUSAND POUNDS (£25,000) STERLING represents compensation for the cost of care incurred during the relevant period and NIL represents compensation for loss of mobility during the relevant period), together with the taxed expenses of process to date, in full of the craves of the initial writ.

IN RESPECT WHEREOF

Solicitor

1 Alcozar Terrace, Glasgow

Agent for the defenders

7. LENNOX v FAZAKERLY PIPELINES LTD

Payment — Damages — Personal injuries — Accident at work — Falling object — Negligence — Breach of statutory duty — Provisional damages — Further damages

a. Initial writ (OCR 36.B1 and 36.12., Form PI1,)

SHERIFFDOM OF GRAMPIAN, HIGHLAND
AND ISLANDS AT PETERHEAD

INITIAL WRIT

(Personal Injuries Action)

in the cause

COSMO LENNOX, residing at 46 Plug Street, Aberdeen AB6 8TD

PURSUER

against

FAZAKERLEY PIPELINES LIMITED, a company registered under the Companies Acts company registration number SC830628 and having its registered office at Aintree Road, Liverpool L9 9GD

DEFENDER

The pursuer craves the court to grant decree:

(a) for payment by the defender to the pursuer of the sum of TWO HUNDRED THOUSAND POUNDS (£200,000) STERLING of provisional damages in terms of the Administration of Justice Act 1982, with interest thereon at eight *per centum per annum* from 15 January 2020 or from such other date and at such other rate as to the court shall seem appropriate; and

(b) alternatively, for payment by the defenders to the pursuer of the sum of TWO HUNDRED AND FIFTY THOUSAND POUNDS (£250,000) STERLING with interest thereon at eight *per centum per annum* from 15 January 2020 or from such other date and at such other rate as to the court shall seem appropriate; and

(c) for the expenses of the action.

STATEMENT OF CLAIM

1. The parties are as designed in the instance. The pursuer was born on 21 August 1966. His National Insurance number is NG 865663 T. He is unemployed. The defender is a company registered under the Companies Acts.

2. The pursuer seeks reparation for loss, injury and damage sustained by him arising from a wrongful act on the part of the defender at Fetterangus. This court has jurisdiction in terms of Section 20 of and Rule 2(c) of Schedule 8 to the Civil Jurisdiction and Judgments Act 1982.

3. On or about 15 January 2020, the pursuer was employed by the defender as a labourer. On said date the defender was engaged in a project to lay a ductile iron concrete lined pipe within a trench traversing fields at Balwherry Farm, Fetterangus, Aberdeenshire.

4. On said date the pursuer was working on the project and on site. He had been instructed by his foreman to assist in the laying of a section of pipe in a deep trench. Two sections of pipe required to be joined, by means of bolting together the flanges at the end of each pipe section. The pursuer required to stand on the base of the trench to receive a crate of such bolts.

5. The pursuer was not wearing head protection. The bolts were lowered in a steel bucket secured to a chain which was fixed to a pulley. The pursuer required to stand beneath the bucket. In around November 2019 a link within the chain had snapped. The adjacent links had been joined using nylon rope. As a result, the chain as so repaired was liable to break or come apart under strain.

6. As the bucket was being lowered, the rope repair suddenly gave way and the chain came apart. Consequently, the bucket fell and struck the pursuer on the head. He thereby sustained serious loss, injury and damage as hereinafter condescended upon.

7. As a result of the accident the pursuer has suffered serious loss, injury and damage. He claims damages under the following heads:

(1) ***Solatium.*** The pursuer sustained in the accident a fractured skull, giving rise to a life-threatening haematoma, and was rendered unconscious. He required surgical and other treatment at Sir Flavius Green Hospital, Aberdeen. The doctor there was Ms Clementine Chandler. The pursuer subsequently attended his General Practitioner, Dr Abel Sharkey, 22 Badenoch Clinic, Aberdeen. He suffered pain in his head, neck and shoulders. He also began to suffer severe headaches. He continues to suffer such pain and headaches and requires painkillers daily. Further, he has developed

a post-traumatic syndrome. He has become irritable and intolerant of noise. He also now suffers from insomnia, vertigo and dizziness on exertion. His condition is likely to be permanent. Further, there is a risk that the pursuer will in future contract epilepsy. This is a serious disease.

(2) **Loss of earnings.** The pursuer has lost and will continue to lose earnings as a result of his injury. At the time of the incident he was earning about £450 net per week. But for the accident he is likely to have worked until the age of 65 years, in 2031. Since the accident he has been unfit for work. He is unlikely to be able to resume work in the future. Details of earnings lost will be provided.

In the circumstances, and in respect that the defenders were insured at the material time, the pursuer seeks provisional damages in terms of Section 12 of the Administration of Justice Act 1982, assessed on the assumption that he will not develop epilepsy, in terms of the first crave. Failing such an award, the pursuer seeks in the alternative damages not assessed on that assumption, in terms of the second crave. In the circumstances, the sums first and second sued for are reasonable.

8. This claim is based on fault at common law and on breach of the duties incumbent upon the defenders by virtue of the Health and Safety Act 1974 and regulation 4(1) of the Construction (Head Protection) Regulations 1989, regulation 5(1) and 12(1) of the Provision and Use of Work Equipment Regulations 1998 and regulation 10 of the Work at Height Regulations 2005. Interest is sought from the date of the incident in terms of the Interest on Damages (Scotland) Act 1958.

PLEAS IN LAW

1) The sum first craved being a reasonable estimate of the loss and damages suffered by the pursuer and predicated upon the assumption that he will not develop the serious disease condescended upon, decree should be granted as first craved in terms of Section 12(2)(a) of the Administration of Justice Act 1982.

2) There being a risk that the pursuer will, as a result of the omission giving rise to his cause of action, develop a serious disease, and the defender being insured in respect of the claim at the time of the omission, all as condescended upon, an order should be made in terms of Section 12(2)(b) of the Administration of Justice Act 1982 that the pursuer may apply for a further award of damages.

IN RESPECT WHEREOF

Solicitor
14 Leopard Drive, Aberdeen
Agent for the pursuer

b. Motion for pursuer to be ordained to submit himself to medical examination and to sist timetable OCR 36.H1

SHERIFFDOM OF GRAMPIAN, HIGHLAND
AND ISLANDS AT PETERHEAD

PHD-A45-23

MOTION FOR THE
DEFENDER

in the cause

COSMO LENNOX, [*designation*]

PURSUER

against

FAZAKERLEY PIPELINES LIMITED,
[*designation*]

DEFENDER

The defender moves the court:

1) to ordain the pursuer to submit himself for medical examination by Mr Brian Duguid, Department of Neurosurgery, Peterhead Clinic, and
2) In terms of OCR 36.H1(1) to discharge the existing timetable and to sist the cause for a period of six weeks or such other period as to the court shall seem reasonable, for that purpose.

IN RESPECT WHEREOF

Solicitor

4 Ocelot Road, Aberdeen

Agent for the defender

c. Minute for further damages (OCR 36.13.(1))

SHERIFFDOM OF GRAMPIAN, HIGHLAND
AND ISLANDS AT PETERHEAD

PHD-A45-23

MINUTE

for the pursuer

in the cause

COSMO LENNOX, [*designation*]

PURSUER

against

FAZAKERLEY PIPELINES LIMITED,
[*designation*]

DEFENDER

The pursuer craves the court:

1. To grant decree against the defender for payment to the pursuer of the sum of FORTY THOUSAND POUNDS (£40,000) STERLING as further damages.
2. To find the defender liable in the expenses of this minute.

STATEMENT OF FACTS

1. By interlocutor dated 16 August 2023 the court granted decree for payment to the minuter of the sum of £150,000 as provisional damages. These were predicated on the assumption that the pursuer would not develop epilepsy. In particular, *solatium* was awarded on that basis. The interlocutor also contained an order in terms of Section 12(2)(b) of the Administration of Justice Act 1982 that the pursuer may apply for a further award of damages.

2. Since that date the minuter has developed epilepsy. On or about 11 December 2023 he had a grand mal seizure and was admitted to Peterhead Clinic for observation and treatment. He is likely to have further seizures. Such will involve pain, suffering and inconvenience. Accordingly, the minuter is entitled to an award of further damages

in respect of *solatium*. The sum craved is a reasonable estimate of his further loss, injury and damage.

3. The defender has been called upon to make further reparation to the pursuer. The defender refuses or at least delays to do so. Therefore, this minute is necessary.

PLEAS IN LAW

1. Provisional damages having been awarded on the assumption that the pursuer would not develop epilepsy and the minuter now having developed epilepsy, further reparation for further damages should be granted.

2. The sum sued for as further damages being a reasonable estimate of the minuter's further loss, injury and damage, decree should be granted as craved.

IN RESPECT WHEREOF

[*designation*]

Agent for the pursuer and minuter

8. MAREK v SOUTH ROXBURGHSHIRE COUNCIL

Payment — Damages — Personal injuries — Occupational disease — Dermatitis — Negligence — Breach of statutory duty

a. Initial writ (OCR 36.B1, Form PI1)

SHERIFFDOM OF LOTHIAN AND BORDERS AT JEDBURGH

INITIAL WRIT

(Personal Injuries Action)

in the cause

LENA MAREK, residing at 51 Hope Street, Roxburgh TD7 8FD (Assisted Person)

PURSUER

against

SOUTH ROXBURGHSHIRE COUNCIL, a local authority having its headquarters at 4 Town Square, Roxburgh

DEFENDER

The pursuer craves the court to grant decree:

(a) for payment by the defender to the pursuer of the sum of FORTY THOUSAND POUNDS (£40,000) STERLING; with interest thereon at eight *per centum per annum* from 1 July 2020 or from such other date and at such other rate as to the court shall seem appropriate; and

(b) for expenses as taxed.

STATEMENT OF CLAIM

1. The parties are as designed in the instance. The pursuer was born on 14 June 1990. Her National Insurance number is GH 675986 F. She is a cleaner. The defender is a local authority constituted under the Local Government (Scotland) Act 1994.

2. The defender is domiciled in Roxburgh. Accordingly, this court has jurisdiction in terms of Section 20 of and Rules 1 and 2(b) of Schedule 8 to the Civil Jurisdiction and Judgments Act 1982.

3. The pursuer was employed by the defender as a cleaner. Her employment started in 2017. Her hours were 7am to 8.30am Monday to Friday and weekends as required. Her duties included cleaning fabrics, such as carpets and curtains, and soft furnishings. In connection with these cleaning tasks she was issued with a product in plastic bottles bearing the name 'Su-PERC-leena'. This was a solvent which the pursuer was required to apply to stained or dirty surfaces in a hand held sprayer or on a rag. She was not issued with a face mask, apron or gloves. She was not given any training on the use of the solvent. She was given no guidance on avoiding skin contact or avoiding inhalation or on hand washing or ventilation. The solvent was tetrachloroethylene.

4. Tetrachloroethylene is a hazardous substance for the purposes of the Control of Substances Hazardous to Health Regulations 2002. It is a known carcinogen and skin irritant. The defender had a duty to prevent or adequately control the pursuer's exposure to such substances. The defender had a duty to replace the tetrachloroethylene with another solvent or cleaning fluid which eliminated or reduced the risk to health. The defender had a duty to carry out a risk assessment. The defender had a duty to provide the pursuer with information, training and guidance to protect her health. The defender failed in all these duties.

5. Whilst she was carrying out cleaning, spray would contact the skin on the pursuer's hands, wrists and forearms. Her hands would touch the solvent soaking the rags used for cleaning. She was constantly aware of the smell and presence in the air of solvent fumes. As a result of such exposure to the substance, in about mid 2021, the pursuer developed a disease, namely contact irritant dermatitis.

6. As a result of said exposure to the substance, the pursuer has suffered loss, injury and damage. She claims damages under the following heads:

(1) ***Solatium.*** The pursuer developed contact irritant dermatitis. She required to consult her General Practitioner, Dr Hannah Flerin, The Health Centre, Kelso. She suffered and continues to suffer raised and weeping sores and rashes on her arms, wrists and hands. These are unsightly and feel prickly. She requires to wear rubber gloves when washing dishes or her hair at home. Her skin nips upon bathing. Her condition is likely to persist indefinitely.

(2) **Loss of earnings.** The pursuer has required to be absent from work for periods of between a day and a fortnight by reason of escalations in her condition. Details of earnings lost will be provided. She will continue to be periodically unfit for work by reason of her dermatitis. The sum sued for is a reasonable estimate of the pursuer's loss, injury and damage

7. This claim is based on fault at common law and on breach of the duties incumbent upon the defenders by virtue of regulations 6(1), 7(1) and 12(1) of the Control of Substances Hazardous to Health Regulations 2002. Interest is sought from the date by which the pursuer had been injured, in terms of the Interest on Damages (Scotland) Act 1958.

IN RESPECT WHEREOF

Solicitor

1 Cheviot Street, Coldstream

Agent for the pursuer

b. Minute of amendment (OCR 18.3.(1))

SHERIFFDOM OF LOTHIAN AND BORDERS AT JEDBURGH

JED-A29-23

MINUTE OF AMENDMENT

in the cause

LENA MAREK, [*designation*]

PURSUER

against

SOUTH ROXBURGHSHIRE COUNCIL, [*designation*]

DEFENDER

ZELENSKY for the pursuer moves the court to allow the record to be opened and amended as follows:

1. By deleting, in the crave, 'FORTY THOUSAND POUNDS (£40,000) STERLING; and substituting therefor SIXTY THOUSAND POUNDS (£60,000) STERLING'
2. By deleting, in Condescendence 1 'she is a cleaner', and substituting therefor the following: 'She is unemployed'; and
3. In Condescendence 6(2) delete 'has'.
4. In Condescendence 6(2) delete 'Details of earnings lost will be provided' and substitute therefor 'As a result of these absences, her employment with the defender was terminated on or about 16 September 2023. She has sought alternative employment, without success.'

IN RESPECT WHEREOF

[*designation*]

Agent for the pursuer

c. Motion for minute of amendment to be received and answered (OCR 18.3.(1)(a) and (b)(ii))

SHERIFFDOM OF LOTHIAN AND BORDERS AT JEDBURGH

JED-A29-23

MOTION FOR THE PURSUER

in the cause

LENA MAREK, [*designation*]

PURSUER

against

SOUTH ROXBURGHSHIRE COUNCIL, [*designation*]

DEFENDER

The pursuer moves the court:

1) To allow the minute of amendment for the pursuer to be received and to form no of process; and
2) To allow 14 days for Answers if so advised; and
3) To allow 14 days for adjustment of the Minute and Answers.
4) To assign a hearing in terms of OCR 18.3.

Part of process lodged with the motion:

Enc; Minute of Amendment

IN RESPECT WHEREOF

[*designation*]

Agent for the pursuer

d. Answers

SHERIFFDOM OF LOTHIAN AND BORDERS AT JEDBURGH

JED-A29-23

ANSWERS

for the defender

to the Minute of Amendment for the Pursuer

in the cause

LENA MAREK, [*designation*]

PURSUER

against

SOUTH ROXBURGHSHIRE COUNCIL, [*designation*]

DEFENDER

Add to the end of answer 5:

'Admitted that the pursuer's employment was terminated by the defender on or about 16 September 2023 under explanation that she was summarily dismissed for misconduct, namely racially abusing another member of staff. The termination was unconnected to her absences from work'.

IN RESPECT WHEREOF

[*designation*]

Agent for the defender

9. LOCHINVAR v LIDDESDALE NHS TRUST

Payment — Damages — Personal injuries — Clinical negligence — Injured person of non-age

a. Initial writ (OCR 36.C1, Form G1)

SHERIFFDOM OF LOTHIAN AND BORDERS AT SELKIRK

INITIAL WRIT

in the cause

JENNIFER LOCHINVAR residing at 16, Reiver Road, Hawick TD9 6ES, suing as legal representative of ROSALIND LOCHINVAR, born on 3 November 2016 and residing with her (Assisted Person),

PURSUER

against

LIDDESDALE NHS TRUST, constituted in terms of the National Health Service and Community Care Act 1990 and having its office at Hermitage Castle Road, Branxholm TD9 5RD

DEFENDER

The pursuer craves the court to grant decree:

(a) for payment by the defender to the pursuer as legal representative of Rosalind Lochinvar of the sum of FIFTY THOUSAND POUNDS (£50,000) STERLING, with interest thereon at eight *per centum per annum* from 1 November 2020 or from such other date and at such other rate as to the court shall seem appropriate; and

(b) for the expenses of the action.

STATEMENT OF CLAIM

1. The parties are as designed in the instance. The pursuer is the mother of Rosalind Lochinvar (hereinafter 'Rosalind'), who was born on 3 November 2016 and who resides with her. The pursuer sues in her capacity as legal representative of Rosalind for the purposes of Section 1(1)(d) of the Children Act 1995. The defender is a health board as defined by Section 2 of the National Health Service (Scotland) Act 1978.

2. The defender is domiciled in Branxholm. Accordingly, Selkirk sheriff court has jurisdiction in terms of Section 20 of and Rules 1 and 2(b) of Schedule 8 to the Civil Jurisdiction and Judgments Act 1982.

3. On or about 1 November 2020 Rosalind fractured her right arm in a fall at her home. The pursuer immediately took her to the Accident & Emergency Department at the Alice of Gloucester Hospital, Buccleuch Road, Hawick. It is owned and operated by the defender.

4. Rosalind was examined by a doctor there. His name is Errol Rait (hereinafter 'the doctor'). The defender is responsible for his acts and omissions in the course of his employment by the defender. The doctor was fully informed as to the circumstances of the accident. The pursuer told him that Rosalind's arm had been fractured.

5. The doctor examined Rosalind's arm. He raised it, whereupon Rosalind complained of pain. The doctor advised that the arm could not be broken because otherwise he would not have been able to raise it. He diagnosed a sprain or strain and recommended paracetamol. The pursuer took Rosalind home.

6. Rosalind continued to suffer pain. She could not sleep. Painkillers failed to make any difference. The arm was swollen and bruised. On the following day the pursuer telephoned the Department and spoke to the doctor. She explained Rosalind's symptoms to him, that she was not happy with the care and treatment provided thus far and that she felt that Rosalind's arm should have been x-rayed.

7. The doctor insisted that the arm was unbroken. He said that it was possible that a muscle or ligament had been damaged. He advised that Rosalind should be encouraged to move the arm after a few days to prevent it stiffening up.

8. At no time did the doctor suggest that Rosalind return to the hospital. He never offered an x-ray of her arm.

9. During the following weeks the swelling subsided and the arm stiffened. Rosalind was reluctant to move it. She was distressed and in pain when changing into or out of clothes or when bathing. In January 2021 Rosalind's father took her to the fracture clinic at the hospital. An x-ray was taken and the existence of a supra-condylar fracture of the arm revealed.

10. Given the circumstances as explained by the pursuer and the symptoms evident on examination no doctor acting with reasonable care

and competence would have failed to have had Rosalind's arm scanned by computed tomography or X-ray. Either would have revealed a fracture.

11. As a result of the doctor's said acts and omissions, Rosalind has suffered loss, injury and damage. The pursuer claims damages on her behalf under the head of ***Solatium***;

12. Had a fracture been diagnosed at the material time, suitable treatment, such as a sling or cast, would have been provided, restricting movement, facilitating healing and minimising pain. Also, it would have reduced the risk and extent of future disability. In the event, Rosalind suffered pain of greater duration and intensity than would otherwise have been the case had such treatment been provided.

She has been left with lasting disabilities. In connection with these she has had to attend her General Practitioner, Dr Ross Macdonald, 14 Scout Street, Hawick many times. Her lower right arm now hangs at an abnormal angle and she has a restricted range of movement.

She has had to give up pony riding and ballet. She has not been able to participate fully in activities with other children. Her right shoulder blade now protrudes, giving an appearance of poor posture, such being compensatory for her reduced arm mobility.

Cosmetic surgery, which could only be carried out once Rosalind has attained the age of 16 years, might improve the shape of the arm but Rosalind would be left with scarring. The sum sued for is a reasonable estimate of Rosalind's said loss, injury and damage.

PLEAS IN LAW

1) In respect that no doctor acting with reasonable care and competence would have failed to have had Rosalind Lochinvar's arm scanned as condescended upon, but the doctor employed by the defender having so failed, he was negligent.

2) The defender being vicariously liable for the acts and omissions and negligence of its employees and contractors, including the doctor condescended upon, is liable to make reparation for any loss and damages resulting therefrom.

3) The sum sued for being a reasonable estimate of the loss, injury and damages of Rosalind Lochinvar, decree should be granted as craved.

IN RESPECT WHEREOF

Solicitor

3 Mecklenburg Place, Edinburgh

Agent for the pursuer

Enc; Draft interlocutor Form PI4.

b. Minute of tender (no recoverable benefits)

SHERIFFDOM OF LOTHIAN AND BORDERS AT SELKIRK

SEL-A25-23

MINUTE OF TENDER

for the defender

in the cause

JENNIFER LOCHINVAR, [*designation*]

PURSUER

against

LIDDESDALE NHS TRUST, [*designation*]

DEFENDER

JACKSON for the defender states that without prejudice to and under reservation of its whole rights and pleas and without admission of liability the defender tenders to the pursuer the sum of TWENTY FIVE THOUSAND POUNDS (£25,000) STERLING, with the taxed expenses of process to date, in full of the craves of the initial writ.

IN RESPECT WHEREOF

Solicitor

1 Abercromby Street, Edinburgh

Agent for the defender

c. Minute of acceptance of tender

SHERIFFDOM OF LOTHIAN AND BORDERS AT SELKIRK

SEL-A25-23

MINUTE OF ACCEPTANCE OF TENDER

for the pursuer

in the cause

JENNIFER LOCHINVAR, [*designation*]

PURSUER

against

LIDDESDALE NHS TRUST, [*designation*]

DEFENDER

MORTON for the pursuer states to the court that the pursuer hereby accepts the tender contained in the minute of tender, no 17 of process, in full of the craves of the initial writ.

IN RESPECT WHEREOF

[*designation*]

Agent for the pursuer

d. Motion for decree in terms of minutes of tender and acceptance of tender

SHERIFFDOM OF LOTHIAN AND BORDERS AT SELKIRK

SEL-A25-23

MOTION FOR THE PURSUER

in the cause

JENNIFER LOCHINVAR, [*designation*]

PURSUER

against

LIDDESDALE NHS TRUST, [*designation*]

DEFENDER

The pursuer moves the court to grant decree in terms of the minute of tender, no 17 of process, and the minute of acceptance of tender, no 18 of process.

IN RESPECT WHEREOF

[*designation*]

Agent for the pursuer

e. Note of objections to auditor's report (OCR 32.4.)

SHERIFFDOM OF LOTHIAN AND BORDERS AT SELKIRK

SEL-A25-23
NOTE OF OBJECTIONS

for the defender

to report by the Auditor of Court on the pursuer's account of expenses

in the cause

JENNIFER EMMA JONES, [*designation*]

PURSUER

against

LIDDESDALE NHS TRUST, [*designation*]

DEFENDER

The defender objects to the report by the auditor of court dated 4 March 2023 upon the pursuer's account of expenses as regards the following item:

Dr Herbert Moreau, for examination and report		
(page 2)	fee paid	£900
	taxed off	£100
	allowed	£800

The defender submits that the fee allowed was excessive and disconform to recent practice; that in so allowing £800, the Auditor exercised his discretion unreasonably; and that the fee allowed should not exceed £400.

IN RESPECT WHEREOF

[*designation*]
Agent for the defender

10. ELDER v BUTTON

Payment — Damages — Defamation — Interest on damages for defamation — appeal — Sheriff Appeal Court Rules 2021, Rule 6.2

a. Initial writ

SHERIFFDOM OF LOTHIAN AND BORDERS AT SELKIRK

INITIAL WRIT

in the cause

JONATHAN ELDER, residing at 16 Angus Gardens, St Ronan's Well, EH45 7YG

PURSUER

against

HUMPHREY BUTTON, residing at 61 Old Vicarage Road, Earlston EH45 3JU

DEFENDER

The pursuer craves the court:

1. To grant decree against the defender for payment to the pursuer of the sum of THIRTY THOUSAND POUNDS (£30,000) STERLING, with interest thereon at the rate of eight *per cent per annum* from 18 July 2021 until payment.
2. To find the defender liable in expenses.

CONDESCENDENCE

1. The parties are as designed in the instance. The pursuer sues as an individual only. He does not sue as a trading entity for the purposes of the Defamation and Malicious Publications (Scotland) Act 2021.

2. This action concerns injury that occurred to the pursuer. The harm occurred at the pursuer's address. This court has jurisdiction in terms of the Civil Jurisdiction and Judgements Act 1982.

3. The pursuer is a butcher. He is 5 feet 2 inches in height. He lives with his sister Kaitlinn Elder at the address in the instance. The defender is a meat supplier. He used to supply game and fish to the pursuer. This stopped in around March 2021 following an argument over the quality of venison provided by the defender. Since then the defender has posted

numerous false and defamatory messages on social media. None of these names the pursuer or his sister but it is clear that they refer to him.

4. On 16 May 2021 the defender posted a message on Facebook. It referred to the 'Dwarf butcher in St Ronans' as 'selling manky sausages again'. On 26 June 2021 another such post stated that 'That insest (sic) butcher should be closed doon'. A post on 18 July 2021 stated 'Avoid wee perverts and buy your meat in Gala'. The defender posted all said messages.

5. The pursuer is the only butcher in or within a 25 mile radius of St Ronan's. He is well below average height for a man of his age, His sister works in his business. The pursuer and his sister are well known in the area. They have traded for over 20 years. Their father previously operated the business until he retired.

6. The said messages are false and malicious. Further, they are clearly directed at the pursuer. They are intended to cause him serious harm to both his personal reputation and to his business.

7. The pursuer has contacted the police. He has attempted to contact Facebook. He instructed solicitors to write to the defender to request that he remove said posts and to refrain from posting any other messages failing which interdict proceedings might be raised. The defender advised that he was not responsible for any such posts and that a person or persons unknown must have accessed his Facebook account without his knowledge. The pursuer does not accept the truth of said explanation.

8. The said social media were made by the defender, were false malicious and defamatory and as the defender well knew, wholly without foundation. The defender had no probable cause for so stating. The said untrue statements defamed the pursuer.

9. As a result of the defender's defamation of him, the pursuer has suffered loss, injury and damage. The defamation occasioned him great distress. The messages were grossly offensive. The message of 26 June 2021 alleged commission of a criminal offence, namely incest. The pursuer's reputation has been injured. In the whole circumstances, the sum sued for is a reasonable estimate of the pursuer's loss, injury and damage.

PLEAS IN LAW

1. The pursuer having suffered loss, injury and damage through being defamed by the defender, is entitled to reparation from him therefor.

2. The sum sued for being a reasonable estimate of the pursuer's loss, injury and damage, decree should be pronounced as craved.

IN RESPECT WHEREOF

Solicitor
18 Princess Street, Traquair
Agent for the pursuer

b. Appeal

Form 6.2
Rule 6.2(1)

APPEAL

to

THE SHERIFF APPEAL COURT

JONATHAN ELDER, [*designation*]

PURSUER and RESPONDENT

against

HUMPHREY BUTTON, [*designation*]

DEFENDER and APPELLANT

The appellant appeals to the Sheriff Appeal Court against the decision of the sheriff at Selkirk to grant decree by default, made on 11 April 2023. The court reference number is SEL-A36-23.

GROUNDS OF APPEAL

1) In granting decree by default the sheriff did not take into account a relevant factor. This factor is that the defender and appellant has a stateable defence, namely that he did not post the defamatory messages and that the sum sued for is grossly excessive.

2) It would not be in the interests of justice to allow the decree to stand given that there is a defence and that the failure to advance it in written Defences was due to oversight by the agent for the defender and appellant and was not the fault of the defender and appellant.

AVAILABILITY OF SHERIFF'S NOTE

The defender and appellant has requested that the sheriff write a note, but the note is not yet available.

INITIAL CASE MANAGEMENT: APPELLANT'S VIEWS

The defender and appellant considers that the appeal should be appointed to procedure before one Appeal Sheriff (Chapter 8 procedure) because:

1) The respondent's agent has represented that the appeal is unopposed. The hearing ought to be brief.
2) The appeal raises no questions of any complexity.
3) The interlocutor under appeal falls within Rule 6.11 (4)(b)(i) as one that it presumed to be appropriate for Chapter 8 procedure absent special circumstances (of which there are none in this case).

IN RESPECT WHEREOF

Malcolm Goldsmith and Co
65 Rhymer Street
Selkirk
Solicitor for Appellant

II COMMON LAW REMEDIES

1. KATHERINE ASHLEY v CHARLOTTE BILL

Count reckoning and payment — Partnership

a. Initial writ

SHERIFFDOM OF GRAMPIAN, HIGHLAND
AND ISLANDS AT ABERDEEN

INITIAL WRIT

in the cause

KATHERINE ASHLEY residing at4 Glebe Street, Cowdenbeath KY4 9HF

PURSUER

Against

CHARLOTTE BILL, residing at4 Jeffrey Place, Aberdeen AB76 FR

DEFENDER

The pursuer craves the court:

1. To ordain the defender to produce within 14 days of intimation the whole books and accounts of the dissolved firm of Iridescence Glass, together with a full account of her intromissions with the assets of the firm, so that the true balance due to the pursuer may be ascertained; and to pay to the pursuer the sum of FORTY TWO THOUSAND POUNDS (£42,000) STERLING or such other sum as to the court may appear to be the true balance due to her, with interest thereon at the rate of eight *per centum per annum* from the date of citation until payment; and, in the event of the defender's failing to produce such account, to grant decree for payment by the defender to the pursuer in the sum of FORTY TWO THOUSAND POUNDS (£42,000) STERLING with interest thereon at the rate of eight *per centum per annum* from the date of citation until payment.
2. To find the defender liable in expenses as taxed.

CONDESCENDENCE

1. The parties are as designed in the instance. The defender has been resident at the address in the instance for at least three months immediately preceding the raising of this action. She is domiciled there. This court accordingly has jurisdiction in terms of the Civil Jurisdiction and Judgments Act 1982.

2. Between about 20 July 2015 and about 13 June 2022 the parties were partners in the firm of Iridescence Glass. The firm was dissolved by an order of this court followed by agreement as at the latter date. Part of the agreement was that that the defender would wind up the affairs of the firm and implement a final settlement of accounts between the parties. She retained the whole books and accounts of the firm for that purpose.

3. The pursuer has called upon the defender to produce an account of her intromissions with the assets of the firm and to make payment of the balance due to her. The defender refuses or at least delays to do so. This action is therefore necessary.

PLEAS IN LAW

1. The defender being bound to account to the pursuer for her intromissions with the assets of the firm and to make payment of the balance due to the pursuer, should be ordained to produce an account as craved.

2. Failing production of an account, decree should be granted against the defender in terms of the alternative crave for payment.

IN RESPECT WHEREOF

Solicitor
17 Whimbrel Place, Dyce
Agent for the pursuer

b. Defences

SHERIFFDOM OF GRAMPIAN, HIGHLAND
AND ISLANDS AT ABERDEEN

ABE-A69-23

DEFENCES

in the cause

KATHERINE ASHLEY, [*designation*]

PURSUER

against

CHARLOTTE BILL, [*designation*]

DEFENDER

ANSWERS

1. Admitted that this court has jurisdiction.

2. Denied. The parties were never in partnership. The defender was a sole trader. The pursuer supplied products to the defender and was paid for so doing. The terms of supply included a clause stating that: 'Any dispute arising shall be referred to the Glass Artisans' Federation Scheme of Arbitration'.

3. The defender is under no duty to account. The action is unfounded and unnecessary.

PLEAS IN LAW FOR THE DEFENDER

1. In respect that the business relationship between the parties, founded upon by the pursuer, refers to arbitration any dispute arising the cause should be sisted to enable arbitration to take place.

2. The pursuer's averments being irrelevant and, separately, lacking in specification, the cause should be dismissed.

3. The pursuer's averments insofar as relevant being unfounded in fact, the defender should be assoilized.

4. The parties never having been in partnership the defender is under no duty to account to the pursuer.

IN RESPECT WHEREOF

Solicitor
21 Flodden Place, Aberdeen
Agent for the defender

c. Adjustments for the pursuer — addition of plea of competent and omitted

SHERIFFDOM OF GRAMPIAN, HIGHLAND
AND ISLANDS AT ABERDEEN

ABE-A69-23

ADJUSTMENTS FOR THE
PURSUER

in the cause

KATHERINE ASHLEY, [*designation*]

PURSUER

against

CHARLOTTE BILL, [*designation*]

DEFENDER

1. Add the following averments to the end of Condescendence 2:

   'With reference to the defender's averments in answer, the parties were pursuer and defender respectively in action number ABE-A267-21. In that action the court found and declared that the defender had been guilty of conduct prejudicial to the carrying on of the parties' business and it dissolved their partnership under Section 35(a)(c) of the Partnership Act 1890. The defence to the present action being founded entirely on averments that no partnership existed and that the parties were seller and purchaser respectively, matters that were competent by way of a defence to the first action but which were omitted from the defence thereto, said averments cannot competently be made and should be excluded from probation.'

2. Add a plea in law:

   '3. The court having determined in action ABE-A267-21 that a partnership existed and the defender having omitted a defence to that position in those proceedings cannot advance same in the defences to the current action and the averments thereof should be excluded from probation and decree granted as craved.'

d. Motion for the pursuer (individual) to be ordained to find caution (OCR 27.2.)

SHERIFFDOM OF GRAMPIAN, HIGHLAND
AND ISLANDS AT ABERDEEN

ABE-A69-23

MOTION FOR THE
DEFENDER

in the cause

KATHERINE ASHLEY, [*designation*]

PURSUER

against

CHARLOTTE BILL, [*designation*]

DEFENDER

The defender moves the court to ordain the pursuer to find caution for expenses in the sum of SEVEN THOUSAND FIVE HUNDRED POUNDS (£7,500) STERLING or such other sum as the court thinks fit within 28 days under certification that if she fails to do so decree of absolvitor will be granted; all on the ground that the pursuer was sequestrated on 5 March 2023 and has not been discharged therefrom.

Document lodged with the motion:

Copy interlocutor of 5 March 2023.

IN RESPECT WHEREOF

[*designation*]
Agent for the defender

e. Minute of abandonment (OCR 23.1.(1)(b))

SHERIFFDOM OF GRAMPIAN, HIGHLAND
AND ISLANDS AT ABERDEEN

ABE-A69-23

MINUTE OF
ABANDONMENT

for the pursuer

in the cause

KATHERINE ASHLEY, [*designation*]

PURSUER

against

CHARLOTTE BILL, [*designation*]

DEFENDER

NORMAN for the pursuer states to the court that the pursuer abandons the cause and seeks decree of dismissal in terms of rule 23.1.(1)(b) of the Ordinary Cause Rules.

IN RESPECT WHEREOF

[*designation*]
Agent for the pursuer

2. PERCY v MELCHETT

Count reckoning and payment — Executry

a. Initial writ

SHERIFFDOM OF SOUTH STRATHCLYDE, DUMFRIES AND GALLOWAY AT AIRDRIE

INITIAL WRIT

in the cause

SHELLEY PERCY, residing at 42 Forth Street, London EC7 4KL

PURSUER

against

GEORGE ALFRED MELCHETT, residing at 22 Hill Place, Airdrie, ML6 8TU executor-nominate of the late Gabriel Percy, who resided latterly at 153 Calderwood Drive, Airdrie ML6 9GS in terms of confirmation granted by the Commissariot of South Strathclyde Dumfries and Galloway at Airdrie on 9 August 2022

DEFENDER

The pursuer craves the court:

1. To ordain the defender to produce a full account of his intromissions as executor-nominate with the estate of the late Gabriel Percy, who resided latterly at 153 Calderwood Drive, Airdrie ML6 9GS, and to pay to the pursuer the sum of THREE HUNDRED THOUSAND POUNDS (£300,000) STERLING or such other sum as may appear to the court to be the true balance due to the pursuer, with interest thereon at the rate of eight *per cent per annum* from the date of citation until payment; and, in the event of the defender failing to produce such account, to ordain the defender to pay to the pursuer the sum of THREE HUNDRED THOUSAND POUNDS (£300,000) with interest as aforesaid.

2. To find the defender liable in expenses.

CONDESCENDENCE

1. The parties are as designed in the Instance.

2. The defender has been resident at the address in the instance for at least three months immediately preceding the raising of this action. He is domiciled there. Airdrie sheriff court has jurisdiction in terms of Section 20 of and Rule 1 of Schedule 8 to the Civil Jurisdiction and Judgments Act 1982. The pursuer is unaware of any proceedings pending before any court which are in respect of the subject matter of this writ.

3. The pursuer is the only child of the late Gabriel Percy who resided latterly at 153 Calderwood Drive, Airdrie and who died on 1 January 2021. By Trust Disposition and Settlement dated 17 August 1997 the deceased bequeathed his estate to his housekeeper, Lily Pinkerton and appointed the defender as his sole executor-nominate.

4. The defender was confirmed as executor by confirmation granted by the Commissariot of South Strathclyde, Dumfries and Galloway at Airdrie on 9 August 2022.

5. The pursuer is entitled to legitim. She is entitled to an accounting from the defender. The defender was called upon on 12 March and on 18 May 2023 to produce an account of his intromissions with the deceased's estate. He has failed to do so. Accordingly, this action is necessary.

PLEAS IN LAW

1. The defender being bound to account to the pursuer for his intromissions with the deceased's estate and to make payment of the balance due to her, should be ordained to produce an account as craved.

2. Failing production of an account, decree should be granted against the defender in terms of the alternative crave for payment.

IN RESPECT WHEREOF

Solicitor

1 Minto Terrace, Airdrie

Agent for the pursuer

b. Defences

SHERIFFDOM OF SOUTH STRATHCLYDE, DUMFRIES AND GALLOWAY AT AIRDRIE

AIR-A22-23

DEFENCES

in the cause

SHELLEY PERCY, [*designation*]

PURSUER

against

GEORGE ALFRED MELCHETT, [*designation*]

DEFENDER

ANSWERS TO CONDESCENDENCE

1. The pursuer's address is not known and not admitted.
2. Admitted.
3. Admitted.
4. Admitted
5. The pursuer is entitled to an accounting of the moveable estate only. Accounts thereof will be produced. The pursuer has no entitlement to an accounting *quoad* the heritable estate. The heritable estate and moveable estate were valued within Form C1 at £270,000 and £30,000 respectively. The sum sued for in the alternative is grossly excessive and reflects the value of the entire estate.

PLEAS IN LAW FOR THE DEFENDER

1. No title to sue.
2. The defender having no duty to account to the pursuer for his intromissions with the deceased's heritable estate decree should not be granted as craved.
3. Sum sued for excessive.

IN RESPECT WHEREOF

Solicitor
36 Dinwoodie Drive, Airdrie
Agent for the defender

c. Note of objections to executor's accounts

SHERIFFDOM OF SOUTH STRATHCLYDE, DUMFRIES AND GALLOWAY AT AIRDRIE

AIR-A22-23

NOTE OF OBJECTIONS

for the pursuer
to accounts produced by the defender
in the cause

SHELLEY PERCY, [*designation*]

PURSUER

against

GEORGE ALFRED MELCHETT, [*designation*]

DEFENDER

The pursuer objects to the accounts produced insofar as:

1. *25 October 2022*. The sum of £890 has been deducted as an expense from the aggregated heritable and moveable estate even although it relates to the heritable estate only.
2. *16 December 2022*. The sum of £500 is debited for travelling expenses. No such expenses required to be incurred. In addition, *t*he sum debited is grossly excessive.
3. *10 March 2023*. The sum of £600 is debited for payment of creditors of the deceased. No specification is given as to the identity of the creditors or the nature of the debt.

IN RESPECT WHEREOF

[designation]
Agent for the pursuer

3. LEONARD & SKINNER v HASTINGS T/A BIRMINGHAM TRUCK SALES AND REPAIRS AND MONTGOMERY

Furthcoming — Arrested funds — Defender's whereabouts not known

Initial writ

SHERIFFDOM OF LOTHIAN AND BORDERS AT JEDBURGH

INITIAL WRIT

in the cause

RONALD LEONARD SSC and CURTIS SKINNER, having a place of business at 73 Alabama Street, Edinburgh, EH3 9HS executors acting under the Trust Disposition and Settlement of the late Robert Jackson dated 18 March 1996 and registered in the Books of Council and Session on 2 October 2019

PURSUERS

against

(FIRST) NORMAN HASTINGS trading as BIRMINGHAM TRUCK SALES AND REPAIRS, having a place of business at 40 Main Square, Roxburgh TD7 8SA

FIRST NAMED DEFENDER AND ARRESTEE

and

FLORENCE MONTGOMERY, whose whereabouts are unknown

SECOND NAMED DEFENDER AND DEBTOR

The pursuers crave the court:

1. To grant decree against the first defender for payment to the pursuers of the sum of SEVEN THOUSAND SIX HUNDRED AND FIFTY POUNDS (£7,650) STERLING or such other sum as may be owing by him to the second defender and arrested in their hands at the instance of the pursuers on 12 January 2023 by virtue of a decree for the sum of £7,000 and expenses in favour of the pursuers against the second defender granted by the Sheriff of Tayside, Central and Fife at Perth on 17 November 2021; and

2. To grant warrant to cite the second defender by displaying on the walls of court, with a copy of the instance and crave of the initial writ, the warrant of citation and a notice in Form G4, by means of display on the Scottish Courts and Tribunals Website; and

3. To find the first defender liable in the expenses of the action in respect that he has necessitated same by his failure to release the funds arrested; and

4. To find the second defender liable in the expenses of the action in respect that she has failed to authorise the release of funds by the first defender.

CONDESCENDENCE

1. The parties are as designed in the instance. The pursuers are solicitors. They are the executors acting under the Trust Disposition and Settlement of the late Robert Jackson dated 18 March 1996 and registered in the Books of Council and Session on 2 October 2019. They have not yet obtained confirmation. The first defender is a sole trader operating a garage business. Believed and averred that he is or has recently been in a relationship with the second defender.

2. The second named defender's current whereabouts are not known and cannot reasonably be ascertained. Her last known residence was at 41 Huntsville Street, Roxburgh TD7 3RD, which she vacated in early 2022 leaving no forwarding address. Attempts by sheriff officers to locate the second defender have been fruitless. The present action is brought to assert the pursuers' right in and to moveable property situated at the first defenders' said branch, namely monies arrested there. This court accordingly has jurisdiction in terms of the Civil Jurisdiction and Judgments Act 1982.

3. On 17 November 2021 the Sheriff of Tayside, Central and Fife at Perth granted decree in favour of the pursuers against the second defender in the sum of £7,000, with interest and expenses. The second defender has made no payments to the pursuers in respect thereof. The total sum now due by him to them, including the cost of the arrestment in execution hereinafter mentioned, is £7,650.

4. On 12 January 2023 the pursuers executed an arrestment in the hands of the first defender for the sum of £7,650, less or more.

5. Believed and averred that there has been attached by virtue of the arrestment a sum of £8,500, or at any rate a sum sufficient to extinguish the second defender's liability to the pursuers.

6. In terms of Section 73J (2) of the Debtors (Scotland) Act 1987 the first named defender ought to have released funds to the pursuers 14 weeks after the arrestment took place. The first defender has failed to do so. The second defender has failed to authorise the release of funds or to provide a mandate therefor. This action is accordingly necessary.

PLEA IN LAW

The pursuers having arrested in the hands of the arrestee the sum due to them by the common debtor, are entitled to have same made furthcoming, so far as necessary, in satisfaction of the said debt.

IN RESPECT WHEREOF

Solicitor

1 Kellas Terrace, St Ronan's

Agent for the pursuers

4. MORAY SANDS NATURE CLUB v FINDHORN PORPOISE SANCTUARY

Declarator of right of way – crave ad factum praestandum – minute of disclamation – solicitor personally liable in expenses

a. Initial writ

SHERIFFDOM OF GRAMPIAN, HIGHLAND AND ISLANDS AT ELGIN

INITIAL WRIT

in the cause

MORAY SANDS NATURE CLUB, having its premises at 3 Moray Sands, Findhorn IV36 3YT and FIONA KING, residing at 16 Weymss Brae, Nairn IV12 6RG, and DENNIS MAGENNIS residing at 3 Moray Sands, Findhorn IV36 3YT respectively the President and Secretary, the whole office bearers of the club as representing the club and as individuals.

PURSUER

against

FINDHORN PORPOISE SANCTUARY a Scottish Charitable Incorporated Organisation in terms of the Charitable and Trustees Investment (Scotland) Act 2005, registered in the Scottish Charities Register under SC009782 and having a place of business at 16 Chesser Avenue, Edinburgh EH4 8TS.

DEFENDER

The pursuer craves the court:

1. To find and declare that there exists over the heritable subjects known as and forming All and Whole the lands and estate of Kinloss Shores, the Murray Estates, East Findhorn Bay in the county of Morayshire more particularly described in the disposition by Duncan Cawdor in favour of the trustees of John Garmouth dated 16 November 1972 and recorded in the Division of the General Register of Sasines for the County of Moray on 2 December 1972 a public right of way for pedestrian traffic by means of the gravel track three metres or thereby in breadth running from the stile located on the stone dyke between 3 Moray Sands and Kinloss Shores, the Murray Estates, East Findhorn Bay around 150 metres inland from the high tide line in East Findhorn Bay and running in a north easterly direction to the westernmost gate on the timber fence delineating Kinloss Shores, the Murray Estates, East Findhorn Bay along the vehicular track between the B366 road and Burghead Farm, Moray.

2. To ordain the defender to remove from the public right of way for pedestrian traffic by means of [*repeat description of route*] the fence and concrete blocks and any other obstructions thereon in order that pedestrian use of the right of way is free and unimpeded; and

3. To find the defender liable in expenses.

CONDESCENDENCE

1. The parties are as designed in the instance. The pursuer is an unincorporated association. The defender is an organisation which has as its stated objective the welfare of cetaceans in the Moray Firth. It is a SCIO, registered with the Office of the Scottish Charity Regulator under number SC009782.

2. This action has as its object rights *in rem* in the heritable subjects known as and forming Kinloss Shores, the Murray Estates, East Findhorn Bay more particularly described in crave 1 (hereinafter 'the subjects'). The subjects are delineated in yellow on the plan number 5/1 of process. The subjects are located in the Sheriffdom of Grampian, Highland and Islands. This court has exclusive jurisdiction in terms of Section 20 and Regulation 5(1)(a) of Schedule 8 to the Civil Jurisdictions and Judgments Act 1982. The pursuer is unaware of any proceedings pending before any court which are in respect of the subject matter of this initial writ.

3. The pursuer is the owner of 3 Moray Sands and the defender is the owner of the subjects. The properties are contiguous. The boundary of 3 Moray Sands is delineated in blue on the plan number 5/1 of process. The contiguous border between the two properties is shown in green. The parties have been owners of the said properties since 1979 and 2021 respectively.

4. Since 1977 at the latest the general public has enjoyed a right of way across the subjects. The route used by the public is by means of [*repeat description of route*] and shown as a red line marked AB on the

Ordnance Survey map number 5/2 of process. For the sake of clarity it is also shown as an orange line on plan number 5/1 of process.

5. The pursuer has walked the route on an average of two days each week since 1977 when she first moved to the Findhorn area from London. She has done so primarily in pursuit of her pastime of ornithology. During that time the route has been used on a virtually daily basis by other members of the public. Many have walked the route for reasons of leisure, exercise and observing birds and other wildlife.

6. The route has been used and enjoyed by the public for walking purposes for a continuous period of 20 years openly, peaceably and without judicial interruption. Said usage has created a public right of way by means of positive prescription.

7. In about December 2022 the defender erected a fence across the route. Also, concrete blocks have been placed next to the fence. According to the defender's website the defender decided to 'prevent public access due to disturbance of breeding harbour porpoises in the waters of Kinloss Shores.' The defender is not entitled to block the right of way.

8. Agents instructed by the pursuer wrote to the defender on 17 January and 18 February 2023 calling for the removal of the fence and blocks. The defender refuses to remove them. Accordingly, this action is necessary.

PLEAS IN LAW

1) A right of way claimed having been enjoyed by the public for a continuous period of 20 years openly, peaceably and without judicial interruption, as condescended upon, the said right is exempt from challenge in terms of Section 3(3) of the Prescription and Limitation (Scotland) Act 1973 and decree should be granted as first craved.

2) The defender having deliberately obstructed the exercise of the said right of way despite having no right to do so and having refused to remove said obstruction, decree should be granted as second craved.

IN RESPECT WHEREOF

Solicitor

Oliphant and Cassell

19 Manse Road, Inverness

Agent for the pursuer

b. Minute of Disclamation

SHERIFFDOM OF GRAMPIAN, HIGHLAND
AND ISLANDS AT ELGIN

ELG-A87-23
MINUTE OF DISCLAMATION

for

DENNIS MAGENNIS

in the cause

MORAY SANDS NATURE CLUB. [*designation*]

PURSUER

against

FINDHORN PORPOISE SANCTUARY, [*designation*]

DEFENDER

SHARPLES for the minuter hereby states to the court that he gave no instructions or authority for his name being included as one of the pursuers in this action and he therefore disclaims the action.

IN RESPECT WHEREOF

Crispin Batters LLP
54 Jacobite Street
Inverness IV1 6TR
Agent for the minuter

c. Motion to have agent personally liable in expenses

SHERIFFDOM OF GRAMPIAN, HIGHLAND
AND ISLANDS AT ELGIN

ELG-A87-23

MOTION FOR THE DEFENDER

in the cause

MORAY SANDS NATURE CLUB, [*designation*]

PURSUER

against

FINDHORN PORPOISE SANCTUARY, [*designation*]

DEFENDER

The defender moves the court:

In respect that he has been unable to produce a mandate from Dennis Magennis, to find Edward Oliphant, solicitor, Oliphant and Cassell, 16 Struan Street, Inverness liable to the defender in the taxed expenses of the cause to the date on which the court approved the Minute of Disclamation number of process, in respect that:

a) In failing to obtain the instructions of the minuter he acted in the proceedings not as an agent for him but as a principal; and

b) the said failure amounts to a serious breach of his duties to the court for the purposes of Section 11 of the Civil Litigation (Expenses and Group Proceedings) (Scotland) Act 2018.

IN RESPECT WHEREOF

Macbeth and Co
1, Cawdor Street
Elgin IV30 8TG
Agent for the defender

5. TWADDLE v RALSTON

Declarator of servitude, interdict, interim interdict

a. Initial writ

SHERIFFDOM OF NORTH STRATHCLYDE AT DUNFERMLINE

INITIAL WRIT

in the cause

ROBERT TWADDLE, residing at 3B Harmony Street, Gowkhall, Fife KY12 8TF

PURSUER

against

WILLIAM RALSTON, residing at 4 Harmony Street, Gowkhall, Fife KY12 8TF

DEFENDER

The pursuer craves the court:

1. To find and declare that there exists over the heritable subjects known as 4 Harmony Street, Gowkhall, Fife KY12 8TF and registered in the Land Register of Scotland under title number FIF7836 a servitude of *ne luminibus officiatur* prohibiting the obstruction of light within the area hatched green on the plan annexed to the Disposition by Alastair Hughes in favour of Gordon Butler dated 12th and recorded in the Division of the General Register of Sasines for the County of Fife on the 14th both dates in October 1936; and
2. To interdict the defender from erecting or instructing the erection within the area [*repeat description of area*] of any storage shed, garage or other structure likely to obstruct the transmission of natural light across the said area, and to grant interim interdict; and
3. To find the defender liable in expenses as taxed.

CONDESCENDENCE

1. The parties are as designed in the instance. They are immediate neighbours. The pursuer resides within the building formerly known as

3 Harmony Street, Gowkhall, Fife KY12 8TF. In around 1979 it was converted into two separate tenements. 3B Harmony Street (hereinafter '3B') is the ground floor tenement.

2. This action concerns rights *in rem* in heritable property at the address in the instance and within the Sheriffdom of Tayside Central and Fife. This court has exclusive jurisdiction in terms of Section 20 and Regulation 5(1)(a) of Schedule 8 to the Civil Jurisdictions and Judgments Act 1982.

3. A plan was annexed to the Disposition by Alastair Hughes in favour of Gordon Butler dated 12th and recorded in the Division of the General Register of Sasines for the County of Fife on the 14th both dates in October 1936.

4. The Disposition created or declared a servitude of *ne luminibus officiatur* prohibiting the obstruction of light within the area hatched green on the plan. The area falls within 4 Harmony Street, Gowkhall, Fife KY12 8TF (hereinafter '4').

5. Title to 4 was registered in the Land Register of Scotland under title number FIF7836. This occurred in May 2018 when 4 was purchased by the defender. Title sheet FIF7836 fails to include any reference to the servitude. This is a manifest inaccuracy for the purposes of Section 65 of the Conveyancing (Scotland) Act 2012. The Keeper has a duty to rectify the inaccuracy. Agents instructed by the pursuer are currently in correspondence with Registers of Scotland. The defender has objected to rectification. He has claimed, *inter alia*, that the servitude lapsed by means of long negative prescription, acquiescence and a change of circumstances, The Keeper has requested further information.

6. Meanwhile the defender has taken steps to erect within the said area a structure which would, if completed, seriously obstruct and interfere with the natural light crossing the area and reaching the kitchen and utility room windows of 3B. Such obstruction would be an infringement of the servitude. The pursuer, as proprietor of the dominant tenement or benefitted property is entitled to prevent any actions taken by the defender which is detrimental to the existence of the servitude.

7. The defender disputes the existence of the servitude right. Builders instructed by him have brought plant and materials to 4. Believed and averred that it is the defender's intention that a timber garage or storehouse be erected within the said area. In addition, believed and averred that the defender lacks planning permission from Fife Council to erect such a structure.

8. The defender has disputed the existence of the servitude and he has evinced an intention to breach the servitude. Accordingly, decree as craved should be granted. This action is necessary.

9. Having regard to the balance of convenience interim interdict should be granted as craved.

PLEAS IN LAW

1) The heritable subjects known as and forming 4 Harmony Street, Gowkhall, Fife KY12 8TF and registered in the Land Register of Scotland under title number FIF7836 being subject to a servitude of *ne luminibus officiatur* prohibiting the obstruction of light within the area [*repeat description of area*] all as condescended upon, decree should be granted as first craved.

2) The defender having evinced an intention to breach the servitude, decree as second craved should be granted.

3) Having regard to the balance of convenience interim interdict should be granted as second craved.

IN RESPECT WHEREOF

Solicitor
Lucilex LLP
20 King James Street
Dunfermline
Agent for the pursuer

6. CHEN v CHEUNG

Declarator and dissolution of partnership

a. Initial writ

SHERIFFDOM OF TAYSIDE, CENTRAL AND FIFE AT FALKIRK

INITIAL WRIT

in the cause

TONY CHEN, residing at 16 Ferry Street, Falkirk FK7 5SL

PURSUER

against

PETER CHEUNG, residing at 18 Walker Brae, Denny FK5 8RG

DEFENDER

The pursuer craves the court:

1. To find and declare that for the purposes of Section 35(e) of the Partnership Act 1890 the business of the partnership between the parties, trading under the name of 'Happy Joy Valley' can be carried on only at a loss; and to grant decree dissolving the said partnership.
2. To find the defender liable in expenses as taxed.

CONDESCENDENCE

1. The parties are as designed in the instance.
2. These proceedings have as their object the dissolution of the partnership between the pursuer and the defender trading under the name of 'Happy Joy Valley'. The partnership was formed under the law of Scotland. Its central management and control is exercised in Scotland. It has its place of business and seat at 77 Forth Street, Falkirk FK1 4RW. The said address is within the Sheriffdom of Tayside Central and Fife. This court has jurisdiction in terms of Section 20 of and Rule 5(1)(b) of Schedule 8 to the Civil Jurisdiction and Judgments Act 1982. There is no agreement to prorogate the jurisdiction of any other court.

3. The partnership was constituted by oral agreement of the parties on or about 7 October 2019. It has a duration of seven years.

4. It has traded since said date at an annual loss each year. Reference is made to the partnership books and accounts produced herewith. The terms thereof are incorporated herein for the sake of brevity. In the six months immediately preceding the raising of this action the partnership suffered a trading loss of around £27,000,

5. There is no prospect of the business of the partnership becoming profitable. It can be carried on only at a loss.

6. The defender refuses to agree to the dissolution of the partnership. Accordingly, this action is necessary.

PLEA IN LAW

The business of the partnership being capable only of being carried on at a loss, decree of declarator and dissolution should be granted in terms of the Partnership Act 1890, as craved.

IN RESPECT WHEREOF

Solicitor
Tsang and Partners
15 Gartnethill Place, Glasgow
Agent for the pursuer

7. EARHART v WILLIAMSON

Declarator of death — Appointment of judicial factor

Initial writ

SHERIFFDOM OF GRAMPIAN HIGHLAND AND ISLANDS AT ABERDEEN

INITIAL WRIT

in the cause

MARJORY EARHART, residing at 22 Zelensky Square, London WC2 7TH (Assisted Person)

PURSUER

against

PETER WILLIAMSON, whose whereabouts are not known

DEFENDER

The pursuer craves the court:

1. To find and declare, in terms of Section 2(1) of the Presumption of Death (Scotland) Act 1977, that PETER WILLIAMSON, whose last known place of residence was at 19 Dee Street, Aboyne AB34 7TW, died on 12 December 2013.

2. To grant warrant for citation of the defender by the publication of an advertisement in Form P1 in the *Aboyne and Ballater Advertiser.*

3. To grant warrant for intimation to: (i) Mrs Emily Williamson, King James IV Care Home, 16 Dolphin Street Elgin IV30 7RD; (ii) Mrs Emily Davison, residing at 17 Almond Road, Pumpherston, West Lothian EH53 8SK; (iii) The Old Constantinople Assurance Company, 2 Antioch Crescent, Birmingham B3 7RN as persons having an interest in the presumed death of the defender; and (iv) Dorothy McBain K.C. the Lord Advocate, 25 Chambers Street, Edinburgh EH1 8YF.

4. In terms of Section 2(2)(c) of the Presumption of Death (Scotland) Act 1977 to appoint Winston Flockhart, Chartered Accountant, 84 Dee

Road, Elgin IV30 9HE or such other person as the court shall think proper, as judicial factor on the estate of the defender.

5. To find any person offering opposition hereto liable in expenses.

CONDESCENDENCE

1. The parties are as designed. The pursuer is one of the defender's two daughters.

2. The defender's location cannot reasonably be ascertained. The pursuer instructed enquiry agents to trace him. They ascertained that he arrived at Newark Airport, New Jersey U.S.A. on 11 December 2006. Thereafter there is no trace of the defender.

3. The pursuer used the UK Missing Persons Unit of the National Crime Agency. She placed advertisements in newspapers both in the *Doric Gazette* in Aberdeen and in the *Hackensack Advertiser*, New Jersey. These attempts to locate the defender have proved fruitless.

4. As at 11 December 2006 the defender was domiciled in Scotland. His address at that date was 19 Dee Street, Aboyne AB34 7TW. That address is within the Sheriffdom of Grampian Highland and Islands. Aberdeen Sheriff Court has jurisdiction in terms of Sections 1(3) and (4) of the Presumption of Death (Scotland) Act 1977.

5. The defender was married. His wife was Emily Williamson. They had two children, namely the pursuer and Mrs Emily Davison. The only other person known to the pursuer to have an interest in the presumed death of the defender is The Old Constantinople Assurance Company. The defender obtained a policy of life insurance, number WIL2976 from the company. All three persons are as designed in the third crave.

6. The defender was born in Peterhead on 18 June 1941. After his marriage to Emily Williamson, on 23 November 1963, he lived with her until they separated in around 2003. He then lived alone at 19 Dee Street, Aboyne AB34 7TW until about 11 December 2006. On that date, he left home in the morning and drove to Glasgow Airport. He boarded a Perrin Airlines flight NE76 to Newark, New Jersey, USA.

7. Since that date neither the pursuer, the three persons designed in the third crave or anyone else known to the pursuer has heard anything from the defender. Believed and averred that the defender has died in the USA or otherwise furth of the United Kingdom. The pursuer seeks declarator as first craved.

8. The defender is believed to have had an interest in a fishing business based in Peterhead or Fraserburgh. It is reasonable and appropriate that a judicial factor be appointed on the estate of the defender. Winston Flockhart, CA is suitable qualified to act. Decree as fourth craved should be granted.

PLEAS IN LAW

1. The defender's last having been known to have been alive on 11 December 2006 decree of declarator should be pronounced as first craved.

2. It being expedient that a judicial factor be appointed to the estate of the defender and Winston Flockhart C.A. being suitably qualified to act decree should be granted as fourth craved.

IN RESPECT WHEREOF

Solicitor
19 Milk Way
Lumphanan
AB31 8RD
Agent for the pursuer

8. CAESAR'S GARAGE LTD v ANTHONY

Payment — Multiplepoinding — Party holding subject in medio ('real raiser') pursuing action — Death of defender pendente lite

a. Initial writ

SHERIFFDOM OF LOTHIAN AND BORDERS AT EDINBURGH

INITIAL WRIT

in the cause

CAESAR'S GARAGE LIMITED, a company registered under the Companies Acts, number SC664927 and having a place of business at Cleopatra Lane Edinburgh EH4 9YW

PURSUER

against

MARK ANTHONY, residing at 3 Actium Way, Edinburgh EH2 6BW

FIRST NAMED DEFENDER

and

JOHN PRESTER residing at 43 Orient Drive, Edinburgh EH5 7JS

SECOND NAMED DEFENDER

The pursuer craves the court:

1. To grant decree for the delivery of a 1968 Daimler V8 250 motor car, registration number VFU 256G or the distribution of the sale proceeds thereof, in favour of the party or parties found entitled thereto, and for the exoneration of the pursuer.

2. To find the defenders liable in the expenses of the action.

CONDESCENDENCE

1. The parties are as designed in the instance. The action is brought to obtain authority for the disposal of moveable property (hereinafter referred to as 'the subject *in medio*') situated in Edinburgh. This court accordingly has jurisdiction in terms of Section 20 of and Rule 2(i) of Schedule 8 to the Civil Jurisdiction and Judgments Act 1982

2. The subject *in medio* is a 1968 Daimler V8 250 motor car, registration number VFU 256G. The defenders are the only persons so far as known to the pursuer having an interest therein.

3. The pursuer has been in possession of the subject *in medio* since about 12 November 2022. It was delivered to the pursuer by the second defender for the purpose of carrying out repairs thereto. The first defender has claimed it on the ground that he owns it. Both defenders have threatened to litigate against the pursuer. This action is accordingly necessary.

PLEA IN LAW

The pursuer being liable only in once and single delivery of the subject *in medio*, and questions having arisen as to the party now in right thereof, decree should be pronounced as craved.

IN RESPECT WHEREOF

Solicitor
Prentice and McGuffey
19 Porteous Square, Edinburgh
Agent for the pursuer

b. Defences Objection and Claim (OCR 35.11.(1))

SHERIFFDOM OF LOTHIAN AND BORDERS AT EDINBURGH

EDI-A611-23

DEFENCES, OBJECTION AND CLAIM

for the second defender

in the cause

CAESAR'S GARAGE LIMITED, [*designation*]

PURSUER

against

MARK ANTHONY, [*designation*]

FIRST NAMED DEFENDER

and

JOHN PRESTER [*designation*]

SECOND NAMED DEFENDER

DEFENCES

Edinburgh Sheriff Court does not have jurisdiction. At the time of raising the action the subject *in medio* was in the pursuer's premises in Dunfermline. The cause should be transferred to the sheriff court in Dunfermline in terms of OCR 26.1.

OBJECTION

The subject *in medio* is a Jaguar Daimler 2.5 V8 saloon, not a V8 250. Insofar as the court's interlocutor will govern title to the vehicle and affect its marketability the distinction is vital and the crave should be amended accordingly.

CLAIM

The second defender owns the subject *in medio*. He purchased it in good faith and for value from Paolo Minto in about February 2022. Minto won it in a wager with the first defender. The first defender maintains that Minto defrauded him. Minto cannot now be located. The first defender disputes that title to the car has passed. In these circumstances, the second defender is to be ranked and preferred to the subject *in medio*.

PLEAS IN LAW

1) No jurisdiction.
2) The subject *in medio* being a Jaguar Daimler 2.5 V8 saloon, decree should be granted accordingly.
3) The second defender being the owner of the subject *in medio*, is entitled to be ranked and preferred thereto

IN RESPECT WHEREOF

Solicitor
17 Godscroft Street, Edinburgh
Agent for the second defender

c. Minute of transference (OCR 25.2.)

SHERIFFDOM OF LOTHIAN AND BORDERS AT EDINBURGH

EDI-A611-23

MINUTE OF TRANSFERENCE

for the pursuers

in the cause

CAESAR'S GARAGE LIMITED, [*designation*]

PURSUER

against

MARK ANTHONY, [*designation*]

FIRST NAMED DEFENDER

and

JOHN PRESTER, [*designation*]

SECOND NAMED DEFENDER

The pursuer craves the court:

To grant leave for the cause, so far as directed against the first defender, to be transferred against Mrs Cleo Anthony, residing at 153 Asp Road, Edinburgh, as representative of the estate of the first defender, now deceased.

STATEMENT OF FACTS

The first defender died on 14 November 2023. The representative of his estate is his widow, Mrs Cleo Anthony, designed in the crave. The pursuer seeks transference of the cause against her, as craved.

PLEA IN LAW

The said Cleo Anthony being the representative of the estate of the first defender, now deceased, the cause should be transferred against her as craved.

IN RESPECT WHEREOF

[*designation*]
Agent for the pursuer

9. JANDOO v RASHID

Exhibition and transumpt of testamentary writings

a. Initial writ

SHERIFFDOM OF TAYSIDE, CENTRAL AND FIFE AT PERTH

INITIAL WRIT

in the cause

DAVINDER JANDOO, residing at 41 Alton View, Dundee DD7 9FW

PURSUER

against

SAHJEED RASHID, residing at 2 Abbey Park, Perth PH3 6RE

FIRST NAMED DEFENDER

and

ABDUL AZIZ KHAN, residing at 4 Black Place, Dundee DD4 3AG

SECOND NAMED DEFENDER

The pursuer craves the court:

1. To ordain the first named defender to exhibit and produce in the hands of the clerk of the court the whole testamentary writings of the late Sanjeed Rahman in order that the same may be judicially transumed, and the transumpts thereof, after being made, collated and authenticated by the sheriff clerk, delivered to the pursuer and
2. To find and declare that the said transumpts, so collated and authenticated to be as sufficient and of effect to the pursuer as if they had been extracts from the books of court, and
3. To find the second named defender liable in expenses.

CONDESCENDENCE

1. The parties are as designed. The pursuer is the son of the late Sanjeed Rahman ('the deceased') who died at Perth on 14 January 2019 and resided latterly at 2 Abbey Park, Perth. That address is currently the residence of the first defender. He was a friend of the deceased.

2. The defender is domiciled in the Sheriffdom of Tayside Central and Fife. This court has jurisdiction in terms of Section 20 of and Rule 1 of Schedule 8 to the Civil Jurisdiction and Judgments Act 1982. The pursuer is unaware of any proceedings pending before any court which are in respect of the subject matter of this writ or the testamentary writings or estate of the deceased.

3. For the purposes of Section 1 of the Administration of Justice (Scotland) Act 1972, civil proceedings are not likely to be brought, for reasons of economy.

4. The first named defender has stated that he is in possession of a will and codicil and informal writings of the deceased, that these collectively appoint the first named defender as executor, and that their effect is that the pursuer is bequeathed family photographs and other personal items, that the second named defender is a legatee and the first named defender is residuary beneficiary. The pursuer is unaware of any other persons having an interest in the said estate. Believed and averred that its value falls below the level at which inheritance tax would be payable.

5. No testamentary writings pertaining to the deceased have ever been registered in the Books of Council and Session. Title to the deceased's heritable estate is still shown by Registers of Scotland as belonging to the deceased. No one has applied for appointment as executor-dative or for confirmation in respect of the deceased.

6. The first named defender has failed to exhibit any testamentary writings of the deceased, or any copies thereof, despite numerous requests to do so. The estate needs to be wound up without further delay. The pursuer is entitled, at least, to legitim. He is entitled to know whether the deceased died testate and, if so, the contents and effect of his testamentary writings.

7. The pursuer cannot obtain extracts of the writings due to the failure of the first named defender to register them. He is therefore under the necessity of seeking to have them produced and for transumpts to be made.

PLEA IN LAW

The pursuer being entitled to a share of the estate of the late Sanjeed Rahman, the first named defender possessing testamentary writings of the late Sanjeed Rahman and having refused to exhibit them, decree should be granted as craved.

IN RESPECT WHEREOF

Solicitor
1 Lucas Street, Dundee
Agent for the pursuer

10. KANDY v TOLPUDDLE AND KANDY

Multiplepoinding — Party not holding fund in medio ('nominal raiser') pursuing action

a. Initial writ

SHERIFFDOM OF NORTH STRATHCLYDE AT DUNOON

INITIAL WRIT

in the cause

JEEVANTHA KANDY, residing at 17 Keaton Avenue, Birmingham B15 7YK

PURSUER

against

JEMIMA TOLPUDDLE, residing c/o Weller Hotel, 44 Stanley Terrace, Dunoon PA23 7TF

FIRST NAMED DEFENDER

and

NADESHA KANDY, residing at 59 Norvell Drive, Sutton Coldfield B72 5DS

SECOND NAMED DEFENDER

The pursuer craves the court:

1) To grant decree for payment of the sum of EIGHT THOUSAND FIVE HUNDRED POUNDS (£8,500) held by the first named defender between the claimants found entitled thereto and, upon payment or consignation thereof, for the exoneration of the first defender.

2. To find the first named defender liable in expenses.

3. To find the second named defender liable in expenses.

CONDESCENDENCE

1. The parties are as designed in the instance. The action is brought to obtain authority for the disposal of funds (hereinafter referred to as 'the fund *in medio*') situated in Dunoon. This court accordingly has jurisdiction in terms of Section 20 of and Rule 2(i) of Schedule 8 to the Civil Jurisdiction and Judgments Act 1982

2. The pursuer and the second defender are spouses. On or about 17 August 2022 the sum of £8,500 was paid to the first named defender towards the price of a family holiday at the Weller Hotel, Dunoon. This event was to celebrate the 20 wedding anniversary of the pursuer and the second defender.

3. On or about 23 March 2023 the pursuer and the second defender separated. Their marriage broke down. They each sought a refund of the £8,500. The pursuer is entitled to same in respect that the funds were paid from her bank account. The second defender claimed, falsely, that the funds were his, held by the pursuer for tax reasons.

4. The first named defender has refused to pay either of the other parties. She claims that the arrangement between the pursuer and the second named defender is a *pactum illicitum*. Also, she has stated that a pending case of interpleader in Birmingham County Court gives rise to a defence of *lis alibi pendens*, although said action refers to different funds. In addition, she is seeking to deduct £4,750 by way of a deposit and alleged outlays concerning catering and excursions. Said sum is excessive and unreasonable.

5. The parties cannot reach agreement either on the amount of the fund *in medio* reasonably to be retained by the first named defender or on how the balance should be distributed. Accordingly, this action is necessary.

PLEAS IN LAW

1) The fund *in medio* being held by the first named defender having been claimed by various parties and the first named defender having refused to make any payment, as condescended upon, the fund falls to be distributed as directed by the court, and decree should be granted accordingly.

2) The pursuer being entitled to the fund *in medio*, decree of payment should be granted in her favour.

IN RESPECT WHEREOF

Solicitor

Prentice and McGuffey

19 Porteous Square, Edinburgh

Agent for the pursuer

11. WYCLIFFE PROPERTIES LTD (IN RECEIVERSHIP) v TYNDALE

Ad factum praestandum — Implement — Missives— Buyer pursuing action

a. Initial writ

SHERIFFDOM OF GRAMPIAN, HIGHLAND
AND ISLANDS AT ABERDEEN

INITIAL WRIT

in the cause

WYCLIFFE PROPERTIES LIMITED (IN RECEIVERSHIP), a company registered under the Companies Acts company registration number SC630962 and having a place of business at 3 Geneva Street, Aberdeen AB2 8DR

PURSUER

against

JAMES TYNDALE Junior, residing at 14 Foxe Street, Aberdeen AB10 6RD

DEFENDER

The pursuer craves the court:

1. To ordain the defenders to implement the missives of sale entered into between the parties dated 5 and 19 June and 10 and 28 August 2022, whereby the pursuer agreed to buy and the defenders agreed to sell at the price of £230,000 the subjects at 17 Quicksilver Circus, Aberdeen AB2 7TY and that by delivering to the pursuer a valid and registrable Disposition and such other deeds as may be necessary to give the pursuer a valid title to the subjects at 17 Quicksilver Circus, Aberdeen AB2 7TY being the heritable subjects registered in the Land Register of Scotland under Title Number ABE2849 and that within 14

days or such other period as to the court shall seem reasonable from the date of decree.

2. Failing implement as aforesaid, to grant decree against the defender for payment to the pursuer of the sum of TWENTY FIVE THOUSAND POUNDS (£25,000) STERLING with interest at eight *per centum per annum* until payment,

3. To find the defender liable in expenses.

CONDESCENDENCE

1. The parties are as designed. The defender resides at 14 Foxe Street Aberdeen AB10 6RD. He was born in July 1993. His father, James Tyndale senior also lives at that address, and he was born in around 1971. This action concerns rights *in rem* in immoveable property situated in Aberdeen. This court accordingly has exclusive jurisdiction in terms of Section 20 of and Rule 5(1)(a) of Schedule 8 to the Civil Jurisdiction and Judgments Act 1982.

2. By concluded missives dated 5 and 19 June and 10 and 28 August, all 2022, the pursuer agreed to buy and the defender agreed to sell the subjects at 17 Quicksilver Circus, Aberdeen AB2 7TY at a price of £230,000 with entry at 11 February 2023. Copies of the missives are produced.

3. The defender failed to give entry at the said date, or subsequently. He has failed to execute and deliver a valid disposition. The pursuer is and has always been willing and able to pay the purchase price.

4. Despite repeated requests, the defender refuses or at least delays to implement the bargain. The pursuer seeks decree for implement as first craved.

5. The pursuer has incurred legal expenses estimated at £3,400 in connection with the conveyancing to date. Also, as at 11 February 2023 the subjects had a market value of at least £250,000. A valuation by Kiki and Hector, chartered surveyors, is produced herewith. The pursuer has suffered loss and damage in the amount second sued for. The sum second craved is a reasonable estimate of the pursuers' loss and damage in the event of the defenders' failure to implement the contract.

PLEAS IN LAW

1. The defender being obliged to implement the missives of sale dated 5 and 19 June and 10 and 28 August – all 2022 – and having failed to do so, decree should be granted as first craved.

2. Alternatively, the pursuer having suffered loss and damage and the sum second sued for being a reasonable estimate thereof, damages ought to be awarded in the sum second craved.

IN RESPECT WHEREOF

Solicitor
Hassle Free Conveyancing LLP
1 Platinum Gardens, Aberdeen
Agent for the pursuer

12. OBERON CREDIT LTD v MINTO

Ad factum praestandum — Delivery — Payment — Damages — Debt — Hire-purchase

a. Initial writ

SHERIFFDOM OF GRAMPIAN, HIGHLAND AND ISLANDS AT LOCHMADDY

INITIAL WRIT

in the cause

OBERON CREDIT LIMITED, a company registered under the Companies Acts company registration number SC773946 and having its head office at 1 Arnold Lane, Cambridge CA37 8TD

PURSUER

against

PAOLO MINTO, residing at The Auld Bothy, Blathaisbhal, North Uist HS6 8TD

DEFENDER

The pursuer craves the court:

1. To ordain the defender to deliver to the pursuer a 1968 Daimler V8 250 motor car, registration number VFU 256G, within 14 days of the date of decree to follow hereon or within such other period as the court thinks fit; and, failing delivery aforesaid, to grant warrant to officers of court to search for and take possession of the said vehicle in any premises occupied by the defender and deliver the same to the pursuer, and to that end, if necessary, to open shut and lockfast places in such premises; and to grant decree against the defender, failing recovery of the car, for payment to the pursuer of the sum of SEVEN THOUSAND POUNDS (£7,000) STERLING.

2. To grant decree against the defender for payment to the pursuer of the sum of FIVE THOUSAND POUNDS (£5,000) STERLING with interest thereon at the rate of eight *per cent per annum* from the date of citation until payment.

3. To find the defender liable in expenses.

CONDESCENDENCE

1. The parties are as designed in the instance.

2. This action concerns a consumer contract for the purposes of the Civil Jurisdiction and Judgments Act 1982. The defender has been resident at the address in the instance for more than three months immediately preceding the raising of this action. He is domiciled there. Accordingly, Lochmaddy sheriff court has exclusive jurisdiction in terms of Section 20 of and Rule 3 of Schedule 8 to the said Act.

3. On or about 15 July 2020 the defender entered into a hire-purchase agreement with the pursuer whereby he hired from the pursuer a 1968 Daimler V8 250 motor car, registration number VFU 256G for 24 months at £500 per month with an option to purchase at the end of that period. Condition 5(i) provides that in the event of a failure by the defender to make payments, the pursuer is entitled to terminate the agreement and recover possession of the car. A copy of the agreement is produced.

4. The defender made payments under the agreement until about 16 January 2022. Since then he has failed to make any payments. By notice dated 16 November 2022 the pursuer terminated the agreement. The pursuer is accordingly entitled to recover possession of the car, failing which to reasonable reparation therefor.

5. The current market value of the car is around £7,000. Accordingly, decree should be granted in terms of the first crave.

6. Further and in any event, the pursuer is entitled to payment of arrears due under the agreement. As at 16 November 2022 the sum due by the defender in that regard amounted to about £5,000, which is the sum second craved.

7. The pursuer has repeatedly called upon the defender to return the car and make payment of the arrears. He refuses or at least delays to do so. This action is accordingly necessary.

PLEAS IN LAW

1. The pursuer having justifiably terminated the parties' agreement, is entitled to recover possession of the car hired thereunder, failing which to reasonable reparation therefor, as first craved.

2. The defender being indebted to the pursuers for arrears due under the agreement, decree for payment should be granted as second craved.

IN RESPECT WHEREOF

Solicitor
ScotClaim Ltd
2 Foxtrot Square, Aberdeen
Agent for the pursuer

b. Motion for warrant for diligence by arrestment on the dependence of the action (OCR 6.A2.(1)(a))

SHERIFFDOM OF GRAMPIAN, HIGHLAND
AND ISLANDS AT LOCHMADDY

LMD-A2-23

MOTION FOR THE PURSUERS

in the cause

OBERON CREDIT LIMITED, [*designation*]

PURSUER

against

PAOLO MINTO, [*designation*]

DEFENDER

The pursuer moves the court to grant warrant for diligence by arrestment on the dependence of the action in terms of Section 15A of the Debtors (Scotland) Act 1987.

Part of process lodged with the motion:

Statement

IN RESPECT WHEREOF

[*designation*]
Agent for the pursuer

c. Statement (Form G4A)

SHERIFFDOM OF GRAMPIAN, HIGHLAND
AND ISLANDS AT LOCHMADDY

DEBTORS (SCOTLAND) ACT 1987, Section 15D

LMD-A2-23

STATEMENT

for the pursuers

in the cause

OBERON CREDIT LIMITED, [*designation*]

PURSUER

against

PAOLO MINTO, [*designation*]

DEFENDER

1. The applicant is the pursuer in the action by Oberon Credit Limited, a company with its head office at 1 Arnold Lane, Cambridge CA37 8TD against Paolo Minto, residing at The Auld Bothy, Blathaisbhal, North Uist HS6 8TD

2. The following persons have an interest: Darien Bank plc, 121 East Boulevard, Aberdeen.

3. The applicant seeks the grant under section 15E(1) of the Debtors (Scotland) Act 1987 of warrant for diligence in advance of a hearing on the application.

4. There is a real and substantial risk that enforcement of any decree in the action in favour of the pursuer would be defeated or prejudiced by reason of the likelihood of the defender removing, disposing of, burdening, concealing or otherwise dealing with all or some of his assets were warrant for diligence not granted in advance of a hearing on the application under section 15F of the Debtors (Scotland) Act 1987. On or about 10 January 2023 the defender made telephone contact with the pursuer. In the course of the conversation with one of the pursuer's

representatives he advised that he would shortly be returning permanently to Italy, of which he is a citizen. He promised to return forthwith the car that is the subject of these proceedings and to pay the arrears under the parties' hire-purchase agreement. He failed however, without explanation, to keep his promises. In these circumstances, the pursuer is justifiably apprehensive that without the protection of diligence of the dependence of this action, it will be unable to satisfactorily enforce any decree in its favour. Further, having regard to the bad faith exhibited by the defender aforesaid, the pursuer is fearful that without the granting of warrant for diligence in advance of a hearing under section 15F of the 1987 Act, the defender will take immediate steps to remove, dispose of, burden, conceal or otherwise deal with the funds held by him in Darien Bank plc, to the pursuer's detriment. The pursuer is unaware of any adverse effect that granting the warrant might have on Darien Bank plc. Granting the present application would be reasonable in all the circumstances.

IN RESPECT WHEREOF

[*designation*]
Agent for the pursuer

d. Motion for recall of arrestment (OCR 6.A4.(1)(a))

SHERIFFDOM OF GRAMPIAN, HIGHLAND
AND ISLANDS AT LOCHMADDY

LMD-A2-23

MOTION FOR THE DEFENDER

in the cause

OBERON CREDIT LIMITED, [*designation*]

PURSUER

against

PAOLO MINTO, [*designation*]

DEFENDER

The defender moves the court to recall the arrestment on the dependence of this action served upon Darien Bank plc, 123 East Boulevard, Aberdeen on 24 January 2023.

IN RESPECT WHEREOF

Solicitor
11 Egypt Avenue, Aberdeen
Agent for the defender

13. PEEBLES v PIERCE

Action ad factum praestandum, no alternative crave – Summary Cause – Sheriff Court (Scotland) Act 1971 Section 35 (1)(c) – defence of personal bar by mora, taciturnity and acquiescence

Summary Cause; Response to the Claim

Admitted that the defender has a duty to produce an account of her intromissions as executrix with the estate, insofar as the duty is imprescribable in terms of Schedule 3 (e) (i) of the Prescription and Limitation (Scotland) Act 1973. However she cannot now produce any account due solely to a lack of evidence and material. Any obligation to make any further payment to the claimant has been extinguished by the operation of long negative prescription in terms of Section 7 of the Act. The crave for provision of the accounts is free standing and with no alternative for payment, so a failure to comply would place her at risk of a finding of contempt of court. In the circumstances the respondent faces unfair prejudice as a result of the *mora*, taciturnity and acquiescence of the claimant and, accordingly, the claimant is barred from bringing this claim.

D1. Background
The respondent was executrix nominate of the late Lance Musgrave, who died on 8 August 2001. Admitted that the claimant is a son of the deceased. The claimant was not mentioned in the deceased's will. He claimed and was paid legitim. The respondent did not use the services of a solicitor in winding up of the estate. She did not require to obtain confirmation and did not do so. The claimant queried his entitlement and the accounts around two years after the death of the deceased but did not do so again until the raising of these proceedings. All statements, receipts and other papers relating to the executry were retained for a reasonable time but have now been destroyed.

D2 The claim should be unsuccessful because the respondent cannot reasonably be ordered to do the impossible and the claimant being personally barred by *mora*, taciturnity and acquiescence from insisting in this claim the cause should be dismissed.

14. DROMEDARY VETERINARY SUPPLIES LIMITED v SAMARAS

Interdict — Breach of contract — Restrictive covenant

Initial writ

SHERIFFDOM OF NORTH STRATHCLYDE AT DUMBARTON

INITIAL WRIT

in the cause

DROMEDARY VETERINARY SUPPLIES LIMITED, a company registered under the Companies Acts, number SC409638 and having its registered office at Bactrian House, Nile Road, Chorley PR2 7YF

PURSUER

against

ZOE SAMARAS, residing at 56 Archimedes Drive, Dumbarton G82 6TY

DEFENDER

The pursuer craves the court:

1. To interdict the defender either solely or jointly with or as manager or agent or officer or employee for any person, firm or company from directly or indirectly carrying on or being engaged or interested in any business supplying veterinary products or equine foodstuffs within a radius of ten miles or such other distance as to the court shall seem reasonable of Unit 2, Vaughan Business Park Industrial Estate, Dumbarton G82 5DG until 28 April 2023; and
2. To grant interdict *ad interim*; and
3. To find the defender liable in expenses.

CONDESCENDENCE

1. The parties are as designed in the instance.

2. The defender has been resident at the address in the instance for at least three months immediately preceding the raising of this action. He is domiciled there. Dumbarton sheriff court has jurisdiction in terms of Section 20 of and Rule 1 of Schedule 8 to the Civil Jurisdiction and Judgments Act 1982. There is no agreement to prorogate the jurisdiction of any other court.

3. The pursuer has a depot at Unit 2, Vaughan Business Park Industrial Estate, Dumbarton G82 5DG. The pursuer carries on business as suppliers of veterinary products and equine foodstuffs. These latter products include aristoda grass, hay, dried cactus, grains and berries. Prior to 16 July 2022 the pursuer employed the defender as manager of the depot. At the commencement of her employment, the defender signed a contract of employment which included the following clause:

> '17. The Employee hereby undertakes to the Company that … (b) … she will not for a period of six months after the termination of her employment hereunder either solely or jointly with or as Manager or Agent or Officer or Employee for any person, firm or company directly or indirectly carry on or be engaged or interested in any business selling goods or services of the kind supplied by the Company within a radius of ten miles of any depot or branch at which the Employee has been employed during the last twelve months of her employment with the Company.'

4. The defender's employment with the pursuer terminated, after notice, on 28 October 2022. Thereafter the defender commenced employment with Alpaca and Llama Food Services Ltd, Leith Street, Dumbarton G82 9KN (hereinafter referred to as 'the company').

5. The company carries on business which is similar to the business of the pursuer. In particular, the company is engaged in the distribution of equine foodstuffs and feed for ruminants, ostriches and emus. These foods include grass, hay and dried fruit.

6. The defender is employed by the company to carry out similar duties to those which she carried out on behalf of the pursuer. These duties are being carried out by the defender within a radius of five miles from the depot at which she was employed during the last 12 months of her employment with the pursuer.

7. The defender has been asked to cease her employment with the company but she refuses to do so. In these circumstances, the defender is in breach of clause 17(b) of the parties' contract and it is likely that she will continue to act in breach thereof.

8. The defender had daily personal contact with the pursuer's customers. She is well placed to solicit business from them for her own purposes. In November 2022 she sought an order for foodstuffs to be supplied to Hull's Alpaca Farm and Fun Park, Renton, Dumbartonshire G82 6TS. The farm and park are within ten miles of the pursuer's depot.

9. In these circumstances, the pursuer is under necessity of seeking an interdict in order to protect its business connections.

10. In the meantime the pursuer seeks interdict *ad interim*, which the balance of convenience favours. If the defender is not so restrained, the pursuer is liable to suffer serious loss of custom and thereby sustain substantial loss and damage.

PLEAS IN LAW

1. The defender being in breach of clause 17(b) of the contract, and the pursuer being justifiably apprehensive that she will continue to act in breach thereof, as condescended upon, interdict should be granted as craved.

2. Having regard to the balance of convenience, *interim* interdict should be granted as craved.

IN RESPECT WHEREOF

Solicitor
1 Gnu Road, Dumbarton
Agent for the pursuer

15. MANDELA STYLE v MANDALA DESIGNS LTD

Interdict — Passing off — Sole trader

a. Initial writ

SHERIFFDOM OF SOUTH STRATHCLYDE DUMFRIES AND GALLOWAY AT LANARK

INITIAL WRIT

in the cause

EDWARD LENNON, residing at 2 Albert Place, Harleyholm and carrying on business under the name of 'MANDELA STYLE' at 35 Grove Street, Lanark PA2 8AB

PURSUER

against

MANDALA DESIGNS LIMITED, a company registered under the Companies Acts company registration number O2398193 and having its registered office at 29 Alva Place, Carlisle CA3 7SK

DEFENDER

The pursuer craves the court:

1. To interdict the defender and all others acting under the defender's authority or on the defender's behalf from trading in Scotland, which failing in the Sheriffdom of South Strathclyde, Dumfries and Galloway, under the name of 'Mandala Style' or any other name colourably similar to that name and thereby passing off such goods supplied by the defender as being produced and sold by the pursuer under the name of 'Mandela Style'; and to grant interdict *ad interim*.

2. To find the defender liable in expenses.

CONDESCENDENCE

1. The parties are as designed. The pursuer carries on business under the name of 'Mandela Style' at 35 Grove Street, Lanark. The defender is a company registered under the Companies Act with its registered office at 29 Solway Place, Carlisle.

2. The pursuer seeks interdict against the defender prohibiting the defender from trading under the name of 'Mandala Style' or any other name colourably similar thereto within Scotland or, failing which, within the Sheriffdom of South Strathclyde, Dumfries and Galloway. The interdict sought would prevent the defender from passing off the defender's goods as being from the range produced by the pursuer under the name of Mandela Style. The action seeks to prevent a delict or quasi-delict the harm of which will otherwise occur at the pursuer's address in Lanark. Accordingly, this court has jurisdiction in terms of Section 20 of and Regulation 2(c) of Schedule 8 to the Civil Jurisdiction and Judgments Act 1982.

3. The pursuer has carried on business at his shop premises at 35 Grove Street, Lanark since about 7 March 2015. He has produced a range of goods labelled with a circular logo in black, green and gold and themed to celebrate the life of the anti-apartheid campaigner and former South African President Nelson Mandela. The range has varied over the years but currently comprises scarves, shirts, sweatshirts, bandanas, beads, bracelets, car stickers, erasers, stationery and keyrings. A 2022 catalogue is produced. Also produced are samples of the merchandise featured in the catalogue.

4. The pursuer supplies said goods to retailers and individuals. His business is largely online although he also attends music festivals, such as the Merry Olde Soul Festival in the Lake District in May 2021. In the tax year 2022/23 his business had a turnover of £27,000.

5. In January 2023 it was drawn to the pursuer's attention by Plunketts, a retailer in Manchester Adelaide Street Market that the defender was advertising products that strongly resemble those produced by the pursuer. The products were waistcoats, hats and flags. In February 2023 another retailer, Excalibur's Bizarre, Broughton, reported that samples of computer mouse mats bearing a virtually identical version of the pursuer's logo had been delivered to their premises. Both these retailers called to enquire whether these products were those of the pursuer.

6. The said waistcoats, hats, flags and mouse mats were produced by the defender. It is evident that confusion and doubt exists as a result of the similarity between the parties' trading names. Believed and averred that the defender has engaged in the sale of such items since July 2021. The defender was incorporated on 11 April 2021.

7. The brand, colour scheme and logo of 'Mandela Style' has acquired a good reputation and a large following with the general public. The pursuer has spent years developing the brand through advertising and promotion. The name of 'Mandela Style' is well known to the public

and to retailers in Scotland and the North of England. In these areas and throughout the U.K. the name, brand, colour scheme and logo are associated in the minds of the public and the retail trade with the pursuer's products. The pursuer has acquired substantial goodwill and business reputation therein.

8. The defender's products are of quality inferior to those made and sold by the pursuer. The former are made of less durable and colour-fast fabrics. The stitching looks irregular and ragged. In addition, unlike 'Mandela Style' the defender's products are not ethically produced. Believed and averred that their manufacture uses badly paid workers in Bangladesh.

9. By emails dated 16 February and 8 March 2023 solicitors instructed by the pursuer alerted the defender to the issues created by the similarity of name. The solicitors sought to enter into a dialogue to ascertain how the parties could continue trading but without confusing the public. It was suggested that the defender trade under a different name. No response has been received to these emails.

10. In these circumstances, the pursuer is justifiably apprehensive that the defender will continue to trade as 'Mandala Style' whilst offering and selling products practically indistinguishable from those of the pursuer. The effect would be to mislead the public. It would also be to the detriment of the reputation and profitability of the pursuer's business. The defender's use of 'Mandala Style' in the course of its supplying goods has misrepresented to customers that they were being supplied with the pursuer's products. In these circumstances, the use by the defender of the name 'Mandala Style' or a colourably similar name in the course of trade would amount to passing off goods supplied by the defender as being those of the pursuer.

11. The pursuer seeks an extended interdict as defined by Section 84 of the Courts Reform (Scotland) Act 2014. In the meantime, he seeks interim interdict. The resulting restraint of trade would be reasonable and proportionate.

PLEAS IN LAW

1. The pursuer being justifiably apprehensive that the defender is passing off and will continue to pass off the defender's goods as his, interdict should be granted as craved.

2. Having regard to the balance of convenience, interdict *ad interim* should be granted.

IN RESPECT WHEREOF

Solicitor

1 High Street, Paisley

Agent for the pursuer

b. Application by prospective lay representative –

SHERIFFDOM OF NORTH STRATHCLYDE AT PAISLEY

PAI-753-23

APPLICATION
FOR A PROSPECTIVE LAY
REPRESENTATIVE TO CONDUCT
PROCEEDINGS

Section 97(2) Courts Reform
(Scotland) Act 2014 and SSI 2016
No 243

in the cause

EDWARD LENNON, [*designation*]

PURSUER

against

MANDALA PRODUCTS LIMITED, [*designation*]

DEFENDER

1) The defender applies for permission for a lay representative to conduct these proceedings on its behalf.

2) The said applicant is a limited company.

3) The applicant is unable to pay for the services of a legal representative because:

a) being a limited company it is ineligible under the Legal Aid (Scotland) Act 1986.
b) the applicant does not possess any policy of insurance that will cover the costs of its defending this action.
c) neither of the company officers has the financial means to risk being found liable in expenses as *dominis litis* by providing funding to the company.

4) The prospective lay representative is Ingo Gunther.

5) Ingo Gunther holds the position of company secretary and one of two directors of the applicant.

6) The applicant has authorised the prospective lay representative. This took place at a directors' meeting on 12 December 2022. A certified except of the minutes of said meeting is annexed hereto.

DECLARATION BY PROSPECTIVE LAY REPRESENTATIVE

A) My responsibility in my position as secretary and director with the applicant does not consist wholly or mainly of conducting legal proceedings.

B) I do not have a personal interest within the meaning of Section 97(5) of the Courts Reform (Scotland) Act 2014 in the outcome of the case.

Ingo Gunther
Secretary and Director
Mandala Products Limited

16. MACDONALD v CAMPBELL

Breach of extended interdict – concurrence of procurator fiscal.

Initial writ

SHERIFFDOM OF TAYSIDE, CENTRAL AND FIFE AT KIRKCALDY

KKD-A385-22
INITIAL WRIT

in the cause

LINDA MACDONALD, residing at 28 Duchess Gardens, Burntisland, Fife, KY3 9DS

PURSUER

against

ARCHIBALD CAMPBELL, residing at 18 Cruachan Street, Cullipool, Luing PA34 4TX

DEFENDER

The pursuer craves the court:

1. To ordain the defender to appear personally at the bar of the court on such day and at such time as the court may determine to answer for a breach of the interdict granted by the sheriff at Oban on 17 November 2022 and in terms of which he was interdicted from molesting the pursuer by abusing her verbally, threatening her, putting her into a state of fear and alarm or distress or using violence towards her anywhere in Scotland; and, failing his appearance, to grant warrant to officers of the court to apprehend the defender and to bring him before the court to answer as aforesaid; and
2. In the event of the charge being admitted or proved, to impose upon the defender such punishment as to the court shall seem just; and
3. To find the defender liable in expenses as taxed.

CONDESCENDENCE

1. The parties are as designed in the instance. This action concerns the enforcement of an interdict granted by the sheriff of North Strathclyde at Oban. The interdict is an extended interdict as defined by Section 84 of the Courts Reform (Scotland) Act 2014. The breach of the interdict occurred in Kirkcaldy, in the Sheriffdom of Tayside Central and Fife. Accordingly, this court has jurisdiction in terms of Section 85(2)(c) of the Act. The pursuer is unaware of any proceedings pending before any court which are in respect of the subject matter of this writ.

2. On 17 November 2022 the sheriff at Oban granted interdict against the defender from molesting the pursuer by abusing her verbally, threatening her, putting her into a state of fear and alarm or distress or using violence towards her anywhere in Scotland. Sheriff officers instructed by the pursuer served the order on the defender. They did so by personal service on 19 November 2022. Their certificate of service is produced.

3. Thereafter, on or about 20 December 2022, the defender approached the pursuer in The Alchemist public house, 28 Pondicherry Lane, Kirkcaldy, Fife KY1 6RT. He walked to within a metre of the pursuer. He shouted 'I ken where you and your maukit boyfriend live.' and 'Watch your back, darling'. These remarks were made in a menacing manner. The pursuer interpreted them as threats. She was reasonably entitled to do so.

4. The defender immediately left the public house in a shaken and distressed state. She was unable to sleep that night due to a fear that the pursuer would attend her home. She required to consult her doctor and to take time off work due to stress. The defender has a history of violence and threats towards the pursuer and her previous partner. Reference is made to the averments in Condescendences 3 to 5 of the principal action. A copy thereof is attached.

5. The defender is in breach of interdict and this action is necessary.

PLEA IN LAW

The defender being in breach of interdict, should be punished therefor.

IN RESPECT WHEREOF

Solicitor

Garden and Maude

1 New Street, Glenrothes KY6 9RE

Agent for the pursuer

Kirkcaldy 12 January 2023

I do not intend to intervene and to that extent I concur in the foregoing writ.

'A. Falkland'

Senior Procurator Fiscal Depute

17. SAELIM V JOHN

Proving the tenor of a lost document

Initial Writ

SHERIFFDOM OF NORTH STRATHCLYDE AT GREENOCK

INITIAL WRIT

in the cause

KANYA SAELIM, residing at 7 Belmont Road, Port Glasgow G48 9RS as an individual and as unconfirmed trustee and executrix nominate of the late Ethelred John acting under and in terms of his Trust Disposition and Settlement dated 11 May 2019

PURSUER

against

ALEXANDER JOHN residing at
14 Haakon Street, Largs KA30 6TY

FIRST NAMED DEFENDER

and

GEORGE JOHN, residing at 16 Sexton Way, Carlisle CA5 8SB

SECOND NAMED DEFENDER

The pursuer craves the court:

1) To find and declare that the lost codicil of the late Ethelred John was of the tenor following;

'Codicil to my Will

I, Ethelred John, residing at 7 Belmont Road, Port Glasgow G48 9RS, the granter of the Trust Disposition and Settlement

dated Eleventh May Two thousand and nineteen do make the following alteration thereto;
I hereby delete clause 7 of my will of 11 May 2019.
Save as hereby amended I confirm my said Trust Disposition and Settlement in its terms. IN WITNESS WHEREOF these presents typewritten on this page are subscribed by me, Ethelred John before this witness Gordon Bennett residing at 15 Mafeking Square, Preston PR4 7TF at Port Glasgow on 22 January 2020.'

2) To find the first named defender liable in expenses as taxed.

3) To find the second named defender liable in expenses as taxed only in the event of his defending these proceedings.

CONDESCENDENCE

1) The parties are as designed in the instance. The late Ethelred John (hereinafter 'the deceased) was born on 12 May 1934 and died on 27 May 2022. Immediately prior to his death the pursuer cohabited with him. The first named defender is the only son of the deceased. He has legal rights in the estate of the deceased in terms of the Succession (Scotland) Act 1964. The second named defender is the brother of the deceased. He and the pursuer are the two residuary beneficiaries in terms of Clauses 2 and 8(a) respectively of the Trust Disposition and Settlement granted by the deceased on 11 May 2019. The second named defender is called for his interest in terms of Ordinary Cause Rule 53.2(1).

2) The second named defender is sued as beneficiary of a trust domiciled in Scotland and created by a written instrument namely the said Trust Disposition and Settlement. The truster was the deceased. The trust came into operation on his death. At that date the deceased was residing with the pursuer at the address in the instance. He was domiciled in the Sheriffdom of North Strathclyde. Greenock sheriff court is the appropriate sheriff court as defined by Section 24A of the Trusts (Scotland) Act 1921 and it has jurisdiction in terms of Section 20 of and Rule 2(g) of Schedule 8 to the Civil Jurisdiction and Judgments Act 1982.

3) The parties are also parties in action number GRE197-22 proceeding in this court. In that action the current pursuer is first named defender, the current first named defender is pursuer and the second named defender is second named defender. The action is one for reduction of the said Trust Disposition and Settlement. There are also craves for interdict. With the exception thereof the pursuer is not aware of any other proceedings pending before any court which are in respect of the subject matter of this writ. There is no agreement to prorogate the jurisdiction of any other court.

4) Clause 7 of the Trust Disposition and Settlement states that:

> 'I hereby bequeath in favour of my son Alexander John my collection of whiskies and all books, glasses and accessories relating thereto.'

5) The deceased had a study in 7 Belmont Road. Within the room he used a desk. Following his death on 27 May 2022, the pursuer located within a drawer in the desk the Trust Disposition and Settlement granted by the deceased on 11 May 2019 and a copy deed headed 'Codicil to my Will' dated 22 January 2020. (hereinafter 'the document'). The document was a copy of a codicil to the Trust Disposition and Settlement.

6) The document states 'I hereby delete clause 7 of my will of 11 May 2019.' The effect thereof is that the said collection would become part of the residue of the estate, to which the pursuer and the second named defender are entitled as residuary beneficiaries. The collection is worth in the region of £30,000.

7) The document is a copy of a deed bearing to have been signed by the deceased. His signature bears to have been witnessed by a friend, Gordon Bennett.

8) Also within the drawer was a letter and invoice from Glanville Crimond, solicitors, Greenock, dated 29 January 2020 'in respect of your codicil, the principal of which we have retained for safe keeping'. Agents instructed by the pursuer emailed the solicitors on 24 August 2022 to ascertain the whereabouts of the principal codicil. They responded to advise that executry staff had been furloughed or working from home during Covid lockdown in 2020 and that they could not locate the codicil 'despite strenuous endeavours'.

9) The document is produced. Its terms are fully set out in crave 1. The codicil is lost. It has not been destroyed *animo revocandi*. The deceased's intention was that it be held in the safe custody of the solicitors. It is necessary that the tenor of the codicil be proved in order that the pursuer as executor nominate of the deceased may obtain confirmation and give effect to the deceased's testamentary intentions as evidenced by both the Trust Disposition and Settlement and the codicil.

PLEAS IN LAW

The codicil of the deceased dated 22 January 2020 having been lost and the tenor of the same being instructed by the copy produced, as condescended upon, decree should be granted as craved.

IN RESPECT WHEREOF

Rodgers and Kossoff
7 Gourock Road, Greenock
Agent for the pursuer

III FAMILY PROCEEDINGS

1. SPOTTISWOODE v SPOTTISWOODE

Divorce — Adultery — Orders for financial provision — Capital sum — Incidental orders — Sale of matrimonial home — Interest

a. Initial writ

SHERIFFDOM OF SOUTH STRATHCLYDE, DUMFRIES AND GALLOWAY AT HAMILTON

INITIAL WRIT

in the cause

LIONEL SPOTTISWOODE, residing at 17 Glencoe Gardens, Airdrie ML6 4WE (Assisted Person)

PURSUER

against

SYBELLA SPOTTISWOODE, residing at c/o Bolland, 73 Pleasant Valley, Hamilton ML3 7JK

DEFENDER

The pursuer craves the court:

1. To divorce the defender from the pursuer on the ground that the marriage between the parties has broken down irretrievably as established by the defender's adultery.
2. To grant warrant in terms of Ordinary Cause Rule 33.7(1)(b) to intimate this writ to Rodney Bolland, 73 Pleasant Valley, Hamilton ML3 7JK, as a person with whom the defender is alleged to have committed adultery.
3. To find the defender liable in expenses.

CONDESCENDENCE

1. The parties are as designed in the instance.
2. The parties were married at Davaar on 19 November 2018. There is one child of the marriage. He is Oliver Spottiswoode born on 16 March 2012. Relative marriage certificate and birth certificate are produced

herewith and referred to for their terms which are incorporated for the sake of brevity.

3. The parties are habitually resident in Scotland. Both parties have been resident within the Sheriffdom of South Strathclyde, Dumfries and Galloway for a period exceeding 40 days immediately preceding the raising of this action. This court has jurisdiction. in terms of the Domicile and Matrimonial Proceedings Act 1973. The pursuer is unaware of any proceedings continuing in Scotland or elsewhere which are in respect of the marriage or which are capable of affecting its validity or subsistence.

4. After their marriage the parties lived together until around 14 March 2022. Since then they have not lived together nor had marital relations.

5. For the purposes of the Divorce (Scotland) Act 1976 Section 1(2) (a) the marriage has broken down irretrievably as established by the defender's adultery. The defender has formed an adulterous relationship with Rodney Bolland. Since about May 2022, they have cohabited at 73 Pleasant Valley, Hamilton ML3 7JK. In particular, they stayed alone overnight at that address on or about 29 May 2022. There is no prospect of a reconciliation. The pursuer seeks decree of divorce.

6. The child resides with the defender and paramour. He attends Cadzow Primary School. He is progressing well. He has his own bedroom at the address in the instance. The pursuer has regular residential contact to him. There is no necessity for any orders in terms of Section 11 of the Children (Scotland) Act 1995.

PLEA IN LAW

The marriage having broken down irretrievably, decree of divorce should be granted as craved.

IN RESPECT WHEREOF

Solicitor

Bain and Gregson

14 Gartcosh Road, Airdrie

Agent for the pursuer

b. Defences (OCR 9.6.(2) & 33.34.(2)(b))

SHERIFFDOM OF SOUTH STRATHCLYDE, DUMFRIES AND GALLOWAY AT HAMILTON

HAM-F62-23

DEFENCES

in the cause

LIONEL SPOTTISWOODE, [*designation*]

PURSUER

against

SYBELLA SPOTTISWOODE, [*designation*]

DEFENDER

The defender craves the court:

1) To grant decree against the pursuer for payment to the defender of a capital sum of TWENTY EIGHT THOUSAND FIVE HUNDRED AND THIRTY FIVE POUNDS (£28,535) STERLING, with interest thereon at the rate of eight *per cent per annum* from 21 July 2022 or such other date as to the court shall seem appropriate until payment.
2) To grant an order for the sale of the heritable property at 17 Glencoe Gardens, Airdrie ML6 4WE; to that end, to grant warrant to Bauld Legal LLP, Solicitors and Estate Agents, 16 Cumbernauld Road, Airdrie, or such other person as the court may think fit, to dispose of the subjects in such manner and under such conditions as the court shall direct; and to ordain the parties to execute and deliver such disposition and other deeds as shall be necessary to give a valid title to the subjects to the purchaser or purchasers thereof, which failing to authorise the sheriff clerk to execute such disposition and deeds, as adjusted at his sight.
3) To grant a pension sharing order in terms of Section 8(1)(baa) of the Family Law (Scotland) Act 1985 in favour of the defender in respect of the pursuer's pension rights in the Owl and Unicorn

Ltd policy number 27496 to the extent of SIXTY THOUSAND POUNDS (£60,000) STERLING or such other sum as the court may consider reasonable; and

4) To grant warrant to intimate these Defences to Owl and Unicorn Ltd, 66 Marmaduke Place, Pimlico, London W2 7RA.
5) To order the pursuer to provide details of his resources, in terms of Section 20 of the Family Law (Scotland) Act 1985.
6) To find the pursuer liable in expenses as taxed.

ANSWERS TO CONDESCENDENCE

1. Admitted.

2. Admitted.

3. Admitted that this court has jurisdiction. The defender is unaware of any such proceedings.

4. Admitted

5. Admitted that the marriage has broken down irretrievably.

6. Admitted that there is no necessity for any orders in terms of Section 11 of the Children (Scotland) Act 1995. The defender seeks a capital sum as craved. At the relevant date the parties had matrimonial property with values as follows:

A) **Owned in equal shares**

I. 17, Glencoe Gardens, Airdrie ML6 4WE: £175,000.
Less secured loan by Merryweather Building Society of £120,000.
Equity: £55,000.

II The furniture and furnishings therein: £2,000.

B) **Pursuer**

I. Current account, number 09764939, Teviot Bank: £2,700.

II Owl and Unicorn Ltd pension fund 27496, proportion of CETV attributable to period between marriage and separation: £75,800.

III 750 5p Ordinary shares in Old Albion Engineering plc: £8,400.

C) **Defender**

I Current account, number 28764, EthicalEarth plc: £2,100.

II Occupational pension, Chatelherault Council, proportion of CETV attributable to period between marriage and separation: £12,000.

Accordingly, the net total value of the matrimonial assets at the relevant date was £158,000. An equal division thereof would be achieved by a transfer by the pursuer to the defender in the sum of £36,400. The pursuer has the resources to make same, namely his share of the equity, his shares and savings.

An equal division would not represent a fair sharing for the purposes of Section 10(1) of the Act. A fair sharing would be whereby the defender receives 65% being £102,700. This would be achieved by a transfer by the pursuer to the defender in the sum of £60,100. The pursuer has the resources to make such transfer, namely his share of the equity, his shares, savings and pension fund.

The defender relies on those principles specified in Sections 9(1)(a), 9(1)(b) and 9(1)(c) of the Family Law (Scotland) Act 1985. She seeks a fair sharing of the net value of the matrimonial property. The pursuer enjoyed a financial advantage and the defender experienced a corresponding economic disadvantage. These were consequences of her having made a career sacrifice to enable the child to be looked after at home while the pursuer obtained promotion at work and higher remuneration.

The defender has no realisable capital resources other than her interest in the matrimonial home. She will not be able to access any pension funds until at least 2033. She is unaware of the pursuer's current resources. In the circumstances, decree should be granted as craved by the defender.

PLEAS IN LAW

1) The sum sued for in terms of crave 1 of the Defences being justified by the principles set out in Section 9 of the Family Law (Scotland) Act 1985 and reasonable having regards to the parties' needs and resources decree should be granted as craved by the defender.

2) The defender as joint proprietor of the heritable subjects at 17 Glencoe Gardens, Airdrie ML6 4WE being entitled to seek the sale thereof and the order sought in terms of crave 2 of the Defences being justified by the principles set out in Section 9 of the Family Law (Scotland) Act 1985 and reasonable having regards to the parties' needs and resources decree should be granted as craved by the defender.

3) The order sought in terms of crave 3 of the Defences being justified by the principles set out in Section 9 of the Family Law (Scotland) Act 1985 and reasonable having regards to the parties' needs and resources decree should be granted as craved by the defender.

IN RESPECT WHEREOF

Solicitor
Forrest and Glen
192 Parliamentary Road, Glasgow
Agent for the defender

c. Statement of financial property (OCR 33.34.(4))

SHERIFFDOM OF SOUTH STRATHCLYDE, DUMFRIES AND GALLOWAY AT HAMILTON

FORM F13A

HAM-F62-23

FORM OF STATEMENT OF FINANCIAL PROPERTY

for the defender

in the cause

LIONEL SPOTTISWOODE, [*designation*]

PURSUER

against

SYBELLA SPOTTISWOODE, [*designation*]

DEFENDER

The Defender's financial position at 14 March 2022 being the relevant date under Section 10(3) of the Family Law Scotland Act 1985:

Assets:

I. One half interest in 17, Glencoe Gardens, Airdrie ML6 4WE which half is worth £87,500.

II Furniture and furnishings which half is worth £2,000.

III Current account, number 28764, EthicalEarth plc: £1,000.

IV Occupational pension, Chatelherault Council, proportion of CETV attributable to period between marriage and separation: £12,000.

Debts;

One half of the secured loan by Merryweather Building Society, which half is £60,000.

I certify that this information is correct to the best of my belief.

Date: 11 April 2023.

d. Note of adjustments for pursuer (OCR 9.8.)

SHERIFFDOM OF SOUTH STRATHCLYDE, DUMFRIES AND GALLOWAY AT HAMILTON

HAM-F62-23

NOTE OF ADJUSTMENTS

for the pursuer

in the cause

LIONEL SPOTTISWOODE, [*designation*]

PURSUER

against

SYBELLA SPOTTISWOODE, [*designation*]

DEFENDER

1. Insert new articles of condescendence:

‘7. At the date of separation the Current account, number 28764, EthicalEarth plc is believed to have been around £2,100. The value of her interest in any pension held through her employment with, Chatelherault Council is not known and not admitted. Accordingly, the net total value of the matrimonial assets at the relevant date is not known and not admitted.

8. The sum craved and order sought in crave 3 of the Defences are not justified by the principles of Sections 9 of the Family Law (Scotland) Act 1985 nor reasonable having regard to the parties’ resources. With reference to Sections 9(1)(a) and 10(1) the net value of the matrimonial property at the relevant date ought to be shared equally.

9. The defender wished to leave her employment after the birth of the parties’ child. The pursuer did not wish her to do so but he respected her choice. Consequently, he had the increased

financial burden and responsibility of being sole earner. The defender has paid nothing towards the parties' loan with Merryweather Building Society since November 2011. The defender also chose to leave the matrimonial home and to live with Rodney Bolland. Believed and averred that he earns around £75,000 *per annum* and that there is no debt secured over 73 Pleasant Valley.

10. The sale of the matrimonial home will compel the pursuer to find new accommodation. He requires a capital sum to fund any purchase. Given his age and state of health he would be able to secure a secured loan of only 10 years. His monthly repayment instalments would be considerable. He has no cohabitant with whom to share his living expenses. In the whole circumstances, no capital sum should be awarded. *Esto* an award of a capital sum is justified and reasonable (which is denied), the sum sued for is excessive. A pension share of £30,000 in favour of the defender would satisfy the principles of the Act and would be reasonable having regard to the parties' resources.

2. Add new pleas-in-law as follows:

'2. The sum sued for in terms of crave 1 of the Defences not being justified by the principles set out in Section 9 of the Family Law (Scotland) Act 1985 nor reasonable having regards to the parties' needs and resources decree should not be granted as craved by the defender.

3. The order sought in terms of crave 3 of the Defences not being justified by the principles set out in Section 9 of the Family Law (Scotland) Act 1985 nor reasonable having regards to the parties' needs and resources decree should not be granted as craved by the defender.

e. Statement of financial property (OCR 33.9.(c))

SHERIFFDOM OF SOUTH STRATHCLYDE, DUMFRIES AND GALLOWAY AT HAMILTON

FORM F13A

HAM-F62-23

FORM OF STATEMENT OF FINANCIAL PROPERTY

for the pursuer

in the cause

LIONEL SPOTTISWOODE [*designation*]

PURSUER

against

SYBELLA SPOTTISWOODE [*designation*]

DEFENDER

The Pursuer's financial position at 14 March 2022 being the relevant date under Section 10(3) of the Family Law Scotland Act 1985.

Assets;

I 17, Glencoe Gardens, Airdrie ML6 4WE. £175,000 (one half share) £87,500.

II The furniture and furnishings therein (one half share) £1,000.

III Current account, number 09764939, Teviot Bank: £2,700.

IV Pension fund, proportion of CETV attributable to period between marriage and separation: £75,000.

V 750 5p Ordinary shares in Albion Engineering plc: £8,300.

Debts;

1) One half of the secured loan by Merryweather Building Society, which half is £60,000.
2) Debt on Penguincard account: £2,400.
3) Debt due to Scottish Legal Aid Board from previous action: £1,600.

I certify that this information is correct to the best of my belief.

Date; 14 April 2023

f. Note of adjustments for defender (OCR 9.8.)

SHERIFFDOM OF SOUTH STRATHCLYDE, DUMFRIES AND GALLOWAY AT HAMILTON

HAM-F62-23

NOTE OF ADJUSTMENTS

for the defender

in the cause

LIONEL SPOTTISWOODE, [*designation*]

PURSUER

against

SYBELLA SPOTTISWOODE, [*designation*]

DEFENDER

In Answer 6 delete from 'The defender seeks a capital sum as craved' to the end of the condescendence and add new Answers:

Answer 7, comprising from 'The defender seeks a capital sum as craved' to 'shares and savings'.

Answer 8, comprising from 'An equal division would not' to 'savings and pension fund'.

Answer 9, comprising from 'The defender relies on' to 'remuneration'.

Answer 10, comprising 'The defender has no realisable capital resources' to 'She is unaware of the pursuer's current resources. In the circumstances, decree should be granted as craved by the defender'.

g. Notice to admit (OCR 29.14.(1))

SHERIFFDOM OF SOUTH STRATHCLYDE, DUMFRIES AND GALLOWAY AT HAMILTON

HAM-F62-23

NOTICE TO ADMIT

for the defender

in the cause

LIONEL SPOTTISWOODE [*designation*]

PURSUER

against

SYBELLA SPOTTISWOODE [*designation*]

DEFENDER

The defender calls upon the defender to admit for the purposes of this action that:

(i) Production 6/1 is a true and accurate copy of a pension statement issued by the Scottish local authority pensions agency on 12 December 2022.
(ii) Production 6/1 correctly states that the CETV of the defender's pension from Chatelherault Council is £97,000 as at the relevant date.
(iii) the proportion of the said CETV attributable to the period between the date of the marriage and the relevant date is £75,000.
(iv) Production 6/2 is a true and accurate copy of a mortgage statement issued by the Merryweather Building Society on 16 November 2022.
(v) Production 6/2 correctly states the source and amount of payments made to the Merryweather Building Society in respect of the parties' secured borrowing.

IN RESPECT WHEREOF

Solicitor

[*designation*]

h. Motion for defender to be appointed to lead at diet of proof, to allow affidavit evidence and for pursuer to provide details of resources. (OCR 33.28.(1)(d))

SHERIFFDOM OF SOUTH STRATHCLYDE, DUMFRIES AND GALLOWAY AT HAMILTON

HAM-F62-23

MOTION FOR THE DEFENDER

in the cause

LIONEL SPOTTISWOODE, [*designation*]

PURSUER

against

SYBELLA SPOTTISWOODE, [*designation*]

DEFENDER

The defender moves the court:

1) To appoint the defender to lead at the diet of proof.
2) To allow affidavit evidence in respect of proof of adultery and the welfare of the parties' child.
3) To order the pursuer to provide details of his resources within 14 days.

IN RESPECT WHEREOF

Solicitor

[*designation*]

i. Affidavit of witness

SHERIFFDOM OF SOUTH STRATHCLYDE, DUMFRIES AND GALLOWAY AT HAMILTON

HAM-F62-23

AFFIDAVIT

of Rodney Bolland

in the cause

LIONEL SPOTTISWOODE, [*designation*]

PURSUER

against

SYBELLA SPOTTISWOODE, [*designation*]

DEFENDER

At Glasgow on the Sixteenth day of April Two Thousand and Twenty Two in the presence of HAZEL FORREST, Solicitor and Notary Public, 192 Parliamentary Road, Glasgow COMPEARED RODNEY BOLLAND residing at 73 Pleasant Valley, Hamilton ML3 7JK, who being solemnly sworn DEPONES as follows:

1. My full name is Rodney Bolland. I was born on 16 January 1991. I am employed as a sales manager at Bagga Bargain, Coatbridge. I have known Sybella Spottiswoode since November 2020.

2. To the best of my knowledge Mrs Spottiswoode separated from her husband in the middle of March 2022 and she has not shared a bedroom or resumed living with him since then. I understand that she lived with her mother for a week in April 2022.

3. Since May 2022, Mrs Spottiswoode and I have cohabited at 73 Pleasant Valley, Hamilton ML3 7JK. I own that house. We are in a stable relationship. We have committed adultery.

4. Mrs Spottiswoode and her husband have a son, Oliver Spottiswoode. He is ten years old. He lives with us at 73 Pleasant Valley. He has his own bedroom there. The accommodation comprises a living room, two

bedrooms, kitchenette and bathroom, which is quite sufficient for us. The property is well furnished and always kept very clean and tidy.

5. Oliver attends Cadzow Primary School where he is in P5. He is performing well academically. He is keen on football and computers. He likes playing games on Xbox. He supports Raith Rovers FC and has attended matches with me and my nephews, with whom he gets on well. He is very fond of his Labradoodle dog, Dexter, who lives with us. Oliver's father has contact with Oliver twice each week. He has contact all day each Saturday and for several hours on a Tuesday or Thursday evening. Oliver has asthma and takes medication to control it. Otherwise he enjoys good health.

All of which is truth as the deponent shall answer to God.

DEPONENT

NOTARY PUBLIC

2. CONNERY v CONNERY

Divorce — Unreasonable behaviour — Vulnerable witness application

a. Initial writ

SHERIFFDOM OF GRAMPIAN, HIGHLAND
AND ISLANDS AT ELGIN

INITIAL WRIT

in the cause

MORVEN CONNERY, residing at 63 Sueno Place, Forres IV36 4SN

PURSUER

against

VERNON CONNERY, residing at 14 Moray Street Forres IV36 2RD

DEFENDER

The pursuer craves the court:

1. To divorce the defender from the pursuer on the ground that the marriage has broken down irretrievably as established by the defender's behaviour.

2. To find the defender liable in expenses as taxed.

CONDESCENDENCE

1. The parties are as designed in the instance.

2. The parties are habitually resident in Scotland. The pursuer has been resident within the Sheriffdom of Grampian, Highland and Islands for a period exceeding 40 days immediately preceding the raising of this action. Elgin sheriff court accordingly has jurisdiction in terms of the Domicile and Matrimonial Proceedings Act 1973. The pursuer is unaware of any proceedings continuing in Scotland or elsewhere which are in respect of the marriage or are capable of affecting its validity or subsistence.

3. The parties were married at Aberdeen on 11 November 2018. The relative certificate of marriage is produced. After the marriage the parties

lived together until about 8 August 2022. Since then they have not lived together nor had marital relations.

4. The defender has behaved in such a manner that the pursuer cannot reasonably be expected to cohabit with him. During the marriage the defender was drunk most evenings. He drank an average of five litres of spirits each week together with extra strength lager and several litres of strong cider. Whilst inebriated he was violent, aggressive and coercive towards the pursuer.

5. At Christmas 2019 the parties were within the matrimonial home. The defender was drunk. He shouted and swore at the pursuer and pushed her into a door, causing bruising to her face and arm. During Covid lockdowns in 2020 and 2021 the defender committed similar assaults at least once every six weeks. In addition, on a weekly basis he was abusive, calling the pursuer a 'fat bitch' and a 'lazy cow'. On at least four occasions in 2021 he locked the pursuer out the matrimonial home, forcing her to sleep in her car. In summer 2022, during a holiday in Tunisia the pursuer grabbed the pursuer by the throat, slapped her face and pushed her onto a glass table which broke causing injuries to the pursuer. These required hospital treatment. As a result of this assault in Tunisia, the pursuer left the defender immediately upon their return to the UK.

6. Following upon the parties' separation, the defender has repeatedly threatened the pursuer with violence. In particular, on or about 17 February 2023, he sent her messages by social media threatening that he would going to 'put her through a glass door' if she did not resume living with him.

7. The marriage has broken down irretrievably. There is no prospect of a reconciliation. Decree of divorce should be granted as first craved.

PLEA IN LAW

The marriage having broken down irretrievably as a result of the defender's behaviour, as condescended upon, and with reference to the Divorce (Scotland) Act 1976 Section 1(2)(b), decree of divorce should be granted as first craved.

IN RESPECT WHEREOF

Solicitor
Charles and Stewart
19 Murray Street, Elgin
Agent for the pursuer

b. Vulnerable witness application

SHERIFFDOM OF GRAMPIAN, HIGHLAND
AND ISLANDS AT ELGIN

Court ref no ELG- F24-23

Form G20 Rule 45.3

VULNERABLE WITNESSES
(SCOTLAND) ACT 2004
Section 12

VULNERABLE WITNESS
APPLICATION

In the cause

MORVEN CONNERY, [*designation*]

PURSUER

against

VERNON CONNERY, [*designation*]

DEFENDER

The applicant is the pursuer in the action by [*designation*] against [*designation*]. She intends to give evidence as a witness. She was born on 18 February 1998. The applicant considers that she is a vulnerable witness under Section 11(1)(b) of the Vulnerable Witnesses (Scotland) Act 2004 for the following reasons:

There is a significant risk that the value of her evidence may be unfairly diminished as a result of fear and distress associated with giving her evidence. With regard to Section 11(2) of the Act the relevant factors are: the domestic relationship between the witness and the defender; the history of violent and abusive behaviour directed by the defender at the pursuer; the traumatic effect that this has had upon her, causing her to be fearful of the defender; the injustice of her having to suffer further trauma of having to give evidence whilst being watched by the defender in open court; the sensitivity of some of the evidence as regards abuse; and the ill-effect on the health and wellbeing of the witness.

The applicant considers that the following special measures are the most appropriate for the purpose of taking her evidence; the most appropriate method would be by means of a live videoconferencing link as envisaged by OCR 32A.1. Failing which, a screen should be erected so that the witness cannot see the pursuer but can be seen by agents and the sheriff.

The reasons that these special measures are considered the most appropriate are as follows; The defender is extremely hostile and is likely to evince that hostility as well as malice and menace towards the witness. Given that she is the pursuer and the first witness and that evidence is unlikely to commence in practice before 10.30am, regardless of the time set down for the proof, the applicant would be waiting in the court building for at least 40 minutes. Family proofs tend to be heard in Courtroom 9, which lacks witness rooms so that parties and witnesses and their friends and family members often wait together in the corridor outside the room. If compelled to give evidence in open court there is a serious risk that she would forget or omit relevant material as a result of being pre-occupied and distracted by the physical presence of the defender. There is minimal prejudice to the defender because the special measures will not impinge upon the sheriff's ability to assess the witness' demeanour and body language, and his agent will have the same opportunity to cross examine as under normal circumstances. The pursuer has expressed to her agents the following views on the special measures that are considered most appropriate;

She is scared of the defender and feels intimidated, ill and nervous at the prospect of giving evidence in his physical presence. This anxiety is beyond that to be expected of any witness ordinarily giving evidence in open court. The pursuer does not wish to see the defender. If she does not have to do so she believes that she will be able to stay more focussed on the questions and more articulate in her answers. Other information considered relevant to this application is as follows; The quality of the evidence of the witness will be far better and the court will be assisted far more in reaching the correct findings in fact if the special measures referred to are implemented.

The applicant asks the court to consider this application and to make an order authorising the measures sought.

IN RESPECT WHEREOF

[*designation*]
Agent for the applicant

3. GASTON v GASTON

Divorce — Unreasonable behaviour — Protective measures — Exclusion order — Property order — Transfer of tenancy — Intimation to landlord of matrimonial home — affidavit of pursuer

a. Initial writ

SHERIFFDOM OF GLASGOW AND STRATHKELVIN AT GLASGOW

INITIAL WRIT

in the cause

SENGA GASTON, residing at Flat 2/34 Pork Market Street, Glasgow G23 7SF (Assisted Person)

PURSUER

against

ANGUS GASTON, residing at Flat 2/34 Pork Market Street, Glasgow G23 7SF

DEFENDER

The pursuer craves the court:

1. To divorce the defender from the pursuer on the ground that the marriage has broken down irretrievably as established by the defender's behaviour.

2. (1) To grant an exclusion order in terms of Section 4 of the Matrimonial Homes (Family Protection)(Scotland) Act 1981 suspending the defender's occupancy rights in the heritable subjects at Flat 2/34, Pork Market Street, Glasgow G23 7SF; (2) to grant warrant for the summary ejection of the defender therefrom; (3) to interdict the defender from entering the subjects without the express permission of the pursuer; and to attach a power of arrest to the interdict; and (4) to interdict the defender from removing, except with the written consent of the pursuer or by a further order of the court, any furniture or plenishings in the subjects, in terms of Sections 4(4) (a),(b) and (c) of the Act; and

3. To grant decree for the transfer of the tenancy of the subjects at Flat 2/34 Pork Market Street, Glasgow G23 7SF from the defender to the pursuer, in terms of Section 13(1) of the Act; and

4. To grant warrant to intimate this initial writ to Odette Burnett Housing Association Ltd, 77 Eisenhower Road, Glasgow G62 8GS as landlord of the matrimonial home at Flat 2/34 Pork Market Street, Glasgow G23 7SF, in terms of Section 13(4) of the Act.

5. To find the defender liable in expenses.

CONDESCENDENCE

1. The parties reside at Flat 2/34 Pork Market Street, Glasgow. They were married at Aberdeen on 11 November 2019. Extract marriage certificate is produced. They have no children. The parties are habitually resident in Scotland. The pursuer has been resident within the Sheriffdom of Glasgow and Strathkelvin for a period exceeding 40 days immediately preceding the raising of this action. Glasgow sheriff court accordingly has jurisdiction in terms of the Domicile and Matrimonial Proceedings Act 1973. The pursuer is unaware of any proceedings continuing in Scotland or elsewhere which are in respect of the marriage or which are capable of affecting its validity or subsistence.

2. Since the date of marriage the defender has behaved in such a way that the pursuer cannot reasonably be expected to cohabit with him. He consumes diazepam and fortified wine most days, causing him to become intoxicated and aggressive. He buys these drugs from dealers, whom he brings to the matrimonial home. On around 12 March, 18 and 22 April 2023 a youth invited to the matrimonial home by the defender stole cash and jewellery. The pursuer himself sells drugs, principally cannabis resin and MDMA. This breaches the defender's tenancy with Odette Burnett Housing Association Ltd and risks their both being evicted for anti-social behaviour.

3. On numerous occasions, including on 2 and 17 March and 4 and 30 April 2023 the pursuer was so drunk he left the front door wide open. At Christmas 2022 and mid-January 2023 he almost caused a house fire late at night by leaving bacon and sausages under a grill and then passing out. He was drunk or drugged. He threatened to expel the defender from the home by force if she objected to his behaviour. The marriage has broken down irretrievably. There is no prospect of a reconciliation. The pursuer seeks decree of divorce.

4. The pursuer seeks an exclusion order and ancillary orders as second craved. The matrimonial home is owned by Odette Burnett Housing Association. The defender is the sole tenant thereof.

5. An exclusion order is necessary for the protection of the pursuer's health. The defender's conduct has adversely affected her mental health. She developed sleep problems, anxiety and depression. She consulted her GP Dr Mukherjee at the Cygnus Health Centre, Glasgow. The doctor

prescribed a daily dose of 20mg fluoxetine anti-depressants. This was increased to 50mg, which is her current dose. In the circumstances, decree should be granted as second craved. Affidavits and a medical report will follow.

6. The ancillary orders should be granted. The defender is habitually drunk. When under the influence of alcohol, which is often, he is frequently unable to control his behaviour. He would be unlikely to possess the self-control to obtemper an interdict. The mere existence of an interdict is unlikely to afford the pursuer sufficient protection. A power of arrest is necessary.

7. An order for the transfer of the tenancy to the pursuer alone would be reasonable and appropriate in the circumstances. The defender has a friend, Jasper Baxter, with whom he has stayed recently.

8. The pursuer is a suitable person to be sole tenant of the subjects. She is in employment as an attendant at Chunky Gibbon Soft Play, Motherwell. She would meet the tenant's obligations under the lease, including paying rent. In the circumstances, decree should be granted as third craved.

PLEAS IN LAW

1. The marriage having broken down irretrievably, decree of divorce should be pronounced.

2. An exclusion order in terms of Section 4 of the Matrimonial Homes (Family Protection) (Scotland) Act 1981 being necessary for the protection of the health of the pursuer from reasonably apprehended conduct of the defender which would be injurious to her health, and the pursuer being entitled to the ancillary orders craved, an exclusion order suspending the defender's occupancy rights in the matrimonial home and orders ancillary thereto should be granted as second craved.

3. The pursuer being a non-entitled spouse and it being just and reasonable that the tenancy of the matrimonial home should be transferred from the defender to the pursuer, decree therefor in terms of Section 13 of the Matrimonial Homes (Family Protection) (Scotland) Act 1981 should be granted as third craved.

IN RESPECT WHEREOF

Solicitor

The Hope Law Centre

13 Neville Street, Glasgow

Agent for the pursuer

b. Affidavit of the pursuer

SHERIFFDOM OF GLASGOW AND STRATHKELVIN AT GLASGOW

AFFIDAVIT FOR THE PURSUER

in the cause

SENGA GASTON, [*designation*]

PURSUER

against

ANGUS GASTON, [*designation*]

DEFENDER

At Elgin the Second day of August Two Thousand and Twenty Two in the presence of CASPER HAUSER, Solicitor and Notary Public, 19 Hobbes Road, Glasgow COMPEARED SENGA GASTON [*designation*] who, being solemnly sworn, DEPONES as follows:

1. My full name is Senga Gaston. I was born on 26 October 1995. am 27 years old. I live at Flat 2/34 Pork Market Street, Glasgow G23 7SF. That property is owned by Odette Burnett Housing Association Ltd. My husband is the sole tenant. I am employed as an attendant at Chunky Gibbon Soft Play, Motherwell.

2. I married Angus Gaston at Aberdeen on 11 November 2019. We have no children. I produce an extract of our Marriage certificate, number 5/1 of process, which I have docquetted and signed as relative hereto.

3. My husband and I are habitually resident in Scotland. I was resident within the Sheriffdom of Glasgow and Strathkelvin for a period exceeding 40 days immediately preceding the raising of this action. I am unaware of any other proceedings continuing in Scotland or elsewhere which are in respect of my marriage or capable of affecting its validity or subsistence

4. Since our marriage my husband has consumed Valium tablets and 'Findo Gask' fortified wine on most days. This has caused him to become drunk and aggressive. He buys these tablets from dealers. He has invited them into our house. I find them intimidating. He knows that because I have told him often. On around 12 March, 18 and 22 April 2023 one of these men stole cash, bracelets and rings. Also, I am concerned that

the presence of drug dealers will get him and me into trouble with the landlord and the police. My husband himself sells drugs. These are mainly cannabis and ecstasy.

5. On numerous occasions, including on 2 and 17 March and 4 and 30 April 2023 my husband was so drunk he left the front door wide open. Anyone could have come in. At Christmas 2022 and in the middle of January 2023 he almost set the house on fire in the middle of the night by leaving food under a grill and then passing out drunk. I have challenged his behaviour but his reaction is always to threaten to throw me out because it is his flat. The marriage has broken down irretrievably. There is no prospect of a reconciliation. I seek decree of divorce.

6. Also, I seek an exclusion order and the other orders in my writ. As a result of my husband's behaviour I developed sleep problems, anxiety and depression. I never had any of these problems before the marriage. I consulted my G.P. Dr Mukherjee at the Cygnus Health Centre, Glasgow. She prescribed a daily dose of 20mg fluoxetine anti-depressants. This was increased to 50mg. I feel, and my doctor agrees, that this medication deals with the symptoms, but not the cause, of my health problems.

7. I do not seek any financial orders. My husband has a friend, Jasper Baxter. He stayed with him last month and could do so again if he had to move out of the flat. I wish to have the tenancy put into my sole name. I can afford to maintain the rent.

All of which is true as the deponent shall answer to God.

DEPONENT

NOTARY PUBLIC

4. RENDALL v RENDALL

Divorce — Two years non-cohabitation — Orders for financial provision — Transfer of property — Capital sum — Pension lump sum — Pension sharing — Incidental orders — Occupation of former matrimonial home — Liability for outgoings — Interest — Intimation to security holders — Intimation to persons responsible for pension scheme — Interim aliment

a. Initial writ

SHERIFFDOM OF GRAMPIAN HIGHLAND AND ISLANDS AT KIRKWALL

INITIAL WRIT

in the cause

EMILY RENDALL residing at 11 Quoyloo Road, Grimbister, Orkney KW15 8YD (Assisted Person),

PURSUER

against

MAGNUS RENDALL, residing at 8 Brodgar Place, Bimbister Orkney KW17 5DF

DEFENDER

The pursuer craves the court:

1. To divorce the defender from the pursuer on the ground that the marriage has broken down irretrievably as established by the parties' non-cohabitation for a period of two years, and;

2. To grant the pursuer interim aliment in the sum of THREE HUNDRED POUNDS (£300) STERLING per week, with interest thereon at 8 *per centum per annum* until payment, and;

3. To set aside the parties' Agreement dated 17 and 22 March 2018, in terms of Section 16(1) of the Family Law (Scotland) Act 1985, and;

4. To grant a property transfer order in terms of Section 8(1)(aa) of the Family Law (Scotland) Act 1985 transferring the defender's whole right,

title and interest in the matrimonial home at 8 Brodgar Place, Bimbister Orkney KW17 5DF and registered in the Land Register of Scotland under title number ZET2756, the furniture, contents and plenishings therein to the pursuer and to ordain the defender within 21 days of decree or within such other period as the court may direct to execute and deliver to the pursuer a valid Disposition of his said right, title and interest in the said matrimonial home and such other deeds as may be necessary to give the pursuer a valid title thereto, which failing to make an order dispensing with such execution and delivery by the defender and directing the sheriff clerk in terms of Section 87 of the Courts Reform (Scotland) Act 2014 to execute such disposition and other deeds, if any, in the pursuer's favour, all as adjusted at his sight, and;

5. In the event of decree being granted in terms of the second or third crave, to find the defender liable, as between the parties, for all sums due after the date of decree herein for such period as the court thinks fit to The Hyperion Building Society, 19 Dempster Road, Ballymena, Antrim BT42 8TS in respect of the loans and the standard security in its favour relative to the matrimonial home at 8 Brodgar Place, Bimbister, Orkney KW17 5DF, and;

6. To grant decree against the defender for payment to the pursuer of a capital sum of THIRTY THOUSAND POUNDS (£30,000) STERLING, with interest thereon at the rate of eight *per cent per annum* from 11 December 2017 or such other date as the court thinks fit until payment, and;

7. To grant warrant to intimate this initial writ to The Hyperion Building Society, 19 Dempster Road, Ballymena, Antrim BT42 8TS as holders of a standard security over the matrimonial home at 8 Brodgar Place, Bimbister, Orkney KW17 5DF

8. To find the defender liable in expenses.

CONDESCENDENCE

1. The parties are as designed in the instance. They were married at Aberdeen on 18 March 1994 and have no children under the age of 16 years. Relative marriage certificate is produced.

2. The pursuer has been resident within the Sheriffdom of Grampian, Highland and Islands for a period exceeding 40 days immediately preceding the raising of this action. This court has jurisdiction in terms of the Domicile and Matrimonial Proceedings Act 1973. The pursuer is unaware of any proceedings continuing in Scotland or elsewhere which are in respect of the marriage or are capable of affecting its validity or subsistence.

3. After their marriage the parties lived together until about 11 December 2017. Since then they have not lived together nor had marital relations. The marriage has broken down irretrievably. There is no prospect of a reconciliation. The pursuer seeks decree of divorce.

4. The defender has been called upon to aliment the pursuer. He refuses or at least delays to do so. Interim aliment should be granted as second craved. Schedules of parties' income, outgoings and resources (insofar as known to the pursuer) are produced.

5. From almost immediately after the parties' separation the defender persistently and relentlessly tried to persuade the defender to enter into a separation agreement. He telephoned and emailed the pursuer every day, often several times a day about the subject. He contacted her at night. The pursuer felt harassed and hounded. The defender presented the pursuer with an agreement that he stated he had drawn up himself. To avoid further pressure and stress, the pursuer signed the agreement. It is dated 17 and 22 March 2018.

6. The agreement should be set aside as being neither fair nor reasonable as at those dates. At no time prior to her signing the agreement had the pursuer had any legal advice. Neither did she know the extent of the defender's resources. The agreement prohibits the pursuer from seeking any financial provision in return for a payment to her of £10,000. Said sum was paid. The payment has been taken into account by the pursuer in terms of the financial provision now sought. The said sum is grossly inadequate and bears no relation to an award which would be justified by the provisions of Section 9 of the Act.

7. The pursuer seeks orders for financial provision as craved. She seeks a fair sharing of the net value of the matrimonial property. The pursuer's property at the relevant date comprised her interest in the matrimonial home at Brodgar Place, Bimbister Orkney KW17 5DF which she owned equally with the defender, company shares, and a current account holding around £1750. Valuations of the house and shares will be produced. The defender's property at that time included his share of the matrimonial home, a controlling interest in a company, Belladonna Herbal Ltd, cryptocurrency and life insurance policies.

8. The matrimonial home is subject to a secured loan by the Hyperion Building Society, 19 Dempster Road, Ballymena, Antrim BT42 8TS

9. The pursuer seeks fair account of economic advantage derived by the defender from contributions by her and of economic disadvantage suffered by her in the interests of the defender and of the family. She gave up her career as a driving instructor to look after the parties' home and children. This enabled the defender to accumulate property whilst she herself had to forego earnings and pension rights. The parties' said property constitutes their current resources. Accordingly, the defender has the resources to meet orders for financial provision as craved. Decree therefor should accordingly be pronounced.

PLEAS IN LAW

1. The marriage of the parties having broken down irretrievably, decree of divorce should be granted as craved.

2. The defender being obliged to provide reasonable support to the pursuer and the sum sued for being reasonable, interim aliment should be granted as craved, in terms of Section 6(1)(b) of the Family Law (Scotland) Act 1985.

3. The parties' Agreement dated 17 and 22 March 2018 being neither fair nor reasonable at the time it was entered into, as condescended upon should be set aside in terms of Section 16(1) of the Family Law (Scotland) Act 1985, and;

4. The orders for financial provision craved being justified by the principles set forth in Section 9(1)(a) and (b) of the Family Law (Scotland) Act 1985 and reasonable having regard to the resources of the parties, should be granted.

IN RESPECT WHEREOF

Solicitor

Calidore Street

Kirkwall, KW15 7TD

Agent for the pursuer

b. Specification of documents (OCR 28.2.(2)(a))

SHERIFFDOM OF GRAMPIAN HIGHLAND
AND ISLANDS AT KIRKWALL

KIR-F12-23

SPECIFICATION OF
DOCUMENTS

in respect of which a commission and
diligence is sought by the pursuer

in the cause

EMILY RENDALL, [*designation*]

PURSUER

against

MAGNUS RENDALL, [*designation*]

DEFENDER

1. All books of account, cash books and ledgers, USB sticks, VAT books, profit and loss accounts and balance sheets, and all other documents kept by or on behalf of Belladonna Herbal Ltd, Scapa Flow House, Kirkwall KW15 7RS so that excerpts may be taken therefrom at the sight of the commissioner of all entries therein showing or tending to show the value of the defender's interest in the company as at 11 December 2017 and as at the date hereof.

2. All lists of investments, stock, share and debenture certificates and dividend counterfoils, bank account statements, building society passbooks, USB sticks, IOUs, bonds, deposit receipts, insurance and assurance policies, pension plans and all other documents kept by or on behalf of the defender so that excerpts may be taken therefrom at the sight of the commissioner of all entries showing or tending to show the extent and value of the defender's moveable property as at 11 December 2017 and as at the date hereof.

3. All title deeds, back letters, valuations and all other documents kept by or on behalf of the defender so that excerpts may be taken therefrom at the sight of the commissioner of all entries therein showing or tending

to show the extent and value of the defender's heritable property as at 11 December 2017 and as at the date hereof.

4. Failing principals, drafts, copies or duplicates of the above or any of them.

IN RESPECT WHEREOF

[*designation*]

Agent for the pursuer

c. Joint minute of agreement (OCR 33.26.)

SHERIFFDOM OF GRAMPIAN HIGHLAND
AND ISLANDS AT KIRKWALL

KIR-F12-23

JOINT MINUTE OF
AGREEMENT

in the cause

EMILY RENDALL, [*designation*]

PURSUER

against

MAGNUS RENDALL, [*designation*]

DEFENDER

TATLOCK for the pursuer and HAIG for the defender state to the court that in the event of decree of divorce being granted and subject to the approval of the court the parties hereby agree as follows:

1. The defender shall repay the outstanding loan secured over the said heritable property in favour of the Hyperion Building Society, 19 Dempster Road, Ballymena, Antrim BT42 8TS within 14 days of the date of decree.

2. The defender shall dispone to the pursuer his whole right, title and interest in the heritable property at 8 Brodgar Place, Bimbister Orkney KW17 5DF and registered in the Land Register of Scotland under title number ZET2756 and shall deliver to the pursuer within one month of the date of decree a valid Disposition of his said right, title and interest in the said heritable property.

3. The sheriff clerk at Kirkwall shall be directed by the court to execute such disposition and other deeds, if any, in the pursuer's favour, all as adjusted at his sight in the event of a Disposition not having been delivered within one month as aforesaid;

4. The defender shall be liable for the expenses of the action as taxed; and

5. *Quoad ultra* the defender shall be assoilzied from the craves of the initial writ.

The parties move the court to interpone authority hereto and to grant decree in terms hereof.

IN RESPECT WHEREOF

[*designation*]
Agent for the pursuer

Solicitor
Saxony Legal (Scotland) LLP
Basement Street, Dundee
Agent for the defender

5. BAZALGETTE v BEAUREGARD

Cessation of cohabitation — Claim under Section 28, Family Law (Scotland) Act 2006.

a. Initial writ

SHERIFFDOM OF GLASGOW AND STRATHKELVIN AT GLASGOW

INITIAL WRIT

in the cause

GERARD BAZALGETTE residing at 103 Sproston Green, Cardiff CF10 6TD

PURSUER

against

FINDLAY BEAUREGARD residing at 16, Vesuvius Hill, Glasgow G5 8DS

DEFENDER

The pursuer craves the court:

1. To grant decree for payment by the defender to the pursuer in the sum of FORTY FIVE THOUSAND POUNDS (£45,000) STERLING with interest thereon at eight *per centum per annum* from 26 March 2022 or from such other date as to the court shall seem fit, in terms of Section 28 of the Family Law (Scotland) Act 2006, and;
2. To find the defender liable in expenses.

CONDESCENDENCE

1. The parties are as designed in the instance. Formerly, they cohabited in a same sex relationship as husband and husband. They did so between 16 March 2019 and 26 March 2022. They were cohabitants as defined by Section 25 of the Family Law (Scotland) Act 2006.
2. Glasgow Sheriff Court is the appropriate court as defined by Section 28(9)(b) of the Act. The pursuer knows of no proceedings continuing in Scotland or elsewhere which are in respect of the subject matter of this initial writ.

3. The defender enjoyed economic advantage as a result of contributions made by the pursuer. The pursuer suffered economic disadvantage in the interests of the defender. The pursuer seeks an order for payment as craved. The pursuer is unemployed and in receipt of benefits. He has no capital. The defender is in full time employment and earning in excess of £65,000 net *per annum*. He is believed to have significant capital. The pursuer was dependent upon the defender for financial support during the cohabitation. Accordingly, decree should be granted as craved.

4. This action is raised to prevent the claim becoming time barred. Further details will follow of the matters narrated in Section 28 of the Act.

PLEA IN LAW

The defender having enjoyed economic advantage as a result of contributions made by the pursuer, the pursuer having suffered economic disadvantage in the interests of the defender, as condescended upon, and the sum sought being reasonable, decree should be granted as craved.

IN RESPECT WHEREOF

Solicitor
85 Chatterton Court, Glasgow
Agent for the pursuer

6. JEFFERSON v BYRD AND LOVE

Declarator of non-parentage and of parentage

a. Initial writ, including minute for decree (Form F27)

SHERIFFDOM OF GRAMPIAN HIGHLAND
AND ISLANDS AT BANFF

INITIAL WRIT

in the cause

GRACE JEFFERSON, residing at 65 Tobacco Road, Portsoy AB45 9TN

PURSUER

against

GENE BYRD, residing at 3 Rhymney Avenue, Portsoy AB45 5RW

FIRST NAMED DEFENDER

and

ARTHUR LOVE, residing at 3 Glendale Boulevard, Turriff AB53 9TE

SECOND NAMED DEFENDER

The pursuer craves the court:

1. To find and declare that Gene Byrd, residing at 3, Rhymney Avenue, Portsoy AB45 5RW is not the father of MARTIN JEFFERSON born on 17 September 2022 and residing at 65 Tobacco Road, Portsoy AB45 9TN, and;

2. To find and declare that Arthur Love, residing at 3, Glendale Boulevard, Turriff AB53 9TE is the father of MARTIN JEFFERSON born on 17 September 2022 and residing at 65, Tobacco Road, Portsoy AB45 9TN, and;

3. To find the first named defender liable in the expenses of the action in the event of opposition thereto, and;

4. To find the second named defender liable in the expenses of the action in the event of opposition thereto.

CONDESCENDENCE

1. The parties are as designed in the instance. The pursuer is the mother of Martin Jefferson (hereinafter referred to as 'the child'). The child was born on 17 September 2022. He was born within the Sheriffdom of Grampian Highland and Islands. He lives with the pursuer at her address in the instance.

2. Said address is within the said Sheriffdom at Portsoy. The child's birth was registered in Banff. He is habitually resident at the pursuer's said address. This court has jurisdiction by virtue of Section 7 of the Law Reform (Parent and Child) (Scotland) Act 1986. Both defenders are domiciled in the said sheriffdom. The pursuer is unaware of any proceedings pending in Scotland or elsewhere which are in respect of the subject matter of this Initial Writ. There is produced herewith an extract of the Certificate of Birth relating to the child.

3. In around Christmas 2021 the pursuer had sexual relations with both defenders. She and the first named defender believed that he was the child's father. Accordingly, the first named defender signed the child's birth certificate to indicate his paternity.

4. The pursuer came to have doubts over whether the first named defender was the child's father. The child and both defenders were the subject of DNA profiling testing. The test report states that the probability of the first named defender's being the child's father is 0% and the probability of the second named defender's being the child's father is 99.99 %, The test reports and relative technical data are produced herewith and referred to for their terms which are produced herewith and referred to for their terms which are incorporated herein for the sake of brevity

5. The first named defender is not the father of the child. Instead, the second named defender is the child's father. The child's birth certificate is incorrect.

6. Solicitors instructed on behalf of the pursuer wrote to the Registrar General for Scotland on 13 January 2023 to request that the Register of Births be corrected. It was submitted that the error was more than a clerical or similar error remediable in terms of Section 42(2) and (3) of the Registration of Births, Deaths and Marriages (Scotland) Act 1965. Instead, a request was made for correction in terms of Section 42(5) of the Act.

7. The Registrar responded in term of a letter of 11 February 2023. The letter advised that in order to remove the first named defender's details from the child's birth entry in the Register the Registrar would require sight of a Declarator of Parentage/Non-Parentage granted by the sheriff.

8. Accordingly, decree is sought as craved. The orders sought are necessary to allow the rectification of the Register of Births, Deaths and Marriages.

PLEAS IN LAW

1) The first named defender not being the father of Martin Jefferson, born on 17 September 2022, decree of declarator should be granted as first craved.

2) The second named defender being the father of Martin Jefferson, born on 17 September 2022, decree of declarator should be granted as second craved.

IN RESPECT WHEREOF

Dryden and MacLean
1 George Street, Banff
Aberdeenshire
AB45 8TR
Agent for the pursuer

BALIN for the pursuer, having considered the evidence contained in the affidavits and other document specified in the schedule hereto and being satisfied that upon the evidence a motion for decree in terms of the first and second craves may properly be made, moves the court accordingly.

IN RESPECT WHEREOF

Agent for the pursuer

SCHEDULE

1. Affidavit of the pursuer.
2. Affidavit of the second named defender.
3. Extract birth certificate of Martin Jefferson.
4. Report from Hesperus Laboratories Ltd, 17 December 2022.
5. Letter dated 11 February 2023.

b. Affidavit of pursuer (OCR 33.28.(2))

SHERIFFDOM OF GRAMPIAN HIGHLAND
AND ISLANDS AT BANFF

BAN-F36-23
AFFIDAVIT OF THE PURSUER

in the cause

GRACE JEFFERSON, [*designation*]

PURSUER

against

GENE BYRD, [*designation*]

FIRST NAMED DEFENDER

and

ARTHUR LOVE, [*designation*]

SECOND NAMED DEFENDER

At Banff on the Eighteenth day of March Two Thousand and Twenty Three in the presence of LEE DRYDEN, Solicitor and Notary Public, 1 George Street, Banff COMPEARED GRACE JEFFERSON, residing at 65, Tobacco Road, Portsoy AB45 9TN who being solemnly sworn, DEPONES as follows:

1. My full name is Grace Jefferson. I was born on 16 May 2001. I am employed as a hairdresser. I reside at 65 Tobacco Road, Portsoy AB45 9TN with my son Martin Jefferson.

2. I went to school with Gene Byrd and Arthur Love. They are the defenders in this case. I was friends with both of them. That remains so. At around Christmas 2021 I went to several parties. I had sexual relations with Gene Byrd on several occasions and once with Arthur Love.

3. On 17 September 2022 I gave birth to my son Martin Jefferson. I refer to the extract of the entry in the Register of Births, no 5/1 of process, which I have docquetted and signed as relative hereto.

4. At first I assumed that Gene Byrd was Martin's father. He believed so too. That is why he signed the birth certificate. Then I had doubts. Both Gene Byrd and Arthur Love agreed to provide DNA so that a paternity test could be undertaken. This test went ahead and I refer to the report from Hesperus Laboratories Ltd, 17 December 2022 no 5/2 of process, which I have docquetted and signed as relative hereto.

5. The report states that the chances of Gene Byrd being Martin's father are 0% and the chances of Arthur Love being Martin's father is 99.99 %. In light of this my view is that the birth certificate is wrong. My solicitor contacted the Register of Births Deaths and Marriages to see if the register could be changed. They responded to say that in order to remove Gene Byrd's details from Martin's birth entry in the Register they would need to see a court order declaring the identity of Martin's true father.

6. I am seeking the declarators sought in my writ so that steps can then be taken to get the Register of Births Deaths and Marriages corrected.

All of which is truth as the deponent shall answer to God.

DEPONENT

NOTARY PUBLIC

c. Affidavit of witness (OCR 33.28.(2))

SHERIFFDOM OF GRAMPIAN HIGHLAND
AND ISLANDS AT BANFF

BAN-F36-23

AFFIDAVIT OF ARTHUR LOVE

in the cause

GRACE JEFFERSON, [*designation*]

PURSUER

against

GENE BYRD, [*designation*]

FIRST NAMED DEFENDER

and

ARTHUR LOVE, [*designation*]

SECOND NAMED DEFENDER

At Banff on the Eighteenth day of March Two Thousand and Twenty Three in the presence of LEE DRYDEN, Solicitor and Notary Public, 1 George Street, Banff COMPEARED ARTHUR LOVE, residing at 3 Glendale Boulevard, Turriff AB53 9TE who being solemnly sworn, DEPONES as follows:

1. My full name is Arthur Love. I was born on 3 January 2001. I am unemployed. I live at 3 Glendale Boulevard, Turriff AB53 9TE
2. I have known Grace Jefferson for many years. At around Christmas 2021 I had sexual relations with her.
3. I knew that in September 2022 she birth to a boy whom she named Martin. I did not consider that I might be his father. In around October she approached me and said that she thought that I might be Martin's father. She asked if I would provide a DNA sample. I did so. A paternity

test took place and I understand that there is an almost 100% likelihood that I am Martin's father.

4. I have seen Martin's birth certificate and it shows Gene Byrd is being Martin's father. I am on friendly terms with Gene, and he told me that he had thought that he was the father, but that the test now shows otherwise.

5. I understand that Ms Jefferson wants to have the birth certificate changed and I am supportive of that. So is Gene.

All of which is truth as the deponent shall answer to God.

DEPONENT

NOTARY PUBLIC

7. REDDITCH v O'REILLY

Children (Scotland) Act 1995 — Section 11 order — Contact

a. Closed Record

SHERIFFDOM OF TAYSIDE CENTRAL AND FIFE
AT STIRLING

STI-F77-23

CLOSED RECORD

In the cause

RYAN REDDITCH, residing at 17 Bladder Road, Bridge of Allan FK9 6RE (Assisted Person)

PURSUER

against

BERNADETTE O'REILLY residing at 58 Watchmakers Gait, Stirling FK8 6RQ (Assisted Person)

DEFENDER

The pursuer craves the court:

1. To make a contact order in terms of Section 11 of the Children (Scotland) Act 1995 in respect of KHALEESI O'REILLY born on 17 March 2016 whereby she is to be with the pursuer each alternate weekend between 5pm on Friday until 3pm on Saturday and each alternate Wednesday from 5pm until 7pm, or during such other period or periods as the court shall think fit,

2. To make a specific issue order in respect of KHALEESI O'REILLY born on 17 March 2016 whereby she should attend the wedding of Gloria Redditch at the Blessed Brian Abbey House, Stirling on Saturday 21 January 2023.

3. To grant warrant to intimate Form 9 in the terms of the draft attached to KHALEESI O'REILLY born on 17 March 2016 as a child to whom the order sought would relate, and;

4. To find the defender liable in expenses as taxed.

CONDESCENDENCE and ANSWERS

1) The parties are as designed in the instance. They were in a relationship from around 2015 to 2021. The parties are the parents of Khaleesi O'Reilly. She was born on 17 March 2016. An extract of the child's certificate of birth is produced herewith.

Ans 1

Admitted.

2) The child is habitually resident in the Sheriffdom of Tayside Central and Fife. Accordingly, this court has jurisdiction in terms of Section 9 of the Family Law Act 1986. The pursuer is unaware of any proceedings continuing or concluded in Scotland or elsewhere which relate to the child. No permanence order (as defined in Section 80(2) of the Adoption and Children (Scotland) Act 2007) is in force in respect of the child.

Ans 2

Admitted.

3) When the parties separated the child was five years old and about to enter P1 at St Ternan's Primary School, Stirling. The parties agreed that they would refrain from arranging a contact schedule until the child was settled at school. Denied that the defender asked the pursuer to discuss contact.

Ans 3

Denied. At the time of the parties' separation the pursuer was in another relationship with a woman at his workplace in Hillington, Glasgow. He wished to spend time with her rather than with the child. The defender repeatedly asked the pursuer to discuss a contact arrangement with her. He refused to do so.

4) In around 2022 the parties discussed contact. It was agreed that the pursuer have contact each Sunday from 12 noon to 6pm and on a Tuesday evening for two hours. Contact operated under this arrangement until 2022 when the defender stopped contact.

Ans 4

Admitted, under explanation that the pursuer consistently failed to adhere to the arrangement or indeed any other arrangement. The parties changed the Tuesday to Wednesday to accommodate the pursuer's work shifts and he failed to adhere to that too.

5) Following the raising of these proceedings the parties reached agreement about interim contact and the court granted an order reflecting the agreed terms. At the continued Child Welfare Hearing on 10 August 2022 interim contact was granted and the cause sisted to monitor it. With reference to the Answer, admitted that the pursuer was late by 30 minutes on Saturday 19 August 2022 under explanation that whilst travelling east the pursuer found himself in traffic congestion on the M8 west of the Kingston Bridge, Glasgow. The pursuer did not have the use of a hands-free telephone

in his car and could not alert the defender to his lateness until he was able to pull off the motorway at Charing Cross. This added to his lateness. Admitted that the pursuer has been late on other occasions and that he has not attended on others under explanation that his work commitments interfered with his ability to adhere to an arrangement. The defender is a car salesman with Bucephalus Autos Ltd. He was based at the company's showroom at Hillington, Glasgow. He was required to work late if necessary and with no notice. Had he not done so he would have lost his job.

Ans 5

Admitted that interim contact was granted on 10 August 2022. On every Saturday thereafter the pursuer was either late or failed to attend at all. In particular, he was late on 3 and 17 September (by over an hour), he failed to attend on 1 October and was late on 15 October. The defender warned the pursuer that if he was late on 29 October she would enroll a motion to terminate interim contact. The defender was late. As a result the child missed a Hallowe'en party. The pursuer agreed not to exercise contact until his work situation stabilized. However, since then the child has been adamant that she does not wish to see the pursuer.

6) The child enjoyed and benefitted from the contact that she had with the pursuer. He regularly took her to hip hop dance classes at the Bremner Centre, Raploch, Stirling. He took her to visit his sister and nieces in Denny.

Ans 6

Admitted that the child enjoyed the contact arranged by agreement until the pursuer began to arrive later or not at all. She then became upset and disappointed. The pursuer become increasingly unreliable to the point where the child no longer wished to suffer the distress and sense of rejection that the pursuer inevitably caused.

7) The pursuer's sister, Gloria Redditch, has invited the pursuer and the child and indeed the defender to attend her wedding at the Blessed Brian Abbey House in Stirling on Saturday 21 January 2023. The child would enjoy the wedding and would benefit from attending it and meeting her wider family.

Ans 7

The defender has asked the child on several occasions whether she wishes to attend the wedding. She does not wish to do so. The child was under four years old when she last met Gloria Redditch. She has little or no connection with her paternal family. This is due to the pursuer's failure to foster any such connection. The specific issue order sought would not benefit the child. It should be refused.

8) It is in the best interests of the child that the orders sought be granted. The pursuer is now in a position to adhere to a structured and regular contact arrangement. In October 2022 he was moved to his employer's showroom at Bonnybridge. The pursuer can reach the defender's address in under 15 minutes and without concerns over traffic

congestion. Accordingly seeks decree as first craved. The child would benefit from attendance at the wedding Accordingly, decree should be granted as second craved.

Ans 8

Denied. An order for contact would not benefit the child. The specific issue order sought would not benefit the child. It should be refused.

PLEA-IN-LAW FOR PURSUER

It being in the best interests of the child that the orders sought be made, decree therefor should be granted as craved.

PLEA-IN-LAW FOR DEFENDER

It not being in the best interests of the child that the orders sought be made, decree therefor should not be granted as craved.

IN RESPECT WHEREOF

solicitor
Cossack Legal
17 Alma Road
Camelon FK1 6WR
Agent for the pursuer

solicitor
Raglan and Cardigan
1 Inkerman Street,
Linlithgow EH49 8GS
Agent for the defender

b. Joint Minute – OCR 33AA.3.(2)

SHERIFFDOM OF TAYSIDE CENTRAL AND FIFE AT STIRLING

STI-F77-23

JOINT MINUTE
of the parties' pre-hearing conference

In terms of OCR 33AA.3.(2)

in the cause

RYAN REDDITCH, [*designation*]

PURSUER

against

BERNADETTE O'REILLY,
[*designation*]

DEFENDER

STATEMENT

1) The conference took place on 11 October 2022 and lasted 30 minutes. The pursuer and his agent Ms Soper met the defender and her agent Mr Lennie. The meeting was by Zoom teleconferencing.

2) The parties discussed settlement of the action. Settlement could not be reached. The defender opposes contact and the child's attendance at the wedding of Gloria Redditch.

3) The parties agreed that some matters are not disputed.

4) The parties discussed the information referred to in OCR 33AA 4.(1). They agreed that the key issue is the pursuer's reliability. The pleadings do not require to be amended given that interim contact has not been exercised since 12 November 2022 and the pursuer has undertaken not to seek to exercise it until the court issues a further direction. Both parties are prepared for proof. Each of them intends to give evidence.

5) The pursuer will speak to his relationship to the child, the problems that caused his lateness and non-attendance for visits and the steps that he will take to be able to exercise contact reliably in future. The defender

will speak to the history of contact visits, the problems that there have been, the effect on this child and why she believes that these would continue were contact to resume. The pursuer has no other witnesses. The defender wishes to call her mother, Mrs Bridget O'Reilly, to speak to the effects on the child of the pursuer's repeated failures to attend for contact visits.

6) Neither party wishes to lodge affidavits. This would not save any significant time. Including cross-examination the evidence of all three witnesses should be concluded in two hours. Parties would then immediately wish to proceed to submissions.

7) The law is simply that the court has to determine what is in the child's best interests. Neither party intends to cite any case law, as each scenario turns on its own merits.

8) The productions are agreed. There is no dispute that the screenshot printouts, 6/1 to 6/14 of process are authentic copies of messages sent.

c. Motion

SHERIFFDOM OF TAYSIDE CENTRAL AND FIFE AT STIRLING

STI-F77-23

MOTION FOR THE DEFENDER

in the cause

RYAN REDDITCH, [*designation*]

PURSUER

against

BERNADETTE O'REILLY, [*designation*]

RESPONDENT

LENNIE for the defender moves the court

1) In terms of OCR 29.18.(1) to dispense with the recording of evidence at the proof assigned for 18 September 2023 on the bases that:

- a) The parties are impecunious and wish to avoid the cost of the attendance of a shorthand writer.
- b) The evidence is likely to be short and simple.
- c) The parties understand and accept that the absence of a record of the proof will be highly detrimental to their ability to appeal, and;

2) With the greatest of respect to the court and on the specific instructions of the defender that Sheriff Tiraspol consider whether he might decline jurisdiction in relation to the proof in respect that the defender considers that his advising her at the Child Welfare Hearings on 12 March 2023 that she was 'a terrible mother' and on 17 April 2023 that she did 'not have the child's interests at heart' demonstrate disfavour towards her such as that it would be preferable to have the proof heard by another sheriff who would approach the matter afresh.

IN RESPECT WHEREOF

[designation]
Agent for the defender

8. MACFARQUHAR v MACFARQUHAR

Matrimonial home — Dispensation with non-entitled spouse's consent to dealing with matrimonial home

a. Initial writ (OCR 33.67.(2))

SHERIFFDOM OF NORTH STRATHCLYDE AT DUMBARTON

SUMMARY APPLICATION
UNDER THE MATRIMONIAL
HOMES (FAMILY PROTECTION)
(SCOTLAND) ACT 1981, s 7

INITIAL WRIT

in the cause

DUNSTAN MACFARQUHAR residing at 23 Stalin Road, Clydebank G81 7RD

PURSUER

against

BRONWEN MACFARQUHAR, residing c/o Leon, 17 Laird's Gate, Cochno G81 5GW

DEFENDER

The pursuer craves the court:

1. To grant decree dispensing with the consent of Bronwen MacFarquhar to the sale of the heritable subjects at 23 Stalin Road, Clydebank G81 7RD by the pursuer to Krish and Aashvi Mukherjee, residing at 16 Burne-Jones Road, Birmingham B29 8DH, in terms of missives dated 12 February and 6 and 18 March, all 2023.
2. To find the defender liable in the expenses of the action.

CONDESCENDENCE

1. The parties are as designed. They are spouses. They separated in summer 2022.

2. This action concerns rights *in rem* in immoveable property at 23 Stalin Road, Clydebank G81 7RD ('the subjects') located in North Strathclyde. This court has jurisdiction in terms of Section 20 and Rule 5(1)(b) of Schedule 8 to the Civil Jurisdiction and Judgments Act 1982.

3. The pursuer is the sole heritable proprietor of the subjects. They are a matrimonial home. In terms of Section 1(7) of the Matrimonial Homes (Family Protection) (Scotland) Act 1981 the defender still has occupancy rights in the subjects.

4. Upon the parties' separation and in terms of an email dated 11 January 2023 the defender advised the pursuer that she had no objection to his selling the subjects. She led him to believe that she would consent. There has been no relevant change in circumstances in the meantime. Section 7(2)(a) of the 1981 Act applies.

5. In reliance upon this representation the pursuer concluded missives dated 12 February and 6 and 18 March, all 2023, the buyers are Krish and Aashvi Mukherjee. They have sold their own property.

6. The defender now refuses to swear a matrimonial homes affidavit, jeopardising the transaction and putting the pursuer in a position where he could be sued for breach of contract. She has failed to explain why.

7. On separation the defender moved to stay with a man named Noel Leon. They are cohabiting. The defender has no need of the subjects. Equity in the subjects is only about £5,000 due to the level of secured debt over it. There are no children of the marriage.

8. In these circumstances, the defender has withheld her consent unreasonably and the court should, in terms of Section 7(1) of the said Act, dispense with the consent of the defender to the pursuer's proposed dealing with the subjects.

PLEA IN LAW

The defender having withheld her consent unreasonably to a proposed dealing, and having regard to the matters specified in Section 3(3) of the Matrimonial Homes (Family Protection) (Scotland) Act 1981 the court should, in terms of Section 7(1) of the said Act, dispense with the consent of the defender to the pursuer's proposed dealing with the subjects

IN RESPECT WHEREOF

solicitor
4 Whisky Grove, Kilmarnock
Agent for the pursuer

IV PAYMENT ACTIONS

1. PICAROON PLATES AND PARTS LTD v CATHAY CLEANSING SYSTEMS LTD

Commercial Action – Payment — Debt — Sale of goods — Damages — Breach of contract — Satisfactory quality and fitness for purpose — Interest on commercial debt — Interest on damages for breach of contract — Retention

a. Initial writ

SHERIFFDOM OF TAYSIDE CENTRAL AND FIFE
AT PERTH

FORM G1A
COMMERCIAL ACTION

INITIAL WRIT

in the cause

PICAROON PLATES AND PARTS LIMITED, a company registered under the Companies Acts, number SC123456, and having a place of business at 17 Walter Street, Glasgow G3 7SL

PURSUER

against

CATHAY CLEANSING SYSTEMS LIMITED, a company registered under the Companies Acts, number SC789112, and having a place of business at 83 Galloway Street, Dundee DD3 7LT

DEFENDER

The pursuer craves the court:

1. To grant decree against the defender for payment to the pursuer of the sum of SIXTEEN THOUSAND NINE HUNDRED AND EIGHTY

FIVE POUNDS FOURTEEN PENCE (£16,985.14) STERLING with interest thereon from 2 August 2022 until payment at the rate of eight *per centum per annum* above the Bank of England's official dealing rate in force as at 30 June 2022, and;

2. To grant decree against the defender for payment to the pursuer of the sum of ONE HUNDRED POUNDS (£100) STERLING as compensation under Section 5A of the Late Payment of Commercial Debts (Interest) Act 1998 as amended, and;

3. To find the defender liable in expenses.

CONDESCENDENCE

1. The parties are as designed in the instance.

2. The defender is domiciled at 83 Galloway Street, Dundee DD3 7LT. That address is within the Sheriffdom of Tayside Central and Fife. Perth sheriff court has jurisdiction in terms of Section 20 of and Rule 1 of Schedule 8 to the Civil Jurisdiction and Judgments Act 1982 and the Sheriff Principal's Practice Note No. 1 of 2020.

3. On about 4 June 2022 the defender requested the supply by the pursuer of 18 A.G. Buccaneer 20 bar steam boilers.

4. On 7 June 2022 the parties entered a written contract therefor. In terms of the contract the agreed price was £16,985.14 inclusive of VAT, payable within 7 days of supply. The pursuer supplied the boilers on 26 June 2022. The pursuer sent an invoice to the defender that same day.

5. The defender has failed to make payment of the said sum, despite repeatedly being called upon to do so. Accordingly, this action is necessary.

6. The contract falls within the scope of Section 2 of the Late Payment of Commercial Debts (Interest) Act 1998 as amended. Interest at the rate craved is payable 30 days from the date on which the debt arose.

PLEAS IN LAW

1) The pursuer having sold and delivered goods to the defender on the order of the defender, is entitled to payment of the price thereof.

2) The sum sued for being the price agreed by the parties, decree should be granted therefor, with expenses.

3) Interest at the rate craved being due by the defender in terms of the Payment of Commercial Debts (Interest) Act 1998 as amended, decree should be granted as craved.

4) Compensation in the sum of £100 being payable by the defender in terms of Section 5A of the Late Payment of Commercial Debts (Interest) Act 1998 as amended, decree should be granted as second craved.

IN RESPECT WHEREOF

Solicitor
Byers and Callaghan
3 French Street, Glasgow
Agent for the pursuer

APPENDIX FOR PURSUER (Ordinary Cause Rule 40.7(2)).

1) Email from Kurt Becker, pursuer's sales manager, 6 June 2022.
2) Copy Agreement dated 7 June 2022.
3) Email from Alistair Blake, defender's administrator, 26 June 2022.
4) Copy invoice, 26 June 2022.

b. Reponing note

SHERIFFDOM OF TAYSIDE CENTRAL AND FIFE AT PERTH

PER-CA1-23
REPONING NOTE

for the defender

in the cause

PICAROON PLATES AND PARTS LIMITED, [*designation*]

PURSUER

against

CATHAY CLEANSING SYSTEMS LIMITED, [*designation*]

DEFENDER

The defender applies to be reponed in terms of Ordinary Cause Rule 8.1(1):

The proposed defence

The goods sold to the defender by the pursuer were not of satisfactory quality nor fit for the purpose for which they were purchased, all as more particularly detailed in the defences and counterclaim produced with this Note. The pursuer is in material breach of contract. That breach has caused the defender loss and damage, as explained in the defences and counterclaim. The defender is entitled to withhold payment of any sum due to the pursuer pending resolution of the counterclaim.

Explanation for the failure to lodge a Notice of Intention to Defend

Service of the initial writ was made upon the defender by recorded delivery post on 8 September 2022. The writ was signed for by an employee of the defender whose employment was terminated several days later for reasons unconnected with this action. The employee left the writ in a desk drawer. Decree in absence passed on 10 October 2022.

By chance, the writ was discovered on 14 October 2022. Steps were then immediately taken to submit this Note.

IN RESPECT WHEREOF

Solicitor
Allan and Irvine
1 March Street, Dundee
Agent for the defender

c. Defences and counterclaim (OCR 19.1.)

SHERIFFDOM OF TAYSIDE, CENTRAL AND FIFE
AT PERTH

PER-CA1-23

DEFENCES AND COUNTERCLAIM

in the cause

PICAROON PLATES AND PARTS LIMITED, [*designation*]

PURSUER

against

CATHAY CLEANSING SYSTEMS LIMITED, [*designation*]

DEFENDER

The defender craves the court:

1. To grant decree against the pursuer for payment to the defender of the sum of TWELVE THOUSAND EIGHT HUNDRED AND EIGHTY FOUR POUNDS TWENTY SIX PENCE (£12,884.26) STERLING, with interest thereon at the rate of eight *per centum per annum* from 28 October 2022 until payment.
2. To find the pursuer liable in the expenses of the counterclaim.

ANSWERS TO CONDESCENDENCE

1. Admitted that the defender has not made payment of the invoice. The goods were boilers each with a capacity of 250 litres. They were manufactured by A.G. Buccaneer Ltd, The boilers were to be installed in the workplaces of customers of the defender for laundry sterilisation purposes. The pursuer was aware of this.
2. It was an implied term of the contract that the boilers should be of satisfactory quality and should be reasonably fit for the purpose of providing steam in laundry sterilisation facilities. Reference is made to the Sale of Goods Act 1979, s 14(2) and (3).

3. The boilers were not of satisfactory quality. They were not reasonably fit for said purpose. This was by reason of the defects as stated in the statement of facts.

4. Accordingly, the pursuer is in breach of contract. As a result, the defender has suffered loss and damage as specified in the statement of facts. The defender is therefore entitled to retain the sum sued for pending resolution of the counterclaim.

STATEMENT OF FACTS

1. The boilers were delivered by the pursuer to the defender. The defender then sold them to customers in whose workplaces they were installed.

2. Thereafter, each boiler leaked steam at the point of its junction with the premises' pipework.

3. The cause of the leakages was the defective manufacture of the boiler valves.

4. According to the specification issued by the valve manufacturers, the walls of the valves ought to have a consistent thickness of 4mm.

5. In the boilers supplied by the pursuer, the thickness of the walls varied from 2.5mm to 4.5mm. The variations occurred over small areas. The surface of the walls were pitted and ridged randomly. The irregularities exceeded normal manufacturing tolerances.

6. As a result of these irregularities, it was impossible to achieve a watertight union of pipes with the boilers. Consequently, the boilers leaked.

7. In these circumstances, the pursuer was in breach of the aforesaid implied terms. The boilers were not of satisfactory quality. They were not reasonably fit for the purpose of safely generating steam for use in laundry sterilisation. They had present in them defects which rendered them liable to leak when pipes were connected to them. As a result, the defender suffered loss and damage.

8. As a consequence of the leakages, damage was caused to the said workplaces. The said boilers required to be repaired. On or about 1 November 2022 the defender paid their customers around £12,884.26 as reparation. This was a reasonable sum.

9. This sum comprised costs of replacing the valves with others made by another manufacturer and in compensating customers for loss of profit sustained as a result of their laundry businesses being inoperative whilst faults were diagnosed and rectified. A schedule of losses will be produced hereafter.

10. The pursuer has been called upon to make reparation to the defender for the defender's loss and damage. The pursuer refuses or at least delays unreasonably to do so. Accordingly, this counterclaim is necessary.

PLEAS IN LAW

1. The defender having suffered loss and damage through the pursuer's breach of contract and being entitled to damages therefor, is entitled to retain any sum due to the pursuer pending resolution of the counterclaim.

2. The defender having suffered loss and damage through the pursuer's breach of contract, is entitled to damages from the pursuer as counterclaimed.

3. The sum sued for being a reasonable estimate of the defender's loss and damage, decree should be pronounced in terms of the first crave of the counterclaim.

IN RESPECT WHEREOF

[*designation*]
Agent for the defender

APPENDIX FOR THE DEFENDER

1) Email from John Edgar Ltd, 26 August 2022.
2) Email from Industrial and Medical Hygiene Ltd, 3 September 2022.
3) Product Specification (2019 ed,) A.G. Buccaneer.
4) Report from Keith Allman, engineer, 18 September 2022.
5) Invoice dated 19 September 2022.
6) Email exchange between parties, 13 July to 24 September 2022 (16 emails).

d. Motion for leave to appeal to the Sheriff Appeal Court (OCR 31.2.)

SHERIFFDOM OF TAYSIDE, CENTRAL AND FIFE
AT PERTH

PER-CA1-23

MOTION FOR THE PURSUER

in the cause

PICAROON PLATES AND PARTS LIMITED, [*designation*]

PURSUER

against

CATHAY CLEANSING SYSTEMS DOUGLAS LIMITED, [*designation*]

DEFENDER

ROSENCRANTZ for the pursuer moves the court for leave to appeal the Interlocutor of 6 December 2022 to the Sheriff Appeal Court, in terms of Ordinary Cause Rule 31.2.

IN RESPECT WHEREOF

[*designation*]
Agent for the defender

e. Motion for summary decree (OCR 17.2.) which failing interim decree

SHERIFFDOM OF TAYSIDE, CENTRAL AND FIFE
AT PERTH

PER-CA1-23

MOTION FOR THE PURSUER

in the cause

PICAROON PLATES AND PARTS LIMITED, [*designation*]

PURSUER

against

CATHAY CLEANSING SYSTEMS DOUGLAS LIMITED, [*designation*]

DEFENDER

ROSENCRANTZ for the defender moves the court:

1) In respect that for the purposes of OCR 17.2. the defender's case has no real prospect of success and there is no compelling reason why decree should not be granted at this stage, to grant decree as craved with expenses as taxed in favour of the pursuer, which failing;

2) In respect that the sum sued for is £16,985.14 and the defence (insofar as relevant) pertains to the sum of £12,884.26 only, to grant interim decree for the sum of £4,100.88.

IN RESPECT WHEREOF

[*designation*]
Agent for the defender

f. Motion for pursuers (limited company) to be ordained to find caution (OCR 27.2.)

SHERIFFDOM OF TAYSIDE, CENTRAL AND FIFE
AT PERTH

PER-CA1-23

MOTION FOR THE DEFENDER

in the cause

PICAROON PLATES AND PARTS LIMITED, [*designation*]

PURSUER

against

CATHAY CLEANSING SYSTEMS LIMITED, [*designation*]

DEFENDER

GUILDENSTERN for the defender moves the court to ordain the pursuer to find caution in the sum of £15,000 or such other sum as the court thinks fit and to sist the proceedings until caution is found, all in terms of Section 726 of the Companies Act 1985, on the ground that it appears by credible testimony, namely the pursuer's own annual accounts and an unpaid decree, that there is reason to believe that the pursuer will be unable to pay the defender's expenses if the defender is successful.

Documents lodged with the motion:

Companies Office documentation

Extract decree for payment

IN RESPECT WHEREOF

[*designation*]

2. THE RHODESIAN BANK v MARQUES AND MARQUES

Payment — Debt — Bank loan — Guarantee — Joint and several liability — Contractual interest on debt — Defenders' whereabouts not known — one defender's whereabouts ascertained after action raised

a. Initial writ

SHERIFFDOM OF TAYSIDE, CENTRAL AND FIFE AT ALLOA

INITIAL WRIT

in the cause

THE RHODESIAN BANK, a company incorporated by Royal Charter, company registration number RC234567 and having its registered office at 65 Salisbury Road, London SW1Y 9DA

PURSUER

against

LOURENCO MARQUES, whose current whereabouts are unknown

FIRST NAMED DEFENDER

and

CAROL MARQUES, whose current whereabouts are unknown

SECOND NAMED DEFENDER

JOINTLY AND SEVERALLY

The pursuer craves the court:

1. To grant decree against the defenders, jointly and severally, for payment to the pursuer of the sum of SIXTY THOUSAND FOUR HUNDRED AND TWELVE POUNDS SIXTEEN PENCE (£60,412.16) STERLING, with interest thereon at the rate of two *per centum per annum* above the pursuer's base rate applicable from time to time from 1 April 2022 until citation and at eight *per centum per annum* from the date of citation until payment.

2. To grant decree against the defenders, jointly and severally, for payment to the pursuer of the sum of FIFTEEN THOUSAND SIX HUNDRED AND TWENTY POUNDS NINE PENCE (£15,620.09) STERLING, with interest thereon at the rate of three *per centum per annum* above the pursuer's base rate applicable from time to time from 1 April 2022 until citation and at eight *per centum per annum* from the date of citation until payment.

3. in respect that the defenders' whereabouts are unknown, to grant warrant to cite the defenders by display on the walls of court as satisfied by the document's being made publicly available through the Scottish Courts and Tribunals Website, all in terms of Ordinary Cause Rule 5.6 and paragraph 1A of Schedule 4 to the Coronavirus (Scotland) Act 2020, which failing by the publication of an advertisement in Form G3 in the *Alloa Spyglass* newspaper.

4. To find the defenders liable in expenses, jointly and severally.

CONDESCENDENCE

1. The pursuer is as designed in the instance. The defenders' whereabouts are not known and cannot reasonably be ascertained. Their last known residence was at 123 Alderbank Drive, Alloa. They removed from that address in about early 2019. They left no forwarding address. Enquiry agents instructed by the pursuer have been unable to locate them.

2. The pursuer claims payment of sums due to the pursuer by the defenders under and in terms of the contracts hereinafter condescended upon. These sums ought to have been paid by the defenders to the pursuer at its High Street, Alloa branch. The said address is within the Sheriffdom of Tayside Central and Fife. Alloa sheriff court has jurisdiction in terms of Section 20 of and Rules 1 and 2(b) of Schedule 8 to the Civil Jurisdiction and Judgments Act 1982. The pursuer is unaware of any other proceedings pending before any court which are in respect of the subject matter of this writ. There is no agreement to prorogate the jurisdiction of any other court.

3. In 2018 the parties entered into a contract whereby the pursuer made available to the defenders banking facilities at its High Street, Alloa branch. The defenders opened a current account there, numbered 261359.

4. The defenders borrowed money from the pursuer on that account. Interest was exigible on sums borrowed by the defenders as individuals

at the rate of two *per centum per annum* above the pursuer's base rate applicable from time to time and applied quarterly. This was in terms of the parties' contract. As at 1 April 2022, when interest was last applied, the total sum borrowed by the defenders was £60,412.16, which is the sum first craved.

5. The pursuer afforded banking facilities at the said branch to a company named Nyassa Enterprises Ltd (hereinafter referred to as 'the company'). The company opened a current account there, numbered 46129.

6. On or about 4 May 2018 the defenders guaranteed full and final payment on demand of all sums for which the company was or would become due or liable for to the pursuer. A copy of the guarantee is produced herewith and its terms repeated for the sake of brevity.

7, Interest was exigible on sums borrowed by the company at the rate of three *per cent per annum* year above the pursuer's base rate applicable from time to time and applied quarterly. The company borrowed money on the account. As at 1 April 2022, when interest was last applied, the total sum borrowed by the company was £15,620.09. This is the sum second craved.

8. The pursuer has repeatedly called upon the defenders to make payment of the sums borrowed and guaranteed, respectively, by them. They refuse or at least delay unreasonably to do so. Accordingly, this action is necessary.

PLEAS IN LAW

1. The defenders having borrowed money from the pursuer and having failed to repay same, decree should be granted as first craved.

2. The defenders having granted a guarantee in favour of the pursuer of payment of all sums for which Nyassa Enterprises Ltd is due or liable for to the pursuer, and the company being due or liable for to the pursuer in the sum second sued for, decree should be granted as second craved.

IN RESPECT WHEREOF

[*designation*]
Agent for the pursuer

b. Minute of amendment (instance) (OCR 18.3.(1))

SHERIFFDOM OF TAYSIDE, CENTRAL AND FIFE AT ALLOA

ALO-A2-23

MINUTE OF AMENDMENT

for the pursuer

in the cause

RHODESIAN BANK, [*designation*]

PURSUER

against

LOURENCO MARQUES, whose current whereabouts are unknown

FIRST NAMED DEFENDER

and

CAROL MARQUES, whose current whereabouts are unknown

SECOND NAMED DEFENDER

JOINTLY AND SEVERALLY

In the instance of the initial writ delete 'CAROL MARQUES whose current whereabouts are unknown' and substitute therefor 'CAROL MARQUES residing at c/o Smith, 461 Alexander Place, Alloa. FK10 5RD'.

IN RESPECT WHEREOF

[*designation*]
Agent for the pursuer

c. Motion for minute of amendment to be received and for amendment in terms thereof and for warrant for re-service (OCR 5.6.(3))

SHERIFFDOM OF TAYSIDE, CENTRAL AND FIFE AT ALLOA

ALO-A2-23

MOTION FOR THE PURSUERS

in the cause

RHODESIAN BANK, [*designation*]

PURSUER

against

LOURENCO MARQUES, whose current whereabouts are unknown

FIRST NAMED DEFENDER

and

CAROL MARQUES, whose current whereabouts are unknown

SECOND NAMED DEFENDER

JOINTLY AND SEVERALLY

In respect that the second named defender's whereabouts have become known to the pursuer following the raising of these proceedings, the pursuer moves the court:

1) to allow the minute of amendment to be received and to form no of process; and

2) to allow the initial writ to be amended in terms thereof; and

3) to grant warrant for re-service of the initial writ, as so amended, upon the Second Named Defender.

Part of process lodged with the motion:

Minute of amendment

IN RESPECT WHEREOF

[*designation*]
Agent for the defender

3. PINKERTON v BEGGS

Payment — Debt — IOU— Death of pursuer during the litigation

a. Initial writ

SHERIFFDOM OF GRAMPIAN, HIGHLAND
AND ISLANDS AT INVERNESS

INITIAL WRIT

in the cause

ALBERT PINKERTON, residing at 3 Market Square, Tain IV19 1BD

PURSUER

against

STEPHANIE BEGGS, residing at 49 New Street, Inverness IV1 1DF

DEFENDER

The pursuer craves the court:

1. To grant decree against the defender for payment to the pursuer of the sum of FIFTEEN THOUSAND EIGHT HUNDRED POUNDS (£15,800) STERLING, with interest thereon at the rate of eight *per centum per annum* from 16 September 2022 until payment; and
2. To find the defender liable in expenses as taxed.

CONDESCENDENCE

1. The parties are as designed in the instance.
2. The defender has been resident at 49 New Street, Inverness. IV1 1DF for more than three months immediately prior to the raising of this action. She is domiciled there. The said address is within the Sheriffdom of Grampian Highland and Islands. Inverness sheriff court has jurisdiction in terms of Section 20 of and Rule 1 of Schedule 8 to the Civil Jurisdiction and Judgments Act 1982.
3. On 1 July 2022 the defender borrowed from the pursuer the sum of £15,800. The loan was repayable on demand.

4. On said date the defender signed and provided an IOU. It is produced herewith.

5 On or about 16 July 2022 the pursuer wrote to the defender demanding that the defender make payment of that sum. The defender has however refused or at least delayed to do so. This action is therefore necessary.

PLEA IN LAW

The defender being indebted to the pursuer in the sum sued for, as condescended upon, decree should be granted as craved.

IN RESPECT WHEREOF

Solicitor
MacIntyre and MacSporran
1 Clachnacuddin Street,
Inverness
Agent for the pursuer

b. Minute of sist of representative (OCR 25.1.)

SHERIFFDOM OF GRAMPIAN, HIGHLAND
AND ISLANDS AT INVERNESS

INV-A3-23

MINUTE OF SIST

for

ALFRED ELLIS, residing at 21 Newby Avenue, Inverness, unconfirmed executor-nominate of the late Albert Pinkerton in terms of the Trust Disposition and Settlement of the said deceased dated 14 February 2008

MINUTER

in the cause

ALBERT PINKERTON, [*designation*]

PURSUER

against

STEPHANIE BEGGS, [*designation*]

DEFENDER

The minuter craves the court:

To be sisted as executor-nominate of the pursuer in terms of the Trust Disposition and Settlement of the late Albert Pinkerton dated 14 February 2008 in substitution for the late Albert Pinkerton who died on 8 October 2022.

STATEMENT OF FACTS

The pursuer died on 8 October 2022. He left a Trust Disposition and Settlement, dated 14 February 2008. In terms thereof he nominated the minuter to be his executor. The minuter duly accepted office. He intends to apply for confirmation to the estate of the pursuer.

PLEA IN LAW

The pursuer having died while this cause is depending, the minuter as his executor nominate is entitled to be sisted as pursuer in his place.

IN RESPECT WHEREOF

[*designation*]
Agent for the minuter

c. Motion for the pursuer

SHERIFFDOM OF GRAMPIAN, HIGHLAND
AND ISLANDS AT INVERNESS

INV-A3-23

MOTION FOR THE PURSUER

in the cause

ALFRED ELLIS, [*designation*]

PURSUER

against

STEPHANIE BEGGS, [*designation*]

DEFENDER

The pursuer moves the court:

To allow the instance to be amended by deletion of 'unconfirmed executor nominate of the late Albert Pinkerton in terms of the Trust Disposition and Settlement of the deceased dated 14 February 2008' and substitution therefor of 'executor nominate of the late Albert Pinkerton conform to confirmation granted in his favour by the commissariot of Grampian, Highland and Islands on 14 December 2022'.

IN RESPECT WHEREOF

[*designation*]
Agent for the minuter

d. Defences

SHERIFFDOM OF GRAMPIAN, HIGHLAND
AND ISLANDS AT INVERNESS

DEFENCES

In the cause

ALFRED ELLIS, executor nominate of the late Albert Pinkerton conform to confirmation granted in his favour by the commisariot of Grampian, Highland and Islands on 14 December 2022

PURSUER

against

STEPHANIE BEGGS, residing at 49 New Street, Inverness IV1 1DF

DEFENDER

ANSWERS

1. The defender's designation is admitted.
2. Admitted that this court has jurisdiction.
3. Denied. On 1 July 2022 the deceased gifted to the defender the sum of £5,800.
4. Denied. The purported IOU is not signed by the defender. The signature thereon is not that of the defender. The document falls to be reduced by way of exception.
5. Admitted that the deceased wrote to the defender demanding that the defender make payment under explanation that it is not due. This action is therefore unnecessary.

PLEAS IN LAW FOR THE DEFENDER

1) The defender not being indebted to the deceased in the sum sued for, as condescended upon, the defender should be assoilzied from the craves of the initial writ.

2) The purported IOU bearing a forgery of the defender's signature falls to be reduced and should be set aside *ope exceptionis.*

IN RESPECT WHEREOF

Solicitor
Wallace and Bruce
3 Ukraine Street,
Inverness
Agent for the defender

4. DUVALIER v ABBOTSINCH HERITAGE LIMITED

Payment — Debt — Hire of services — Foreign pursuer — Foreign currency — Company limited by guarantee

a. Initial writ

SHERIFFDOM OF NORTH STRATHCLYDE
AT PAISLEY

INITIAL WRIT

in the cause

ERNESTO DUVALIER, having a place of business at 3/219 Rasputin Square, Casco Viejo, Panama City, Panama

PURSUER

against

ABBOTSINCH HERITAGE LIMITED a company limited by guarantee, Company number SC173947, and having a place of business at 231 Govan Road, Paisley PA7 3TF

DEFENDER

The pursuer craves the court:

1. To grant decree against the defender for payment to the pursuer of the sum of ONE HUNDRED AND FORTY SEVEN THOUSAND THREE HUNDRED US DOLLARS ($147,300), with interest thereon at the rate of eight *per centum per annum* from the date of citation until payment, or the sterling equivalent of the said sum and interest at the date of payment or the date of extract whichever is the earlier.

2. To find the defender liable in expenses as taxed.

CONDESCENDENCE

1. The pursuer is a lawyer with a place of business in the Republic of Panama. The defender is a company limited by guarantee under the law of Scotland, where its central management and control is exercised.

2. The defender has a place of business at 231 Govan Road, Paisley. The defender is domiciled there. Paisley sheriff court has jurisdiction in terms of Section 20 of and Rule 1 of Schedule 8 to the Civil Jurisdiction and Judgments Act 1982. The pursuer is unaware of any proceedings pending before any court which are in respect of the subject matter of this writ. There is no agreement to prorogate the jurisdiction of any other court.

3. In about March 2021, the defender instructed the pursuer in connection with a proposed investment transaction.

4. The pursuer duly provided legal advice and other legal services to the value of 147,300 US dollars conform to the professional table of fees established by the Bar Association of Panama and referred to in the pursuer's letter of engagement.

5. The said sum is a reasonable charge. It remains unpaid, despite requests. This action is therefore necessary.

PLEAS IN LAW

1. The pursuer having rendered services to the defenders, is entitled to payment at a reasonable rate therefor.

2. The sum sued for being a reasonable fee for the services provided by the pursuer decree should be granted as craved.

IN RESPECT WHEREOF

Solicitor
Taylor and Noriega
23 Reagan Street, Glasgow
Agent for the pursuer

b. Motion for pursuer to be ordained to sist a mandatary

SHERIFFDOM OF NORTH STRATHCLYDE
AT PAISLEY

PAI-A4-23

MOTION FOR THE DEFENDER

in the cause

ERNESTO DUVALIER, [*designation*]

PURSUER

against

ABBOTSINCH HERITAGE LIMITED,
[*designation*]

DEFENDER

In respect that the pursuer is resident outwith the United Kingdom the defender moves the court to ordain the pursuer to sist a mandatary within 28 days or within such other period as to the court shall seem reasonable.

IN RESPECT WHEREOF

Solicitor
Jones and Kilcoyne
6 Queen's Drive, Paisley
Agent for the defender

c. Minute of sist of mandatary (OCR 14.2.)

SHERIFFDOM OF NORTH STRATHCLYDE
AT PAISLEY

PAI-A4-23

MINUTE OF SIST

for

MAXWELL MONBODDO, solicitor, residing at 41 Largs Road, Glasgow G64 8TF

MINUTER

in the cause

ERNESTO DUVALIER, [*designation*]

PURSUER

against

ABBOTSINCH HERITAGE LIMITED, [*designation*]

DEFENDER

The minuter craves the court:

To grant the minuter leave to be sisted as mandatary for the pursuer.

STATEMENT OF FACTS

In respect that the interlocutor of 20 November 2022 ordained the pursuer sist a mandatary within 28 days the minuter has been instructed by the pursuer so to act. The minuter is a solicitor enrolled in Scotland. He has held a full practising certificate since 2006. He resides and practices only in Scotland. He is solvent.

PLEA IN LAW

The minuter being a suitable person to act as the pursuer's mandatary and being instructed by him so to act should be sisted as craved.

IN RESPECT WHEREOF

[*designation*]
Agent for the minuter

5. WATERMAN v ALEXANDER

Payment — Debt — Unjustified enrichment — Repetition — Claim against deceased person's estate where no known executor — Constitution and payment and constitution cognitionis causa tantum

Initial writ

SHERIFFDOM OF SOUTH STRATHCLYDE, DUMFRIES AND GALLOWAY AT HAMILTON

INITIAL WRIT

in the cause

HORACE WATERMAN, residing at 21 Riverside View, Hamilton ML3 5RW

PURSUER

against

DOROTHY ALEXANDER, residing at 2 Monteith Place, Hamilton ML7 9DS, as representative of the late Gordon Alexander, who resided latterly at that address

DEFENDER

The pursuer craves the court:

1. To find and declare that the sum hereinafter craved, together with interest and expenses, is a just and lawful debt due to the pursuer by the late Gordon Alexander and that the pursuer is a just and lawful creditor for the same and has an interest in the means and estate of the late Gordon Alexander for payment thereof, the sum being that of FIVE THOUSAND FIVE HUNDRED POUNDS (£5,500) STERLING with interest thereon at the rate of eight *per centum per annum* from the date of citation until payment; to ordain the defender as next of kin of the late Gordon Alexander and duly charged to confirm as executor as such to pay to the pursuer the aforesaid sum together with interest as aforesaid and with the expenses of process as taxed; or otherwise, and if the defender shall produce a valid renunciation of her right to

the moveable estate of the late Gordon Alexander, to find and declare *cognitionis causa tantum* that the said sum with interest and expenses aforesaid is a just and lawful debt resting owing by the late Gordon Alexander to the pursuer and that the pursuer is a just and lawful creditor for the same and has an interest in the estate of the late Gordon Alexander for payment thereof.

2. To find the defender liable in expenses as taxed.

CONDESCENDENCE

1. The parties are as designed in the instance. The defender is sued as representative of the late Gordon Alexander who was the defender's father and resided latterly with the defender at 2 Monteith Place, Hamilton ML7 9DS. He died on 8 December 2018. He was intestate. He was a self-employed builder

2. Believed and averred that no one was confirmed as executor to the deceased's estate. The defender has been resident at the said address, in the Sheriffdom of South Strathclyde, Dumfries and Galloway for at least twelve months immediately preceding the raising of this action. The defender is domiciled there. This court has jurisdiction in terms of Section 20 of and Rule 1 of Schedule 8 to the Civil Jurisdiction and Judgments Act 1982. The pursuer is unaware of any proceedings pending before any court which are in respect of the subject matter of this writ or in connection with any confirmation.

3. This is a construction litigation as defined in the Association of Commercial Attorneys scheme in force from 18 June 2019. Reference is made to the Act of Sederunt (Sections 25 to 29 of the Law Reform (Miscellaneous Provisions) (Scotland) Act 1990) (Association of Commercial Attorneys) 2009.

4. On or about 15 May 2018 the pursuer and the deceased entered into a contract for the execution of building works by the deceased at the pursuer's business premises.

5. At that time the pursuer made a cash payment to the deceased in the sum of £5,500. The payment was an advance in respect of necessary building materials for the contract works.

6. On or about 29 May 2018 the pursuer's business premises were destroyed by fire. Performance of the contract was thereby frustrated. The deceased was enriched to the extent of the cash payment. In these circumstances, the pursuer seeks repayment thereof.

7. The deceased was called upon to make repetition of the sum sued for. He refused to do so. This action is therefore necessary.

PLEAS IN LAW

1. The pursuer having made payment as an advance for an anticipated consideration which has not been received through frustration of his

contract with the deceased, and the deceased having been enriched thereby, is entitled to repetition of that payment.

2. The deceased having been enriched to the extent of the sum sued for, decree should be pronounced as craved.

3. The pursuer being a creditor of the deceased and the defender being his next of kin and duly charged to confirm, the pursuer is entitled to decree for payment as craved.

4. Alternatively, and in the event of the defender renouncing her rights to the estate of the deceased, the pursuer is entitled to decree *cognitionis causa tantum*.

IN RESPECT WHEREOF

Commercial Attorney

1 Charlotte Street, Hamilton
Member of the Association of Commercial Attorneys
Agent for the pursuer

6. MONTGOMERY v SMITHERS

Payment — Debt — Unjustified enrichment — Recompense – Pursuer's Offer

a. Initial writ

SHERIFFDOM OF NORTH STRATHCLYDE AT PAISLEY

INITIAL WRIT

in the cause

PETER MONTGOMERY, residing at 56 Drinkwater Green, Linwood PA3 7TF

PURSUER

against

ARMITAGE SMITHERS, residing at 2 Marlin Street, Paisley PA5 8TR

DEFENDER

The pursuer craves the court:

1. To grant decree against the defender for payment to the pursuer of the sum of TWELVE THOUSAND POUNDS (£12,000) STERLING, with interest thereon at the rate of eight *per centum per annum* from the date of citation until payment.
2. To find the defender liable in expenses as taxed.

CONDESCENDENCE

1. The parties are as designed in the instance. The defender is domiciled in Paisley. This court has jurisdiction in terms of Section 20 of and Rule 1 of Schedule 8 to the Civil Jurisdiction and Judgments Act 1982. The pursuer is unaware of any proceedings pending before any court which are in respect of the subject matter of this writ.

2. The pursuer is a piano tuner. He provided services to Walter Piper. On or about 15 January 2020, Mr Piper (hereinafter 'the deceased') died.

By will dated 11 December 1976 the deceased left his entire estate to the pursuer. Such included the deceased's yacht, named 'Salty Dog'.

3. The pursuer duly took possession of the yacht. It required extensive repair and refurbishment. In particular, the hull had sustained storm damage. The sails were in poor condition. The interior fixtures and fittings had become dilapidated. The pursuer duly funded the necessary works to restore the yacht. This was at a total cost of £12,000.

4. Thereafter, the pursuer was informed that a codicil by the deceased, dated 23 November 1981, had been discovered. It had the effect whereby the sole beneficiary of the estate is the defender. He was the deceased's gardener. The pursuer required to deliver the yacht to the defender. He did so.

5. The pursuer has suffered loss in the sum of £12,000. He expended that amount upon property, namely the yacht, in the *bona fide* but erroneous belief that it was his own. He would not have expended that money otherwise. He had no intention of making a gift thereof to the defender.

6. The defender has been enriched by the pursuer's expenditure. The value of 'Salty Dog' has been increased by the amount expended aforesaid. In these circumstances, the pursuer is entitled to be recompensed by the defender in the sum sued for.

7. The defender has been called upon to recompense the pursuer but he refuses or at least delays to do so. This action is therefore necessary.

PLEAS IN LAW

1. The pursuer having expended funds upon property in the *bona fide* but erroneous belief that it was his own, without intention to enrich the defender, and the defender having been enriched thereby, the pursuer is entitled to recompense therefor.

2. The defender having been enriched to the extent of the sum sued for, decree should be pronounced as craved.

IN RESPECT WHEREOF

Solicitor
Ambersons
12 Granton Avenue, Paisley
Agent for the pursuer

b. Pursuer's Offer (OCR 27A.)

SHERIFFDOM OF NORTH STRATHCLYDE AT PAISLEY

PAI-A47-23

MINUTE OF OFFER TO SETTLE

for the pursuer

in the cause

PETER MONTGOMERY, [*designation*]

PURSUER

against

ARMITAGE SMITHERS, [*designation*]

DEFENDER

AMBERSON for the Pursuer hereby states that, for the purposes of Chapter 27A of the Act of Sederunt (Sheriff Court Ordinary Cause Rules) 1993 the Pursuer hereby offers to settle the Action in respect of his claim by accepting the sum of NINE THOUSAND POUNDS (£9,000) STERLING, inclusive of interest thereon to date, together with the expenses of process as taxed to date, in full and final satisfaction of both craves of the initial writ, all without prejudice to, and under reservation of the Pursuer's whole rights and pleas.

IN RESPECT WHEREOF

[*designation*]
Agent for the pursuer

7. BROWN AND CHEYNIE v SHOLTO DOALTY & CO

Payment — Damages — Breach of contract — Negligence — Professional negligence — Surveyor — Interest on damages for negligence and breach of contract — Limited liability partnership

a. Initial writ

SHERIFFDOM OF SOUTH STRATHCLYDE, DUMFRIES AND GALLOWAY AT AYR

INITIAL WRIT

in the cause

RAYMOND BROWN, residing at 195 Irvine Road, Ayr AY3 9DG

FIRST NAMED PURSUER

and

BRUCE CHEYNIE, residing at 195 Irvine Road, Ayr AY3 9DG

SECOND NAMED PURSUER

against

SHOLTO DOALTY & CO, a limited liability partnership incorporated under the Limited Liability Partnerships Act 2000 and having a place of business at 16 Doune Street, Ayr AY8 6FS.

DEFENDER

The pursuers crave the court:

1. To grant decree against the defender for payment to the first named pursuer of the sum of FIFTY SEVEN THOUSAND FIVE HUNDRED POUNDS (£57,500) STERLING, with interest thereon at the rate of eight *per centum per annum* from the date of citation until payment.

2. To grant decree against the defender for payment to the second named pursuer of the sum of FIFTY SEVEN THOUSAND FIVE HUNDRED POUNDS (£57,500) STERLING, with interest thereon at the rate of eight *per centum per annum* from the date of citation until payment.

3. To find the defender liable in expenses as taxed.

CONDESCENDENCE

1. The parties are as designed in the instance. The pursuers are spouses. The defender is a limited liability partnership of chartered surveyors. The defender is incorporated under the Limited Liability Partnerships Act 2000.

2. The defender is domiciled in Ayr. This court accordingly has jurisdiction. Ayr sheriff court has jurisdiction in terms of Section 20 of and Rule 1 of Schedule 8 to the Civil Jurisdiction and Judgments Act 1982.

3. In May 2022 Denise Stoddart (hereinafter 'the seller') owned and wished to sell the dwellinghouse at 195 Irvine Road, Ayr (hereinafter 'the subjects'). She obtained a Home Report. Reference is made to Section 98 of the Housing (Scotland) Act 2006. The purpose of such a report is primarily to enable prospective purchasers to make informed choices about whether to offer to buy heritable property and the price that ought to be offered. Surveyors, including the defender, are well aware of this.

4. On or about 18 May 2022, the seller's solicitors, Alvin Irthing instructed the defender to prepare and provide a Home Report, Such a report was issued on 27 May 2022 (the Report) and it was made available to several prospective buyers, including the pursuers. A copy of the Report is produced herewith and referred to for its terms which are incorporated herein for the sake of brevity.

5. Therein the defender stated: 'There is no visible evidence of dampness or timber defect or infestation … and 'We are of the opinion that the property under report has a present fair open market value of £423,000'.

6. The pursuers acquired a copy of the Report. They read it carefully. They assumed that it was substantially correct and accurate. Relying upon the Report they instructed Jasrindra Law to note interest on the pursuers' behalf. Thereafter, and again in reliance upon the Report, the pursuers instructed Jasrindra Law to submit an Offer to Buy for £440,000. This was sent on 18 June 2022. Missives were concluded on 29 August 2022. That was also the date of settlement, when a Disposition was delivered, the price was paid, keys were handed over and the pursuers took entry.

7. On or around 18 September 2022 the pursuers discovered defects in the property. In particular:

a) There was Japanese Knotweed present behind the shed at the bottom of the garden. This had been present for at least a year.

b) The garden shed was roofed with material which included a sheet of corrugated asbestos.

c) There is knob and tube electrical wiring in the garage, indicative of a system which is at least 70 years old and which, more importantly, presents a fire hazard.

d) The conical roof above the main bedroom is affected by rotted timber joists and panels. This compromised the integrity of the roof and allowed rainwater penetration which caused staining to the ceiling of the said bedroom.

All of these defects had and have a material bearing on the value of the subjects. They all ought to have been obvious to the defender's surveyor.

8. The pursuers have sustained loss and damage as hereinafter condescended on.

9. The pursuers' loss and damage were caused by a breach of the defender's duty of care to the pursuers as persons falling within a class of persons, namely prospective buyers, to whom the defender owed a duty. The purpose of Home Reports is that such persons may rely on them and do not require to obtain their own survey reports as occurred prior to the 2006 Act. The defender knew, or ought to have known, that the pursuers relied upon the Report.

10. The pursuers assumed, and were entitled to assume, that the defender as an LLP of chartered accountants would exercise the degree of care and skill to be expected of reasonably competent members of their profession. In so doing it was the defender's duty to carry out a proper visual inspection of the property. It was their duty to have regard to defects apparent upon such an inspection. It was their duty to include these in the Report. It was their duty to reflect the same in their assessment of the open market value of the property. No surveyor of ordinary skill would have failed to have so acted. In all these duties, the defender failed and accordingly were in breach of their duty of care. But for the defender's said breach the pursuer's loss and damage would not have occurred.

11. As a result of the defender's breach of duty, the pursuer has suffered loss and damage. Had the defender produced a correct and accurate Home Report the pursuers would not have offered to buy the subjects for any sum at all. The property at the date of her purchase thereof, taking into account the said defects, was worth about £325,000. Reference is made to the valuation and the estimate of the cost as at the date of purchase of eliminating the said defects, produced herewith. As hereinbefore averred, they in fact paid the sum of £440,000 therefor. In the circumstances, the sums sued for represent a reasonable estimate of the pursuers' loss and damage.

12. The defender has been called upon to make reparation to the pursuers for their loss and damage. The defender refuses or at least delays to do so. This action is accordingly necessary.

PLEAS IN LAW

1. The pursuers having suffered loss and damage through the defender's fault and negligence, are entitled to reparation from the defender therefor.

2. The sum sued for being a reasonable estimate of the pursuers' loss and damage, decree should be pronounced as craved.

IN RESPECT WHEREOF

Solicitor
49 Arran View Street,
Ayr
Agent for the pursuers

b. Motion for remit to person of skill (OCR 29.2.)

SHERIFFDOM OF SOUTH STRATHCLYDE, DUMFRIES AND GALLOWAY AT AYR

AYR-A22-23

MOTION FOR THE DEFENDER

in the cause

RAYMOND BROWN, [*designation*]

FIRST NAMED PURSUER

BRUCE CHEYNIE, [*designation*]

SECOND NAMED PURSUER

against

SHOLTO DOALTY & CO, [*designation*]

DEFENDER

The defender moves the court:

1) to discharge the Options Hearing assigned for 10 February 2023; and

2) to appoint Cyril Doke chartered surveyor, 18 Flower Street, Thornliebank, East Renfrewshire G78 6RD as a person of skill; and

3) to remit for his determination of:

   a) whether no chartered surveyor acting with reasonable care and competence would have failed to have identified the matters condescended upon in Condescendence 4 or failed to have recommended the instruction of more specialist inspection; and

   b) the market value of the subjects as at 29 August 2022; and

4) to sist the cause for the person of skill to report; and

5) to reserve meantime all questions of expenses as between the parties.

IN RESPECT WHEREOF

Solicitor
29 Jarvis Road, Ayr
Agent for the defender

8. FLOYD v BRENNAN AND DECKER

Payment — Damages — Breach of contract — Negligence — Professional negligence — Solicitor — Prescription of obligation — Interest on damages for negligence and breach of contract —Dissolved firm

a. Initial writ

SHERIFFDOM OF TAYSIDE CENTRAL AND FIFE AT DUNDEE

INITIAL WRIT

in the cause

LUCY FLOYD residing at 1, The Farmhouse, Old Vagrant Street, St Andrews, Fife KY16 4TF (Assisted Person),

PURSUER

against

BRENDAN BRENNAN, residing at 14 George Terrace, Ayr and DECLAN DECKER, residing at 239 Afton Grove, Dundee, the whole partners of the now dissolved partnership of BRENDECKLAW formerly having a place of business at 13 East Regent Street, Dundee DD4 9YH

DEFENDERS

The pursuer craves the court:

1. To grant decree against the defenders for payment to the pursuer of the sum of TWELVE THOUSAND FIVE HUNDRED POUNDS (£12,500) STERLING, with interest thereon at the rate of eight *per cent per annum* from 15 June 2015 until payment.
2. To find the defenders liable in expenses.

CONDESCENDENCE

1. The parties are as designed in the instance. The defenders were the partners of a firm known as Brendecklaw. The firm was dissolved

in December 2022 in terms of the Partnership Act 1890. The defenders' obligations *qua* partners continue in relation to the firm's liability to the pursuer. Reference is made to Section 38 of the Act.

2. The second named partner has been resident in Dundee for at least 12 months immediately preceding the raising of this action. He is domiciled there. This court accordingly has jurisdiction.

3. On or about 15 June 2015 the pursuer was at a Country and Western music event known as 'Remember the Alamo'. The event was staged at a public house known as Crockett's Saloon, 17 Great West Road, Dundee DD4 7RE.

4. At around 11pm the pursuer walked to the lavatory. As she did so her right foot came into contact with a spillage of beer or a similar fluid. Her heel slipped and she lost her footing She fell and sustained injury. The incident was caused by the fault of the public house manager. It was the duty of the manager to take reasonable care for the safety of customers, such as the pursuer. It was the manager's duty to take reasonable care to clean up spillages within a reasonable time. Believed and averred that the fluid on which the pursuer slipped was present for at least 30 minutes before the incident. Said period of time was unreasonable. In all these duties the manager failed. Said failures caused the incident. But for said failures in duty the incident would not have occurred.

5. As a result of the said fault, the pursuer suffered loss, injury and damage. She fractured her left ankle. She required to attend Seven Sisters' University Trust Hospital and her General Practitioner, Dr Al-Zahrawi, Cordoba Medical Centre, Dundee. She suffered much pain and inconvenience. Her fracture was slow to heal and she required to use crutches for several weeks. She was left with continuing discomfort and restriction of movement in her ankle. She required to be absent from work for some months and lost earnings, as will be vouched. She received necessary services from her husband over a prolonged period. He required to assist her with dressing and undressing and with getting in and out of the bath. He also required to take over domestic duties for several weeks, in particular washing, cooking, shopping and housework.

6. On or about 2 September 2015, the pursuer consulted Brendecklaw. The firm accepted her instructions to pursue settlement negotiations and if necessary to raise proceedings against the manager of Crockett's Saloon for loss, injury and damage sustained by her as a result of her accident.

7. Settlement negotiations were fruitless. Brendecklaw failed to raise court proceedings within a period of three years from the date of the incident. As a result, the pursuer's action was time-barred in terms of section 17 of the Prescription and Limitation (Scotland) Act 1973. Consequently, the pursuer has suffered loss and damage as hereinafter condescended upon.

8. The pursuer's loss and damage was caused by breach of contract on the part of the defenders. It was an implied term of the parties' contract that the defenders would exercise the degree of care and skill to be expected of reasonably competent members of their profession. Had they done so they would have raised an action within three years from the date of the accident. In the foregoing duties the defenders failed and in so doing they caused the pursuer to suffer loss and damage. But for their failures in duty, the pursuer would not have suffered loss and damage.

9. Separately, the pursuer's loss and damage was caused by the defenders' fault. It was their duty, having accepted instructions from the pursuer, to exercise the degree of care and skill to be expected of reasonably competent members of their profession. It was their duty to raise an action within a period of three years from the date of the incident. In these duties the defenders failed and by their failures so caused the pursuer to suffer loss and damage. But for their failures in duty, the pursuer would not have suffered loss and damage.

10. Had the said action been raised timeously, the pursuer would have been wholly successful and would have recovered substantial damages or at any rate had excellent prospects of so doing.

11. An award of damages is reasonably estimated at about £14,000, with interest at the rate of eight per cent a year from the date of decree until payment. Decree would have been granted by about late 2022 at the latest. In any event, the pursuer had very good prospects of obtaining an extra-judicial settlement representing the bulk of the value of her claim. In the whole circumstances, the sum sued for is a reasonable estimate of the pursuer's loss and damage.

12. The defenders have been called upon to make reparation and to compensate the pursuer for her loss and damage. The defenders refuse or at least delay to do so. This action is therefore necessary.

PLEAS IN LAW

1. The pursuer having suffered loss and damage through the defenders' breach of contract and separately fault, is entitled to reparation from them therefor.

2. The sum sued for being a reasonable estimate of the pursuer's loss and damage, decree should be pronounced as craved.

IN RESPECT WHEREOF

Solicitor
Sue4U
14 Telegraph Road,
Dundee EH52 6SD
Agent for the pursuer

b. Defences

SHERIFFDOM OF TAYSIDE CENTRAL AND FIFE AT DUNDEE

DUN-A29-23

DEFENCES

in the cause

LUCY FLOYD, [*designation*]

PURSUER

against

BRENDAN BRENNAN and DECLAN DECKER, of BRENDECKLAW, [*designation*]

DEFENDERS

ANSWERS TO CONDESCENDENCE

1. Admitted.
2. Admitted that this court has jurisdiction.
3. Not known and not admitted.
4. The circumstances in which the pursuer came to have an accident are not known and not admitted. The nature, extent and consequences of any loss, injury and damage thereby sustained by her are not known and not admitted. The cause of the accident is not known and not admitted. *Quoad ultra* denied. Explained and averred that *esto* the accident occurred as averred by the pursuer, it was partly caused by her own fault. It was her duty to take reasonable care for her own safety. It was her duty to take reasonable care to look where she was placing her feet. It was her duty to take reasonable care to avoid treading on fluids. In these duties the pursuer failed and by her failures so partly caused the accident.
5. Not known and not admitted.
6. Admitted that on the said date the pursuer consulted the defenders regarding her accident. Admitted, subject to explanation following, that they failed to raise an action within a period of three years from the date of the pursuer's accident. *Quoad ultra* denied. Explained and averred that no instructions were ever received to raise such an action. The

pursuer failed to respond to correspondence after her consultation with the defenders.

7. Denied. Explained and averred that the defenders fulfilled all duties incumbent upon them.

8. Denied. Explained and averred that the defenders fulfilled all duties incumbent upon them.

9. The nature and extent of any loss and damage sustained by the pursuer are not known and not admitted. *Quoad ultra* denied. Explained and averred that the sum sued for is in any event excessive.

10. Denied that the action is necessary. Explained and averred that *esto* any obligation to make reparation to the pursuer has been incumbent upon the defenders as a result of breach of contract or fault on their part (which is denied), such obligation has subsisted for a continuous period of five years from the date of expiry of the triennium without any relevant claim having been made in relation to the obligation and without the subsistence of the obligation having been relevantly acknowledged. The service copy of the writ was received on 16 June 2023. Accordingly, any such obligation has been extinguished by operation of prescription.

PLEAS IN LAW

1. The pursuer's averments being irrelevant and separately being lacking in specification, the action should be dismissed.

2. Any obligation incumbent upon the defenders to make reparation to the pursuer as a result of any breach of contract or fault on their part having prescribed in terms of section 6 of the Prescription and Limitation (Scotland) Act 1973, decree of absolvitor should be pronounced.

3. The pursuer's averments, so far as material being unfounded in fact, the defenders should be assoilzied.

4. The pursuer not having suffered loss and damage through any breach of contract or fault on the part of the defenders, decree of absolvitor should be pronounced.

5. The sum sued for being in any event excessive, decree should not be pronounced as craved.

IN RESPECT WHEREOF

Solicitor
Duff and Co
29 Bathgate Street, Glasgow
Agent for the defenders

c. Motion for certification of junior counsel and for transfer

SHERIFFDOM OF TAYSIDE CENTRAL AND FIFE AT DUNDEE

DUN-A29-23

MOTION FOR THE DEFENDERS
SSI 2019/75, Rule 5.4(2)

in the cause

LUCY FLOYD, [*designation*]

PURSUER

against

BRENDAN BRENNAN and DECLAN DECKER, of BRENDECKLAW, [*designation*]

DEFENDERS

DUFF for the defenders moves the court:

1) To certify the proceedings as being suitable for the instruction of junior counsel in respect that it is reasonable to do so having regard to the factors enumerated in Section 108 of the Courts Reform (Scotland) Act 2014:

(a) The cause is likely to be difficult and complex. It concerns a standard loss of opportunity case where the court must assess the likelihood of success but also an issue of time bar of this action.

(b) The case raises the question of a solicitor's honesty and integrity. These are of the utmost importance to the defender. If the court finds that there has been impropriety the defenders could be prosecuted before the Scottish Solicitors' Discipline Tribunal and struck off the roll of solicitors. They could face criminal proceedings. The pursuer has alleged that Mr Brennan fabricated file entries which are false or misleading. In fairness to him as a witness, he ought to be questioned by counsel rather than by another solicitor, especially one practising in Dundee.

(c) Consistent with a recognition that the matter is unduly complex the pursuer has instructed Quinton Swinton, counsel. He has long experience in professional negligence cases, including appeals before the Inner House. Having regard to equality of arms and Mr Quinton's particular expertise, sanction should be granted lest the pursuer gain unfair advantage.

2) In terms of OCR 26.1. to transfer the cause to the sheriff court at Perth or Kirkcaldy or elsewhere in respect that Mr Brennan appears regularly at Dundee Sheriff Court and it is likely that the sheriffs there may feel it appropriate to decline jurisdiction to hear a proof.

IN RESPECT WHEREOF

[*designation*]
Agent for the defender

d. Minute of abandonment (OCR 23.1.(1)(a))

SHERIFFDOM OF SOUTH STRATHCLYDE, DUMFRIES AND GALLOWAY AT AYR

DUN-A29-23

MINUTE OF ABANDONMENT

for the pursuer

in the cause

LUCY FLOYD, [*designation*]

PURSUER

against

BRENDAN BRENNAN and DECLAN DECKER, of BRENDECKLAW, [*designation*]

DEFENDERS

MONTEITH for the pursuer states to the court that the pursuer abandons the cause and consents to decree of absolvitor in terms of rule 23.1(1)(a) of the Ordinary Cause Rules.

IN RESPECT WHEREOF

[*designation*]
Agent for the pursuer

9. BARNES v SNISHIVAL GOLF CLUB

Reparation – Breach of Contract – No jurisdiction – Prescription of rights — Club

a. Initial writ

SHERIFFDOM OF GRAMPIAN HIGHLAND
AND ISLANDS AT STORNOWAY

INITIAL WRIT

in the cause

FENTON BARNES, residing at 14 Lothian Avenue, Newton Mearns, East Renfrewshire G86 2YS

PURSUER

against

SNISHIVAL GOLF CLUB, An Carra Road, Snishival, South Uist HS8 5RW

FIRST NAMED DEFENDER

and

TRISTAN CLITHEROE, residing at Baleshare Cottage, Claddach, North Uist HS6 5ES, CAPTAIN, office bearer of the Club, as representative of the club and as an individual.

SECOND NAMED DEFENDER

and

CORMACK SUILLEABHAIN, residing at 14 Main Street, Griminish, Benbecula HS7 8SD14 SECRETARY AND TREASURER, office bearer of the Club, as representative of the club and as an individual.

THIRD NAMED DEFENDER

JOINTLY AND SEVERALLY

The pursuer craves the court:

1. To grant decree against the defenders, jointly and severally, for payment to the pursuer in the sum of SIX THOUSAND FIVE HUNDRED AND TWENTY POUNDS (£6,520) STERLING with interest thereon at the rate of eight *per centum per annum* from the date of citation until payment, and;
2. To find the defenders liable, jointly and severally, in expenses as taxed.

CONDESCENDENCE

1. The parties are as designed in the instance. The first named defender is an unincorporated association. It was formed in around 1934. It is formed under the law of Scotland. Its central management and control is exercised in Scotland. It has a place of business at Carra Road, Snishival, South Uist HS6 5ES. The first named defender is domiciled there.
2. The second and third named defenders are the only office-bearers of the first named defender. They reside at the addresses in the instance.
3. All defenders are domiciled in the Sheriffdom of Grampian Highland and Islands. The wrongful act with which this action is concerned occurred at the first named defender's premises. This court has jurisdiction in terms of Schedule 8 of the Civil Jurisdiction and Judgements Act 1982.
4. The defenders manage Snishival golf course. its clubhouse and car park. All these areas are within the control of the defenders
5. On or about 17 November 2017 the pursuer and a friend, Jeremy Wishart, played a round of golf at the club. They finished their round at about 4.40pm. They placed their clubs in the boot of the pursuer's car. The boot and the car were locked and secure. The pursuer and Mr Wishart visited the clubhouse. They consumed several soft drinks.
6. At around 6.15pm they left the clubhouse and went to the pursuer's car. They found that entry to the car had been forced. Their clubs, together with other belongings, had been removed by an unknown person or persons.

7. The pursuer immediately reported the incident to the barman within the clubhouse. Since that date there has been correspondence between the pursuer and the second defender in order to resolve the matter. This has been fruitless.

8. The pursuer's car sustained damage to its driver's door and boot. This damage cost £780 to repair, including VAT. An invoice from James Hawkins Motors is produced and referred to for its terms which are incorporated herein for the sake of brevity. The items belonging to the pursuer and stolen from his car comprised;

a) a set of golf clubs worth around £1,200;
b) a camera and accessories, worth around £3,500;
c) a laptop worth around £950;
d) shoes worth around £90.

9. At the time of the incident the defenders had a duty of care towards those using the club facilities, including the pursuer. The security of the car park, the presence of adequate fencing and lighting were the responsibility of the defenders. The defenders failed to meet said duty. The car park was inadequately fenced. Anyone could enter it. It was inadequately lit. There were no security lights. Closed circuit television would have detected intruders and would have acted as a deterrent to criminals. No CCTV was installed. The defenders failed to take reasonable precautions to protect vehicles and their contents within the car park. But for said failures the pursuer's vehicle would not have been subjected to a break in and the pursuer's property would not have been damaged or stolen.

10. The pursuer has suffered loss for which the defenders are responsible. The defenders are liable to make reparation therefor. They have failed to do so. This action is necessary.

11. Separately, the parties contracted for the provision of services, namely the use of a golf course and ancillary facilities including the use of a car park. It was an implied condition of the contract that the car park would be reasonably safe and secure for the parking of cars, including the pursuer's car. The defenders are in breach of contract by reason of the failures already referred to. The pursuer is entitled to damages in the sum sued for.

PLEAS IN LAW

1. The defenders having a duty of care towards the defender and having breached that duty the defenders are liable, jointly and severally, to the pursuer to make reparation therefor.

2. The parties having contracted for the provision of services and the defenders having breached that contract are liable to the pursuer in damages.

3. The sum sued for being a reasonable estimate of the reparation and damages due to the pursuer by the defenders decree should be granted accordingly.

IN RESPECT WHEREOF

Solicitor
Pimlico Legal Services
(Scotland) LLP, 18 London Way,
Glasgow Agent for the pursuer

b. Defences

SHERIFFDOM OF GRAMPIAN HIGHLAND
AND ISLANDS AT STORNOWAY

STO-A6-23
DEFENCES FOR THE FIRST
NAMED DEFENDER

in the cause

FENTON BARNES, [*designation*]

PURSUER

against

SNISHIVAL GOLF CLUB, [*designation*]

FIRST NAMED DEFENDER

and

TRISTAN CLITHEROE, [*designation*]

SECOND NAMED DEFENDER

and

CORMACK SUILLEABHAIN, [*designation*]

THIRD NAMED DEFENDER

JOINTLY AND SEVERALLY

ANSWERS TO CONDESCENDENCE

1. The pursuer's designation is not known and not admitted.

2. Denied. Tristan Clitheroe was club captain as at 17 November 2017 but has since retired from that role. The captaincy of the first named defender is currently vacant. The vice-captain is Raymond Bolland. He owns a holiday home in South Uist but resides at 16 Royal Oak Street, Sutton Coldfield B74 9HS. The club secretary and treasurer on 17 November 2017 and currently is Cormac O' Suilleabhain, not Cormack Suilleabhain.

3. Admitted that the first defender is domiciled in the Sheriffdom of Grampian, Highland and Islands under explanation that it is located within the sheriff court district of Lochmaddy, not Stornoway. These proceedings ought not to have been raised in this sheriff court district. *Forum non conveniens.*

4. Denied that Tristan Clitheroe currently manages Snishival golf course. its clubhouse or its car park. No-one named Cormack Suilleabhain has ever done so.

5. Believed to be true that on or about 17 November 2017 the pursuer and a companion visited the club. Believed and averred that both visitors consumed alcohol in the clubhouse and that the volume consumed would have rendered them unfit to drive. *Quoad ultra* not known and not admitted.

6. Not known and not admitted.

7. Admitted that an alleged vehicle break-in was reported on the evening of 17 November 2017 Admitted that there has been correspondence under explanation that it was and was stated to be without prejudice to the defenders' rights and pleas and is not to be founded upon.

8. Not known and not admitted. The invoice is referred to for its terms beyond which no admission is made.

9. There was full compliance with any duties of care towards those using the club facilities, including the pursuer. The security of the car park was reasonable and adequate. There was sufficient fencing and lighting. CCTV was unnecessary. *Quoad ultra* denied.

10. Denied. Any rights of reparation have prescribed in terms of Section 6 of and Schedule 1 to the Prescription and Limitation (Scotland) Act 1973.

11. Denied. Any rights to damages have prescribed in terms of Section 6 of and Schedule 1 to the Prescription and Limitation (Scotland) Act 1973.

PLEAS IN LAW FOR THE FIRST NAMED DEFENDER

1. *Forum non conveniens.*

2. The pursuer's averments being irrelevant and, separately, being lacking in specification, the action should be dismissed.

3. The pursuer's right to reparation having prescribed in terms of Section 6 of and Schedule 1 to the Prescription and Limitation (Scotland) Act 1973 the first named defender should be assoilzied.

4. The pursuer's right to damages having prescribed in terms of Section 6 of and Schedule 1 to the Prescription and Limitation (Scotland) Act 1973 the first named defender should be assoilzied.

5. The pursuer's averments so far as relevant being unfounded in fact, the first named defender should be assoilzied from the craves of the initial writ.

IN RESPECT WHEREOF

Solicitor
Chieftain Law
16 Somerled Road
Stornoway
Agent for the first named defender

V ACTIONS CONCERNING HERITABLE PROPERTY

1. ALCATRAZ PROPERTIES LTD v CHITTAGONG LTD

Declarator and removing — Irritancy of lease — Payment — Debt — Rent arrears

a. Initial writ

SHERIFFDOM OF NORTH STRATHCLYDE
AT CAMPBELTOWN

INITIAL WRIT

in the cause

ALCATRAZ PROPERTIES LIMITED, a company registered under the Companies Acts, company registration number SC635497, and having its registered office at 1 Lancaster Place, Glasgow G4 6KH

PURSUER

against

CHITTAGONG LIMITED, a company registered under the Companies Acts, company registration number SC497254, and having a place of business at 44 Spice Road, Campbeltown PA28 9YF

DEFENDER

The pursuer craves the court:

1. To find and declare that the defender, having allowed the rent in respect of 44 Spice Road, Campbeltown PA28 9YF to remain unpaid for 21 days after 1 March 2023, being the day appointed for payment thereof, has in terms of the lease granted to the defender by the pursuer of the heritable subjects known as and forming 44 Spice Road, Campbeltown PA28 9YF, dated 5 and 17 March and 4 April and registered in the Books of Council and Session on 15 April all dates in 2022, thereby incurred an

irritancy of the lease; that the lease, with all that has followed thereon, is at an end, and that the parties thereto and their successors are no longer bound thereby; and that the pursuer is entitled to enter upon possession of the said subjects, and to dispone thereof at pleasure; and

2. To ordain the defender summarily to flit and remove itself, its employees and officers, contractors, agents and sub-tenants, with their goods, gear and whole belongings from the heritable subjects known as and forming 44 Spice Road, Campbeltown PA28 9YF, and to leave the same void and redd, that the pursuer may enter thereon and peaceably possess and enjoy the same and, failing removal as aforesaid, to grant warrant for the summary ejection of the defender, its employees and officers, contractors, agents and sub-tenants from the subjects; and

3. To grant decree against the defender for payment to the pursuer of the sum of SIX THOUSAND POUNDS (£6,000) STERLING, with interest thereon at the rate of eight *per cent per annum* from the date of citation until payment; and

4. To find the defender liable in expenses as taxed.

CONDESCENDENCE

1. The parties are as designed in the instance.

2. This action has as its object a tenancy of heritable property situated at 44 Spice Road, Campbeltown PA28 9YF ('the subjects'). This address is within the Sheriffdom of North Strathclyde. This court has exclusive jurisdiction in terms of Section 20 of and Rule 5(1)(a) of Schedule 8 to the Civil Jurisdiction and Judgments Act 1982. The pursuer is unaware of any proceedings pending before any court which are in respect of the subject matter of this writ. There is no agreement to prorogate the jurisdiction of any other court.

3. The pursuer is heritable proprietor of the subjects. By lease dated 5 and 17 March and 4 April and registered in the Books of Council and Session on 15 April, all dates in 2022, the pursuer let the subjects to the defender. The rent payable thereunder was £24,000 per year payable in advance by quarterly instalments at 1 January, 1 April, 1 July and 1 October. Clause ELEVENTH of the lease provided, *inter alia,* that if at any time during the currency thereof the defender should allow a quarter's rent to be in arrears for 21 days (whether demanded or not), the landlord at its option by notice in writing might bring the lease to an end.

4. The defender failed to pay to the pursuer the quarterly instalment of rent due at 1 April 2023. On or about 8 April 2023 the pursuer served a notice upon the defender for the purposes of Section 4 of the Law Reform (Miscellaneous Provisions) (Scotland) Act 1985. The notice required the defender to make payment of £6,000 in terms of the lease within 14 days immediately following service of the notice.

5. The notice stated that if the defender failed to comply with this requirement the lease might be terminated. The defender did not make

any payment. Accordingly, by notice of termination of the lease dated 2 May 2023 the pursuer exercised its option in terms of said clause ELEVENTH to bring the lease to an end.

6. Notwithstanding the notice, the defender has failed to remove from the subjects. The quarterly instalment of rent due at 1 April 2023 remains unpaid. Accordingly, this action is necessary.

PLEAS IN LAW

1. The defender having incurred an irritancy of the lease, decree of declarant or should be granted in terms of crave one.

2. The defender having failed to remove from the subjects, decree of removing which failing ejection should be granted in terms of crave two.

3. The quarterly instalment of rent due as at 1 April 2023 remaining unpaid, decree should be granted in terms of crave three.

IN RESPECT WHEREOF

Solicitor
Spencer and Gill
4 Chester Avenue, Kilmarnock
Agent for the pursuer

2. STEVENSON v THE OCCUPIERS

Ejection — Unnamed occupiers vi, clam aut precario – violent profits

SUMMARY CAUSE SUMMONS

Action for Recovery of Possession of Heritable Property

Sheriff Court (Scotland) Act Section 35(1)(c)

ALEXANDER STEVENSON, residing at 46 Kingsmill Lane, Manchester M5 6AF against THE OCCUPIERS, residing at Greylands Farm Cottage, Greylands, Oban PA34 7TD.

Claim; to grant decree removing the defenders from the heritable subjects known as and forming Greylands Farm Cottage, Greylands, Oban PA34 7TD and to grant warrant to officers of court to eject the defenders, their families and dependents, their belongings and possessions from the said subjects; and to grant decree against the defenders for payment to the pursuer in the sum of £4000 in respect of violent profits; and to grant decree for expenses as assessed and in terms of SCR 4.5.(3) to reduce the period of notice to 48 hours or such other period as to the court shall seem appropriate, on the basis that the defenders are unlawful occupiers.

SERVICE COPY

The pursuer claims that, in the circumstances described in the statement contained in this copy Summons, he is entitled to recover possession of the property at Greylands Farm Cottage, Greylands, Oban PA34 7TD being the heritable subjects registered in the Land Register of Scotland under Title No. ARG166357, and that you refuse or delay to remove from the said property. The pursuer therefore asks the court to grant a decree against you, removing you, and your families, occupants and dependants (if any) with your and their goods and possessions from the property. The pursuer also claims from you the sum of £4,000 in respect of violent profits and he claims the expenses of bringing the action.

STATEMENT

1. The pursuer is the sole proprietor of the heritable subjects known as and forming Greylands Farm Cottage, Greylands, Oban PA34 7TD ('the subjects'). The defenders are the occupiers of the subjects. Their identity is to the pursuer unknown.

2. This action has as its object rights *in rem* in the subjects. They are within the Sheriffdom of North Strathclyde. This court has exclusive jurisdiction in terms of Section 20 of and Rule 5(1)(a) of Schedule 8 to the Civil Jurisdiction and Judgments Act 1982.

3. This action does not concern a tenancy, licence to occupy or any other contract or gratuitous right or obligation existing between the

parties. The First Tier Tribunal (Property Chamber) has no jurisdiction over the subject matter of the cause. The defenders took possession of the subjects *vi clam aut precario.* They have never had authority to occupy the subjects.

4. The defenders arrived unannounced at the subjects in around September 2022. They are persons who have never had title or other right to occupy the subjects. They are and have always been in occupation of the subjects without the pursuer's consent and they have ignored requests to leave. This action is therefore necessary.

5. The pursuer seeks decree against the defenders for payment to the pursuer in the sum of £4000 in respect of violent profits. The pursuer has been deprived of the ability to lease the subjects due to the defenders' presence. In 2020 he leased them to a charity known as Perfect Ponies for the Disabled at a much reduced annual rent of £2,500. The sum of £4,000 is a reasonable estimate of loss.

3 SKELLING v MACFEETERS

Heritable Securities (Scotland) Act 1894 — Conveyancing and Feudal Reform (Scotland) Act 1970 – Calling-up notice

a. Initial writ

SHERIFFDOM OF GLASGOW AND STRATHKELVIN
AT GLASGOW
SUMMARY APPLICATION

Act of Sederunt 1999/929, as amended by the

ACT OF SEDERUNT (SHERIFF COURT RULES) (ENFORCEMENT OF SECURITIES OVER HERITABLE PROPERTY) 2010

INITIAL WRIT

in the cause

MAVIS SKELLING, residing at 1 Villiers Terrace, London W4 9TS

PURSUER

against

SUSAN MACFEETERS, residing at 3 Silk Road, Crossmyloof, Glasgow G44 8TD

DEFENDER

The pursuer craves the court:

1. To find and declare that the defender is in breach of the Standard Security over the heritable subjects known as and forming 3 Silk Road, Crossmyloof, Glasgow G44 8TD which security was granted by the defender on 4 November 2020 and registered in the Land Register of Scotland under Title Number GLA28756 on 6 November 2020, said breach being the defender's failure to comply with the calling up notice served on her on 15 August 2022; and

2. To find and declare that the pursuer is entitled to exercise the rights of ejection, sale and all ancillary rights under the Heritable Securities (Scotland) Act 1894 and the Conveyancing and Feudal Reform (Scotland) Act 1970 in respect of the heritable subjects known as and forming 3 Silk Road, Crossmyloof, Glasgow G44 8TD, Title Number GLA28756; and

3. To grant warrant for service of Form 11D on Dawn Elgood, residing at 3 Silk Road, Crossmyloof, Glasgow G44 8TD as an entitled resident; and

4. To grant decree for the summary ejection of the defender and her family, tenants and entitled residents from the subjects; and

5. To find the defender liable in expenses.

CONDESCENDENCE

1. The parties are as designed in the instance. The pursuer is an individual. She was born in 1951. The defender (hereinafter 'the debtor') is the sole owner of 3 Silk Road, Crossmyloof, Glasgow G44 8TD ('the security subjects'). The security subjects are registered in the Land Register of Scotland under Title Number GLA 28756.

2. The pursuer has a son named Melvin Skelling. He and the debtor were in a relationship from around 2016 to 2021. The debtor was in need of financial assistance for her taxidermy business in Glasgow. Mr Skelling persuaded the pursuer to lend the debtor funds interest free. The pursuer agreed to do so with a repayment period of 12 years so that repayment in full would occur by her 80th birthday. Also, she agreed to lend only with the protection of a standard security. The debtor and Mr Skelling's relationship ended acrimoniously in around July 2021.

3. Believed and averred that Dawn Elgood is the debtor's cohabitant. She lives with the debtor in the security subjects. To the pursuer's knowledge she is the only entitled resident for the purposes of the Home Owner and Debtor Protection (Scotland) Act 2010 and the security subjects are not a matrimonial home. The security subjects are believed to be the defender's sole residence.

4. The present proceedings concern security subjects located in Glasgow. Accordingly, this court has jurisdiction in terms of Section 29 of the Conveyancing and Feudal Reform (Scotland) Act 1970.

5. The pursuer is the holder of a standard security over the security subjects. It was granted by the debtor on 4 November 2020 and registered in the Land Register of Scotland on 6 November 2020 in respect of all sums due to the pursuer.

6. On or about 4 November the debtor borrowed the sum of £86,400 from the pursuer, repayable in 144 monthly instalments of £600 with no interest. She paid the initial 14 instalments in full, totalling £8,400. Since February 2022 the debtor has failed to make any full monthly payments.

7. On 15 August 2022 agents instructed by the pursuer served upon the debtor a notice calling up the standard security under Section 19 of the 1970 Act. The calling up notice details the sums due by the debtor to the pursuer. Also on 15 August 2022 the agents served notice in Form BB on Dawn Elgood. Copies of the notices are produced. Their terms are incorporated herein for the sake of brevity.

8. In addition, the agents served upon;

a) The debtor Form E of Schedule 6 to the 1970 Act.
b) Dawn Elgood Form F of Schedule 6 to the 1970 Act.
c) Glasgow City Council, City Chambers, George Square, Glasgow, notice that a calling up notice had been served upon the debtor. The said council is the local authority within whose jurisdiction the debtor and said Dawn Elwood reside.
d) Analogous notices under Section 5A(2) of the Heritable Securities (Scotland) Act 1894.

Copies are produced. Their terms are incorporated herein.

9. The pursuer has complied with the pre-action requirements as set out in the 1894 Act and in the 1970 Act and in the Applications by Creditors (Pre-Action Requirements)(Scotland) Order 2010. Form 11C is lodged herewith.

10. The debtor failed to comply with the calling up notice. She is thereby held to be in default in terms of Standard Condition 9(1)(a) of Schedule 3 to the 1970 Act. Since February 2022 she has failed to make monthly payments at all or in full. Payments were as follows;

1 February 2022; due; £600. Paid; zero. Arrears; £600
1 March 2022; due; £600. Paid; zero. Arrears; £1,200
1 April 2022; due; £600 Paid; £200 Arrears; £1,600
1 May 2022; due; £600. Paid; zero. Arrears; £2,200
1 June 2022; due; £600. Paid; £100. Arrears; £2,700
1 July 2022; due; £600. Paid; £100. Arrears; £3,200
1 August 2022; due; £600 Paid; zero Arrears; £3,800
1 September 2022; due; £600. Paid; zero. Arrears; £4,400
1 October 2022; due; £600. Paid; zero. Arrears; £5,000.

11. The reason for the non-payment of agreed monthly instalments is not known. In pre-action correspondence the debtor advised that her business was struggling financially due to increased overheads including utility costs and a lack of demand for her services due to Covid. However, she also advised that a large business order was due and that she would be able to clear all arrears by the end of June 2022.

12. Believed and averred that as evidenced by the increase in arrears the debtor is no longer able to afford to repay the loan, and that any postponement of the grant of decree will simply lead to a further escalation of arrears. This would be unreasonable.

13. The pursuer has attempted to assist the debtor by sending her on 17 October 2022 a 'We want to help!' information brochure published by Prospecthill Citizens' Advice Bureau for people struggling with debt. The brochure suggested budgeting techniques, switching mortgage products and where to obtain debt and legal advice. The pursuer also advised her about Glasgow's Advice and Information Network service.

14. Whether the debtor or Dawn Elgood are able to obtain alternative accommodation is not known. However, the security subjects have a current market value of around £140,000 and were

decree to be granted and implemented the sum due to the pursuer will, after the addition of charges, be in the region of £80,000, leaving equity of around £60,000 which ought to be enough to enable the debtor to purchase alternative accommodation or to be able to rent. There are no other secured loans.

15. The pursuer has taken all reasonable steps to avoid requiring to seek to exercise her rights under the Heritable Securities (Scotland) Act 1894 and the Conveyancing and Feudal Reform (Scotland) Act 1970 as amended. She is now entitled to exercise said rights, and decree should be granted as craved.

PLEA IN LAW

The debtor being in breach of the Standard Security over the heritable subjects known as and forming 3 Silk Road, Crossmyloof, Glasgow G44 8TD which security was granted by the debtor on 4 November 2020 and registered in the Land Register of Scotland on 6 November 2020, the said breach being the defender's failure to comply with the calling up notice served on 15 August 2022, and the pursuer being entitled to exercise the rights of ejection and sale and all ancillary rights under the Heritable Securities (Scotland) Act 1894 and the Conveyancing and Feudal Reform (Scotland) Act 1970 decree should be granted as craved.

IN RESPECT WHEREOF

Solicitor
Lanigan Smith
2 Gray Street, Glasgow
Agent for the pursuer

Document attached; Form 11C

4. FRAZER v DALTON

Division and sale

a. Initial writ

SHERIFFDOM OF LOTHIAN AND BORDERS
AT EDINBURGH

INITIAL WRIT

in the cause

ABIGAIL DALTON, residing at 16 Craigs Avenue, Edinburgh EH12 7TD

PURSUER

against

DONALD FRAZER, residing at 12, Cowan Way, Gilmerton, Edinburgh EH4 3WJ

DEFENDER

The pursuer craves the court:

1. To find and declare that the pursuer is entitled to insist in an action of division or sale of All and Whole those heritable subjects known as and forming 12, Cowan Way, Gilmerton, Edinburgh EH4 3WJ, and described in the disposition granted by the trustees of Graeme Ballantyne in favour of James Percy dated 17th, 21st and 22nd and recorded in the Division of the General Register of Sasines applicable to the County of Edinburgh, now Midlothian, on the 29th, all days of July 1926; and

2) In terms of OCR 47.2., to appoint Roger Pooter, solicitor, 17 Unity Gardens, Edinburgh EH3 7TR or such person as the Court shall think proper to dispose of the subjects, heritably and irredeemably, by public roup or private bargain, in such manner and under such conditions as the court shall direct;

3) To ordain the defender to execute and deliver such deeds, affidavits, declarations and writings as may be necessary to grant a marketable title to the purchaser and complete the disposition of the subjects, which failing to dispense with such execution and delivery and to direct the Sheriff Clerk to execute such deeds and writings as may be necessary

aforesaid, all as adjusted at his sight as shall be necessary aforesaid, in terms of Section 87 of the Courts Reform (Scotland) Act 2014; and

4) To find and declare that the net free proceeds of sale after deduction of any debts or burdens affecting the same and following the deduction of all legal and administrative fees, costs and outlays, including the fees of any estate agent or surveyor, the expense of any advance notice, legal report, coal report, property enquiry report and all other necessary reports, searches and documents be divided equally between the parties.

5) To find the defender liable in expenses as taxed.

CONDESCENDENCE

1. The parties are as designed in the instance. They are former cohabitants. They separated in around July 2020.

2. This action has as its object rights *in rem* in 12 Cowan Way, Gilmerton, Edinburgh EH4 3WJ (hereinafter 'the subjects'). The subjects are located in the Sheriffdom of Lothian and Borders. Edinburgh sheriff court has exclusive jurisdiction in terms of Section 20 of and Rule 5(1)(a) of Schedule 8 to the Civil Jurisdiction and Judgments Act 1982. The pursuer is unaware of any proceedings pending before any court which are in respect of the subject matter of this writ. There is no agreement to prorogate the jurisdiction of any other court.

3. The parties are one half *pro indiviso* heritable proprietors of the subjects by virtue of a disposition in their favour granted by Major Iain Harcourt on 5 June 1979 and recorded in the Division of the General Register of Sasines applicable to the County of Midlothian on 9 June 1979.

4. The pursuer seeks division or sale thereof as craved. The defender refuses or at least delays to agree to such. Accordingly, this action is necessary.

5. The subjects comprise a two bedroom mid terrace dwellinghouse. They have a market value of around £140,000. They are not divisible in any practical or expedient manner. Accordingly, a remit to determine the question of division is not sought.

PLEA IN LAW

The parties being *pro indiviso* proprietors of the subjects and the pursuer being entitled to insist in the division or sale thereof and division being impractical and inexpedient decree should be granted as craved.

IN RESPECT WHEREOF

Solicitor
Swinton and McGhie
22 Castle Drive, Edinburgh
Agent for the pursuer

b. Defences

SHERIFFDOM OF LOTHIAN AND BORDERS
AT EDINBURGH

EDI-A457-23

DEFENCES

in the cause

ABIGAIL DALTON, [*designation*]

PURSUER

against

DONALD FRAZER, [*designation*]

DEFENDER

ANSWERS

1. Admitted.

2. Admitted that this court has jurisdiction.

3. Denied. The *pro indiviso* heritable proprietors of the subjects are the parties and by virtue of the said disposition granted by Major Iain Harcourt and an as yet unregistered disposition by the defender dated 19 March 2023 disponing one half of his half to the aforementioned Walter Elphinstone.

4. Denied that this action is necessary. The pursuer is personally barred from pursuing it. On or around August 2022 the parties and Walter Elphinstone, 14 Trelawny Crescent, Musselburgh agreed that the defender would pay the pursuer the sum of £55,000 in return for her one half share of the subjects. The defender is willing to pay the sum in exchange for a disposition of said half share. Separately, the defender made payments of household overheads well in excess of those made by the pursuer.

5. Admitted that the subjects comprise a two bedroom mid terrace dwellinghouse. *Quoad ultra* not known and not admitted.

PLEAS IN LAW

1) The parties having settled the claim on 18 August 2022 and the defender being willing and able to implement the terms of settlement the pursuer is personally barred from pursuing the action, which should be dismissed.

2) All parties not called.

3) The pursuer's averments being unfounded in fact the defender should be assoilzied from the craves of the initial writ.

4) The pursuer not being entitled to insist in the division or sale of the subjects the defender should be assoilzied from the craves of the initial writ

IN RESPECT WHEREOF

Solicitor
Swinton and McGhie
22 Castle Drive, Edinburgh
Agent for the defender

c. Rule 22 Note for the pursuer

SHERIFFDOM OF LOTHIAN AND BORDERS
AT EDINBURGH

EDI-A457-23

RULE 22 NOTE FOR THE
PURSUER

in the cause

ABIGAIL DALTON, [*designation*]

PURSUER

against

DONALD FRAZER, [*designation*]

DEFENDER

The pursuer wishes to insist in her preliminary plea, number 1, that the defender's pleadings being irrelevant and, separately, lacking in specification decree should be granted as craved, in respect that:

1) An unregistered disposition does not transfer ownership; Land Registration (Scotland) Act 2012 Section 50(3).

2) The averments of an alleged settlement are so lacking in specification as to be irrelevant in that they fail to state how or where the agreement was reached. Even the date is unspecific. There is a fundamental lack of fair notice.

3) The averments of payments towards household overheads are equally unspecific and while they may have been relevant to a claim – which is now time barred – under Section 28 of the Family Law (Scotland) Act 2006 they are irrelevant insofar as constituting a defence to an action of division and sale. The pursuer as co-owner is entitled to the remedy sought; *Upper Crathes Fishings Ltd v Bailey's Executors* 1991 SLT 747.

IN RESPECT WHEREOF

Threepwoods LLP
36 Maris Drive
Glasgow G38 6TD
Agent for the pursuer

5. CALDER AND CALDER v BURNS

Damages – Breach of Missives – Simple Procedure

D1. Claim; Paper Apart

By missives dated 23 February, 6 March and 20 March, all 2023, the claimants agreed to buy and the respondents agreed to sell the house at 68 Blackberry Way, Kirkcudbright, DG6 8RD. The missives incorporated the Scottish Standard Clauses, edition 5 (August 2022).

Clause 4.1 states that any central heating system be 'in working order commensurate with age at the Date of Settlement'. Clause 4.2 states that any defect will be 'made good if intimated within 5 working days'.

Settlement was on Friday 20 March 2023. Over the weekend the claimants tried to operate the central heating system. Prior to 9am on the Saturday the first claimant operated the 'On' switch on the boiler control board. Within half an hour the control panel was too hot to touch. The first claimant switched off the system, using oven gloves. The second claimant operated the 'On' switch that afternoon. Within 20 minutes there was a smell of burning. There was also substantial vibration and a sound of repeated and loud 'knocks' emanating from the outlet from the water pump located next to the boiler. There was no heat in any radiators. There was no hot water flowing from any taps.

On Monday 23 March 2023 agents acting for the claimants emailed the respondents' agents intimating that the central heating system was defective. The respondents' agents were unable to obtain instructions. On 15 April they withdrew from acting. They suggested that the claimants write to the respondents directly. The claimants did so. They met with no response.

The claimants instructed T Breen Heating Engineers Ltd to inspect the system. They did so on 25 March, and again on 7 April. On the former occasion Tam Breen advised the claimants not to use the system as it was a fire hazard and would not heat water. Mr Breen produced a report and quotation. A copy is attached. The system was obsolete, clogged with sludge and appeared never to have been serviced.

The claimants have a 4 year old daughter. Due to a lack of heating and hot water in the house the family stayed with the second claimant's mother until the system was repaired or replaced.

The report recommended replacement. The claimants posted a copy to the respondents on 9 April and gave them 7 days to respond. No response was received. The claimants instructed the recommended work. This was carried out and an invoice issued on 19 April 2023. The claimants paid it. It was for £5,450 including VAT. A copy of the invoice and a printout of the claimants' bank statement showing payment are produced. The claimants are willing to restrict their claim to £5,000 in order to use Simple Procedure.

D7. My claim should be successful because:

The respondents are in breach of contract. We gave them the opportunity to put matters right and they failed to respond. We had to rectify the defective central system ourselves. The sum claimed represents the damages we are due, modified down to enable us to bring the claim under Simple Procedure.

VI ACTIONS CONCERNING TRUSTS

1. BRICE, PETITIONER

Appointment of new trustee under Section 22, Trusts (Scotland) Act 1921.

a. Petition

SHERIFFDOM OF LOTHIAN AND BORDERS AT LIVINGSTON

PETITION

of

ELIZABETH BRICE, residing at 11 Ratho Wynd, Livingston, West Lothian EH52

for

Appointment of a new trustee to act under the Trust Disposition and Settlement of the late Raymond Lincoln dated 11 November 1999 and registered in the Books of Council and Session on 5 January 2001

The petitioner craves the court:

To appoint this petition to be intimated on the walls of court and to be served on Arthur Watts, residing at 68 Berkeley Mews, London WC5 7SH and on Victor Welland, 11 Canal Way, Broxburn and to ordain them and all other parties interested to lodge answers, if so advised, within 21 days after intimation; thereafter, upon resuming consideration hereof, with or without answers and after such inquiry if any as may be thought necessary, to appoint Gordon Hawksley, Solicitor, 14 Queen Street, Livingston, or such other person as the court thinks fit, to be a trustee acting under the Trust, Disposition and Settlement of the late Raymond Lincoln dated 11 November 1999 and registered in the Books of Council and Session on 5 January 2001, with all the powers incident to that office; and to find the petitioner entitled to the expenses of this petition and the procedure to follow hereon out of the trust estate.

STATEMENT OF FACTS

1. By the Trust Disposition and Settlement of the late Raymond Lincoln dated 11 November 1999 and registered in the Books of

Council and Session on 5 January 2001 Raymond Lincoln (hereinafter referred to as 'the truster') appointed Arthur Watts to be his trustee and conveyed to him his whole means and estate, heritable and moveable, real and personal, in trust for the purposes therein specified. A copy of the Trust Disposition and Settlement is produced. The truster died at St John's Hospital, West Lothian on 10 November 2019. At that date, which was the date of the coming into operation of the trust, he resided at 66 Florence Avenue, Livingston. He was domiciled there, in the Sheriffdom of Lothian and Borders. This court accordingly has jurisdiction.

2. The beneficiaries of the trust estate are the petitioner and her brother, Victor Welland, 11 Canal Way, Broxburn. There are no other persons with an interest therein.

3. Arthur Watts, having accepted office as sole trustee aforesaid, has disappeared for a period of at least six months. He was last seen in London at Christmas 2021. His whereabouts are not known. He has not assumed any other person to act as trustee. The petitioner is therefore under necessity of bringing this petition for appointment of a new trustee, in terms of the Trusts (Scotland) Act 1921, section 22. She respectfully suggests that Gordon Hawksley, Solicitor, 14 Queen Street, Livingston is a suitable person for the office of trustee.

PLEA IN LAW

The sole trustee of the trust estate having disappeared for a period of at least six months, a new trustee should be appointed as craved.

IN RESPECT WHEREOF

Solicitor
14 Queen Street, Bathgate
Agent for the petitioner

2. FRY, PETITIONER

Removal of trustee – Section 23, Trusts (Scotland) Act 1921.

a. Petition

SHERIFFDOM OF TAYSIDE, CENTRAL AND FIFE
AT FORFAR

PETITION

In respect of

The Trusts (Scotland) Act 1921, section 23

By

CONSTANCE FRY, residing at 11 Shantung Avenue, Newcastle Upon Tyne NE2 6YF

The petitioner craves the court:

To appoint this petition to be intimated on the walls of court and to be served on Eustace Pye, c/o Basil Carter Memorial Hospital, Lunanhead, Angus DD8 5RS and Florence Spye, residing at 11 Stonehenge Court, Salisbury SP1 8FE; to ordain them and all other parties interested to lodge answers, if so advised, within 21 days after intimation and service; thereafter, upon resuming consideration hereof, with or without answers and after such inquiry if any as may be thought necessary, to remove Eustace Pye from the office of trustee acting under the Trust Deed of Cyril Pye dated 11 February 1996 and registered in the Books of Council and Session on 9 January 2023; and to find the petitioner entitled to the expenses of this petition and the procedure to follow out of the capital of the trust estate.

STATEMENT OF FACTS

1. By Trust Deed dated 11 February 1996 and registered in the Books of Council and Session on 9 January 2023 Cyril Pye (hereinafter 'the truster') appointed the petitioner and Eustace Pye, now c/o Basil Carter Memorial Hospital, Lunanhead, Angus DD8 5RS to be his trustees.

2. He conveyed to them certain property in trust for the purposes therein specified. A copy of the Trust Deed is produced. The trust came

into operation on 4 November 1999. As at that date, the truster was domiciled in the Sheriffdom of Tayside, Central and Fife. This court accordingly has jurisdiction.

3. The sole beneficiary of the trust is Florence Spye, residing at 11 Stonehenge Court, Salisbury SP1 8FE. There are no other persons with an interest in the trust.

4. Eustace Pye has become incapable of acting as trustee aforesaid by reason of dementia. Medical certificates from Dr McCune and Dr Smith are produced herewith.

5. Accordingly, the petitioner seeks removal of Eustace Pye from the office of trustee. This is in terms of the Trusts (Scotland) Act 1921, section 23.

PLEA IN LAW

The trustee having become incapable of acting as trustee by reason of mental disability, she ought to be removed from the office of trustee in terms of Section 23 of the Trusts (Scotland) Act 1921,

IN RESPECT WHEREOF

Solicitor
7 Pictish Avenue
Forfar
Agent for the petitioner

3. LINKLATER, PETITIONER

Completion of title to trust property by beneficiary of lapsed trust – Trusts (Scotland) Act 1921, section 24.

a. Petition

SHERIFFDOM OF GRAMPIAN, HIGHLAND AND ISLANDS
AT LERWICK

PETITION

In respect of

The Trusts (Scotland) Act 1921, section 24.

By

ELSPETH LINKLATER residing at 3 Muness Castle Road, Clivocast, Unst, Shetland ZE2 6TR

The petitioner craves the court:

To appoint this petition to be intimated on the walls of court; to ordain all parties interested to lodge answers, if so advised, within 21 days after intimation; thereafter, upon resuming consideration hereof, with or without answers and after such inquiry if any as may be thought necessary, to authorise and grant warrant to the petitioner to complete a title in her own name to the heritable subjects All and Whole that dwellinghouse being the southmost flat on the ground floor of the tenement number 8 Eriksson Street, Hamnavoe, Burra, Shetland ZE2 7GS in the County of Zetland, being the dwellinghouse described and disponed in the disposition by Symond Laurenson in favour of Ingabar Eunson dated 9 August 1961 and recorded in the Division of the General Register of Sasines for the County of Zetland on 17 August 1961, together with all rights exclusive, common and mutual thereto, fixtures and fittings therein and parts and pertinents thereof described in the disposition; and to find any person opposing this petition liable in expenses.

STATEMENT OF FACTS

1. By Trust Disposition and Settlement dated 11 March 1977 and registered in the Books of Council and Session on 8 January 2023,

Ragnar Larsen (hereinafter referred to as 'the truster') appointed Senga Gahan, then residing at 66 Cemetery Lane, Aberdeen AB4 7TF to be his trustee. He conveyed to her his whole means and estate, heritable and moveable, real and personal, in trust for the purposes specified in the Trust, Disposition and Settlement. A copy is produced. The truster died at Scalloway, Shetland on 4 September 2020. At that date, which was the date of the coming into operation of the trust, he was domiciled in the Sheriffdom of Grampian, Highland and Islands. Accordingly, this court has jurisdiction.

2. The petitioner is the sole beneficiary of the trust. There are no other persons with an interest therein.

3. The truster was at the date of his death proprietor of the heritable subjects All and Whole that dwellinghouse being the southmost flat on the ground floor of the tenement number 8 Eriksson Street, Hamnavoe, Burra, Shetland ZE2 7GS in the County of Zetland being the dwellinghouse described and disponed in the disposition by Symond Laurenson in favour of Ingabar Eunson dated 9 August 1961 and recorded in the Division of the General Register of Sasines for the County of Zetland on 17 August 1961 together with all rights exclusive, common and mutual thereto, fixtures and fittings therein and parts and pertinents thereof described in the disposition. Senga Gahan, having accepted office as sole trustee aforesaid, died on 11 December 2022 without having assumed any other person to act as trustee. The trust has therefore lapsed. The petitioner is desirous of completing title to the heritable subjects in her own name. She therefore brings this petition for authority and warrant to do so, in terms of the Trusts (Scotland) Act 1921, section 24.

PLEA IN LAW

The petitioner being the sole beneficiary of a lapsed trust, should be granted the authority and warrant of the court to complete title to trust property in her own name, as craved.

IN RESPECT WHEREOF

solicitor
2 Jarlshof Way
Lerwick
Solicitor for the petitioner

VII EXPENSES

1. WOLFSON v SUTHERLAND

Minute to find dominis litis liable in expenses

SHERIFFDOM OF GRAMPIAN, HIGHLAND AND ISLANDS
AT WICK

GLW-A674-22

MINUTE

To have *dominis litis* found liable in expenses in the cause

FELIX WOLFSON trading as AMICABLE ATTORNEY and having a place of business at 16 Harbour Road, Staxigoe Caithness KW1 8ER

MINUTER

against

ALLAN SUTHERLAND, care of SUTHERLAND FINANCIAL ADVICE HUB LIMITED having its registered office at 11 Norse Park, Paxigoe Caithness KW1 9HW

RESPONDENT

The minuter craves the court to find the respondent personally liable in the expenses of the cause as taxed.

CONDESCENDENCE

1) The parties are as designed. The respondent is the sole director of and shareholder in the company known as Sutherland Financial Advice Hub Limited and having its registered office at the address in the instance (hereinafter 'the company'). In respect of the cause the respondent is *dominis litis*.

2) The company instructed the minuter to act on its behalf in respect of a dispute between the company and a former employee. The minuter charged fees for his services. These were unpaid and the minuter required

to raise these proceedings against the company. The company's defence of this cause has been dilatory. Proceedings were raised on 10 July 2022. A Notice of Intention to Defend was lodged. Skeletal Defences were lodged on the last day permitted. These were never adjusted. On 27 August the company's agents emailed the defender's agents to advise that a motion would be enrolled for summary decree. On 29 August the company's agents withdrew from acting. A peremptory diet was assigned.

3) New agents appeared for the company. They withdrew from acting after less than a week. A third firm of solicitors commenced acting for the company.

4) On 27 September the minuter and the company agreed a joint remit to the Auditor of Court. The cause was sisted for the purpose of such a remit. A remit took place. The Auditor was provided with the minuter's file. The Auditor's report was to the effect that he had undercharged. On 19 November the third firm wrote to advise that the company had 'now ceased trading', that the solicitors would be withdrawing from acting and that 'there would be no further defence offered, the company regrettably being without funds to meet any outstanding debts.

5) A peremptory diet was assigned. There was no appearance for the company. The court granted decree and continued consideration of the minuter's motion to have the respondent found personally liable in expenses as *dominis litis*. The matter was continued to 18 December 2022. On 16 December Finn Sharkey, solicitors advised that they were acting for the respondent

6) The respondent has acted in bad faith in respect of the company's defence of the proceedings. As the respondent was well aware, there was never a stateable defence to the claim. Had he believed that there was a defence he would, in his capacity as company director, have directed that the company continue to defend the cause until its conclusion. He has never applied to be allowed to represent the company in terms of Section 97 of the Courts Reform (Scotland) Act 2014.

7) The company has been insolvent for the entire duration of this litigation. Reference is made to the company's accounts for the year ended 31 July 2022 approved by the respondent on 9 November 2022. The respondent is a financial advisor. He was well aware of the company's financial situation.

8) Believed and averred that the company was never in a position to meet any decree granted in favour of the minuter.

9) The party with a real interest in defending these proceedings has been the respondent. He has continued to derive a financial benefit from the company. The accounts state that under its pension scheme the company makes contributions to the Fund of the sole director'.

10) The company is a nominal defender. The respondent, as *dominis litis*, has a direct and personal interest in the subject matter of the cause and has controlled the company's defence of the proceedings. The

respondent, having caused the minuter to have incurred the expenses of proceeding with his claim should be found personally liable in those expenses.

PLEA IN LAW

The respondent being *dominis litis* in the cause, as condescended upon, should be found personally liable in the expenses thereof as taxed.

IN RESPECT WHEREOF

Rankine Steen
17 Groats Street
Wick
Agent for the minuter

2. TOMAHAWK v THE ARMADALE WORKING MEN'S CLUB AND INSTITUTE

Motion for interest on expenses – motion to have expenses to solicitor as agent disburser

Motion

SHERIFFDOM OF LOTHIAN AND BORDERS
AT LIVINGSTON

LIV-A876-23

MOTION FOR THE DEFENDER

in the cause

JOHNNY TOMAHAWK residing at 12 Hotspur Street, Bathgate EH48 9HG

PURSUER

against

THE ARMADALE WORKING MEN'S CLUB AND INSTITUTE, a registered society under the Co-operative and Community Benefit Societies Act 2014 and registered in the Mutuals Public Register under number 28764R and and having a place of business at 66 Linlithgow Road EH48 5RD

DEFENDER

PIPER for the defender moves the court:

In respect that the interlocutor of 17 March 2023 constituted a final judgment finding the defender entitled to expenses, the defender lodged an account with the sheriff clerk on 19 April 2023 in terms of Ordinary Cause Rule 32.1A and on 2 May 2023 the auditor transmitted to the sheriff clerk a statement of the taxed expenses and the taxed account, as required by OCR 32.3A.

1. To grant decree for expenses as taxed together with interest at the rate of 8 *per centum per annum* from 19 May 2023 until payment or from such other date no earlier than 28 days after 19 April 2023, the date on which the account of expenses was lodged. Reference is made to OCR 32.5.

2. In terms of OCR 32.2. to allow the decree for expenses to be extracted in the name of Desiree Piper, solicitor, 36 Maris Drive, Glasgow G38 6TD, agent for the defender in the conduct of the cause.

IN RESPECT WHEREOF

Charlotte Edward LLP
36 Maris Drive
Falkirk FK2 6TD

3. COLLINGWOOD v VILLENEUVE

Motion for percentage increase in fees – Taxation of Judicial Expenses Rules 2019

SHERIFFDOM OF NORTH STRATHCLYDE AT OBAN

OBA-A71-23

MOTION

In terms of Rule 5.1, SSI 2019/75

in the cause

SAMUEL COLLINGWOOD, residing at 16 Marlin Place, Kilsyth G65 6TW

PURSUER

against

ODETTE VILLENEUVE, residing at 114 Rue Jean Moulin, 34200 Saint-Malo, France

DEFENDER

JELLICOE for the defender moves the court:

1) To increase by 80% or by such other percentage as to the court shall seem reasonable the fee charges to be allowed at taxation, in respect that with regard to the factors enumerated at Rule 5.2(6) of the Taxation of Judicial Expenses Rules 2019:

(a) The cause was unduly complex and raised a number of difficult or novel questions; the action concerned a collision between a floating timber fishing platform or raft owned by the pursuer and the defender's yacht Hermione. The cause was raised as a standard action for reparation. However, the defences asserted that the two vessels were ships as defined by Section 48 of the Administration of Justice Act 1956 and since the action concerned a collision the cause ought to have been an Admiralty action *in personem* and governed by the specialized and unique procedure specified in Ordinary

Cause Rule 49. Reference was made to numerous authorities on the definition of 'ship' including Lord Marnoch's review of case law in *Global Marine Drilling Company v Triton Holdings Ltd* (1999)

In addition, there was a dispute over jurisdiction (with reference to Section 45 of the 1956 Act and Section 40 of the Courts Reform (Scotland) Act 2014) insofar as the collision occurred within the Sound of Mull, around 1 mile east of Tobermory and on the boundary between this sheriffdom and that of Grampian Highland and Islands.

(b) The solicitor required to deploy unusual skill, time, labour and specialised knowledge. The defender cannot speak English. An interpreter was required in order to enable the solicitor to take instructions. In addition, the means of propulsion of the pursuer's platform/raft, and the use of oars has a significant bearing on whether the vessel is defined as a ship for the purposes of the 1956 Act. The defender's solicitor has considerable experience of maritime collision cases.

(c) The solicitor required to peruse documents concerning the purpose and design of the platform/raft and her use as a vessel propelled by oars, engine or sail.

(d) The solicitor was instructed three days before the expiry of the period of notice following service of the Initial Writ and required to consider whether lodging a NID would imply acceptance of the form of procedure chosen by the pursuer. Instructions had to be taken on whether caution for expenses should be sought. Also, the solicitor and an interpreter had to visit the defender at a guest house on Mull to take instructions.

(e) The proceedings were of significant importance to the client in that Hermione was damaged and was rendered unseaworthy and there was a concern over whether she would be arrested in Tobermory harbour where she had been towed to await repairs.

(f) Hermione has a value of around 18,500 Euros (£18,000) and the defender had been depending on returning to her home in France by sailing the vessel back there.

(g) Considerable steps were taken by the defender's solicitor to settle the cause, including corresponding with insurers, including those in France, and negotiating the disposal of the cause and reaching agreement to use alternative dispute resolution (Timothy Nelson, Nautical Arbiter) to determine the outcome of the parties' dispute.

IN RESPECT WHEREOF

Jeremy Jellicoe
1815 Trafalgar Street
Glasgow G1 6TF
Agent for the defender

VIII MISCELLANEOUS SUMMARY APPLICATIONS

1. MONTAGUE v CAPULET

Suspension of charge

Initial writ

SHERIFFDOM OF NORTH STRATHCLYDE AT PAISLEY

SUMMARY APPLICATION UNDER THE SHERIFF COURTS (SCOTLAND) ACT 1907, s 5(5)

INITIAL WRIT

in the cause

HAZEL MONTAGUE, residing at 18 Mirren Avenue, Paisley G49 Porteous Place, Glasgow G52 9AJ

PURSUER

against

ANNE-MARIE CAPULET residing at 8 White Cart Grove, Bishopton, PA7 5GE

DEFENDER

The pursuer craves the court:

1. To suspend a pretended charge served by the defender upon the pursuer on 11 January 2023, founded on a decree of this court for payment dated 3 December 2022 in action PAI-A576-22 and extracted on 7 January 2023, and any diligence following thereon.

2. To interdict the defender and any other person acting on her instructions from taking any action of enforcement, diligence, sequestration or any other steps or processes on the basis of the pretended charge served by the defender on the pursuer on 11 January 2023, founded on a decree of this court for payment dated 3 December 2022 in action PAI-A576-22 and extracted on 7 January 2023 and to grant interdict *ad interim.*

3. To find the defender liable in expenses.

CONDESCENDENCE

1. The parties are as designed in the instance. This action concerns the enforcement against the pursuer at her address in the instance and within the Sheriffdom of North Strathclyde of a decree granted by this court. This court has jurisdiction in terms of Section 5(5) of the Sheriff Courts (Scotland) Act 1907 and Section 20 of and Rule 5(1)(d) of Schedule 8 to the Civil Jurisdiction and Judgments Act 1982.

2. The pursuer has had signetted but has not yet served an action in the Court of Session for the reduction of the charge which is the subject matter of this initial writ. With the exception of that action the pursuer is unaware of any proceedings before any court which are in respect of the subject matter of this writ.

3. A decree of this court for payment, dated 3 December 2022 and extracted on 7 January 2023 in action PAI-A576-22 was granted against the pursuer by this court. The decree was for payment to the defender in the sum of £24,483, together with interest and expenses.

4. The pursuer made payment to the defender of all sums due to her, including interest and expenses. She did so on or about 17 December 2022. She did so by bank transfer. She emailed the defender that day to state that payment was being made. Copies of the bank transfer statement and email are produced herewith.

5. Notwithstanding payment, on 11 January 2023 a pretended charge for payment of £25,173, together with interest, was served on the pursuer by sheriff officers instructed by the defender.

6. The days of charge will expire on 25 January 2023. This would render the pursuer vulnerable to diligence and to a claim that she was apparently insolvent for the purposes of Section 16 of the Bankruptcy (Scotland) Act 2016. This application is therefore necessary. Having regard to the balance of convenience, interim interdict ought to be granted.

PLEAS IN LAW

1) The defender's decree for payment having been satisfied, the charge and diligence following thereon should be suspended as craved.

2) The defender having instructed the service of a charge despite the extinction of the pursuer's debt and the pursuer being reasonably apprehensive that the defender will pursue wrongful diligence or sequestration interdict as craved is necessary.

3) Having regard to the balance of convenience decree of interdict should be granted *ad interim.*

IN RESPECT WHEREOF

Solicitor
Dodson and Fogg
20 Pickwick Road, Glasgow
G2 6TY
Agent for the pursuer

2. ORZECHOWSKI v OTCASEK

Warrant to cite witnesses and havers in arbitration

Initial writ

SHERIFFDOM OF GLASGOW AND STRATHKELVIN AT GLASGOW

SUMMARY APPLICATION UNDER THE ARBITRATION (SCOTLAND) ACT 2010, s 7

INITIAL WRIT

Scottish Arbitration Rule 45

in the cause

GREG ORZECHOWSKI, residing at 78 Easton Street, Glasgow G9 7BD.

PURSUER

against

CANDY OTCASEK residing at 79 Elliot Row, Glasgow G4 8YD.

DEFENDER

The pursuer craves the court:

To order Desmond Edmonds, residing at 14 Scythia Gardens, Bridge of Weir PA11 6DR and Ermentrude Orleans, 15 Main Street, Bride of Cally PH10 5RD to appear before Abraham Atuahene, arbiter in the arbitration between the pursuer and the defender in terms of the deed of submission dated 7 August and registered in the Books of Council and Session on 19 December 2022, said appearance to be on 18 July 2023 at 11am at Oattes Hall, Falstaff Road, Glasgow G3 7RJ and on such other occasion and at such other places as the arbiter may appoint for diets of proof in the said arbitration, to give evidence to the arbitration for the pursuer and also to produce all documents in their possession or control falling within the terms of the specification of documents annexed hereto; and in the event of any such witness or haver failing to appear after due citation to grant warrant for the issue of letters of second diligence in common form against them at the instance of the pursuer.

CONDESCENDENCE

1. The parties are as designed in the instance.

2. By deed of submission dated 7 August and registered in the Books of Council and Session on 19 December 2022 the parties agreed to submit a dispute to arbitration. They nominated and appointed as arbiter Abraham Atuahene, 16 Windsor Avenue, Glasgow G12 7TD. He accepted office. He did so by email dated 15 February 2023.

3. For the purposes of Section 20 of and Rule 6 of Schedule 8 to the Civil Jurisdiction and Judgments Act 1982 the parties agreed in the deed of submission that this court has jurisdiction. In terms of Section 7 of the Arbitration (Scotland) Act 2010 the arbitration is subject to the Scottish Arbitration Rules. Rule 45 thereof authorises this court to grant the order sought.

4. The arbiter: (1) allowed proof of the parties' claims in the arbitration and appointed same to be heard at James Hall, James Street, Glasgow on 30 November 2022 at 10am and on such other occasions and at such other places as he might thereafter appoint; and (2) approved the specification of documents annexed hereto. He did so in terms of the order dated 2 November 2022.

5. Copies of the deed, email and order are produced herewith and referred to for their terms.

6. Desmond Edmonds, residing at 14 Scythia Gardens, Bridge of Weir PA11 6DR and Ermentrude Orleans, 15 Main Street, Bride of Cally PH10 5RD are essential witnesses for the pursuer. The pursuer sent messages to them on 16 September and 2 November 2022 requesting that they attend the hearing. Desmond Edmonds stated that he was 'too busy'. Ermentrude Orleans advised that she would not attend under any circumstances. The hearing had to be adjourned, to 18 July 2023.

7. In these circumstances, the order sought is necessary.

PLEA IN LAW

The persons named in the crave being essential witnesses for the pursuer and having failed to attend the arbitration hearing already assigned, the order sought should be granted in terms of Scottish Arbitration Rule 45.

IN RESPECT WHEREOF

Solicitor
Nymph and Shepherd
24 Balfour Street, Glasgow
Agent for the pursuer

3. TODE v SLAMANNAN COUNCIL

Civic government appeal — Taxi licence — Licensing authority erring in law

Initial writ

SHERIFFDOM OF TAYSIDE, CENTRAL AND FIFE AT FALKIRK

SUMMARY APPLICATION UNDER THE CIVIC GOVERNMENT (SCOTLAND) ACT 1982, Sch 1, para 18

INITIAL WRIT

in the cause

GRAHAME TODE, residing at 1, Hall Street, Slamannan FK1 6RE

PURSUER

against

SLAMANNAN COUNCIL, a licensing authority having its offices at 1 Mannan Square, Slamannan FK1 6RE

DEFENDER

The pursuer craves the court:

1. To reverse the decision of the defender made on 1 April 2023 to refuse the application by the pursuer for a taxi licence, and to grant the application; or to make such other order as the court thinks fit.
2. To find the defender liable in expenses.

CONDESCENDENCE

1. The parties are as designed in the instance. The defender is a licensing authority with its offices at 1 Mannan Square, Slamannan. It is domiciled there. Accordingly, this court has jurisdiction.
2. The pursuer submitted an application for a taxi licence. On 1 April 2023 the defender considered it and refused it. It purported to find a ground for refusal, namely that set forth in Schedule 1, paragraph 5(3)(a)

(ii), which so far as material provides: '… the applicant … is … not a fit and proper person to be the holder of the licence.'

3. Thereafter the defender issued to the pursuer a statement of its reasons. A copy is produced and its terms held as repeated herein for the sake of brevity. In particular, the defender purported so to find on the basis that the pursuer had a number of convictions for having driven at excessive speed.

4. In arriving at its decision, the defender erred in law. Such convictions have no relevance to the issue of whether or not a taxi licence should be granted. The defender therefore took into account an irrelevant consideration.

5. In these circumstances, the defender's decision should be reversed and the pursuer's application granted.

PLEA IN LAW

The defender in arriving at its decision having erred in law, insofar as having taken into account an irrelevant consideration. Its decision should be reversed and the pursuer's application granted, as craved.

IN RESPECT WHEREOF

Solicitor
16 Badger House,
Slammanan
Agent for the pursuer

4. WATSON v COMHAIRLE NAN EILEAN SIAR

Education appeal — Refusal of placing request

Initial writ

SHERIFFDOM OF GRAMPIAN, HIGHLAND
AND ISLANDS AT PORTREE

SUMMARY APPLICATION UNDER THE EDUCATION
(SCOTLAND) ACT 1980, s 28F(1)

INITIAL WRIT

in the cause

SEBASTIAN WATSON, residing at 77 Fiosgabhaig, Skye IV47 8FS

PURSUER

against

COMHAIRLE NAN EILEAN A CHEO, an education authority having its headquarters at Cuillin House, Uig, Isle of Skye IV51 7RS,

DEFENDER

The pursuer craves the court:

1. To reverse the decision of the defender's appeal committee made on 30 January 2023; and

2. To refuse to confirm the decision of the defender dated 7 February 2023 refusing the written request by the pursuer that the defender place his child, Jeremy Watson, born on 23 April 2014, in Florigarry Primary School, Matthew Henson Road, Skye; and to require the defenders to give effect to the pursuer's placing request of 17 November 2022.

3. To find the defender liable in expenses.

CONDESCENDENCE

1. The parties are as designed in the instance. The pursuer and his son Jeremy Oscar Watson, born on 23 April 2014 (hereinafter 'Jeremy') moved to Skye from Surrey in 2022. The defender is an education authority. It manages Florigarry Primary School. The school is located within the jurisdiction of this court. Accordingly, Portree Sheriff Court has jurisdiction.

2. On 17 November 2022 the pursuer made a written request to the defender that Jeremy be placed in the said school. On 30 January 2023, the defender made a decision refusing the request. The defender purported to be satisfied that a ground of refusal existed in terms of Section 28A(3)(a)(i) of the Education (Scotland) Act 1980.

3. The purported ground was that granting the request would compel the defender to employ an additional teacher at Florigarry Primary School and that, therefore, its duty to place Jeremy there does not apply. Reference is made to the defender's statement of reasons. It is produced and its terms repeated herein for the sake of brevity.

4. The defender offered Jeremy a place at Ketill Primary School, Merkadale, Skye IV47 8ST.

5. The pursuer thereafter referred the decision to an appeal committee of the defender, which confirmed the defender's decision on 7 February 2023.

6. It is denied that the placing of Jeremy at Florigarry Primary School would require the employment of an additional teacher there. There are 21 children in primary 7, the year appropriate for Jeremy given his age.

7. No ground of refusal exists in respect of the placing request. The defender's decision should not be confirmed. In any event, it is in all the circumstances inappropriate that the decision should be confirmed.

PLEA IN LAW

There existing no ground of refusal in respect of the placing request, and in any event it being in all the circumstances inappropriate to do so, the decision should not be confirmed.

IN RESPECT WHEREOF

Solicitor
The Law One
Unit 14
Longman Industrial Estate
Inverness IV1 1RT
Agent for the pursuer

5. SCOTTISH MINISTERS v MCAVEETY

Proceeds of Crime Act 2002 – Answers to Summary Application

Answers

SHERIFFDOM OF NORTH STRATHCLYDE
AT KILMARNOCK

KIL-B732-23

ANSWERS

in causa

THE SCOTTISH MINISTERS,
Civil Recovery Unit,
25 Chambers Street, Edinburgh

PURSUER

against

PHILLIP McAVEETY, residing at 30 Annetyard Drive Skelmorlie PA17 5BN

DEFENDER

ANSWERS

1. The pursuers' designation is not known and not admitted.
2. Admitted that this court has jurisdiction.
3. Admitted that on or about 11 October 2022 officers from Police Scotland attended the said premises. The basis on which they did so, the nature and source and the reliability of the information that led to their doing so and the identity of the officers who attended is not known and not admitted.
4. Admitted that the officers searched the premises. An officer stated that he and his colleague had a warrant to search the premises on the basis that there was reasonable cause to believe that illegal activity was being conducted from there, namely that persons were concerned in the supply of a controlled drug contrary to Section 4 of the Misuse of Drugs Act

1971. Admitted that the officers found cash wrapped in plastic clingfilm and secreted inside a mattress in a bedroom. Admitted that the officers seized the cash. Its current whereabouts is unknown. It is the property of the defender. The sum seized totalled £3,400.

5. Denied that the defender has ever been concerned in the supply of any drug. Admitted that he has a conviction for the possession of drugs under explanation that the offence related to his possession of a small quantity of cannabis resin intended for personal use only. The conviction was on 19 March 2011. Since then the defender has had no convictions.

6. Denied that the cash is property obtained through unlawful conduct.

7. The cash was derived from a number of sources all of which are lawful. Firstly, the defender has an uncle, John Fagin, who resides at Springburn, Glasgow. He kept cash in a rucksack. He did not trust banks, especially after the financial crisis of 2008. His home had been the subject of a break-in in 2015 when valuables had been stolen. He felt vulnerable. He entrusted the rucksack to the defender.

8. The defender inherited a sum of around £2,500 from George Hardie, a friend of his uncle. Mr Hardie died on 18 June 2020. He left his cash to the defender.

9. The defender was the owner of a bull terrier named Buster. In return for cash payments he made Buster available for breeding purposes. This occurred on various occasions between summer and about 18 November 2021. The defender provided Buster to a man known to him only as 'Cammy'. He would take Buster to the Burach Bar in Springburn, Glasgow. The dog would be taken away for several nights then returned to him at the bar. Bull terrier pups sell for around £900 each. The defender would receive cash payments averaging £500 for each breeding session. This occurred on around seven separate occasions. The defender no longer owns Buster. He sold him for a cash payment of £1,000 in November 2021. The buyer was a man who gave his name as 'Norrie'. The defender does not hold a dog breeders' licence.

10. In addition, during summer 2022 the defender assisted his cousin Hugh Butcher with delivering Chinese meals. He received a share of his cousin's earnings. The total of sums received was around £500 over approximately 3 months.

11. The defender accumulated savings that had been intended to fund a holiday abroad. Due to Covid lockdowns these savings were not expended by him.

12. The defender did not open a bank account. He found it too inconvenient to produce identification and to use online application processes. The defender shared his uncle's distrust of banks. Due to recent thefts from his residence by visitors, including family members, the defender felt it necessary and appropriate to place his savings in a secure location within his home.

PLEA IN LAW

The cash seized by Police Scotland from the defender's premises not being property obtained through unlawful conduct, forfeiture should not be granted as craved.

IN RESPECT WHEREOF

Steele and Hyde
Hamiltonhill Road
Glasgow
Agent for the defender

6. BLAKE v THE ADVOCATE GENERAL FOR SCOTLAND

Road traffic appeal — Restoration of driving licence

a. Initial writ

SHERIFFDOM OF NORTH STRATHCLYDE AT GREENOCK

SUMMARY APPLICATION UNDER THE ROAD TRAFFIC ACT 1988, s 100(1)

INITIAL WRIT

in the cause

AMADEUS BLAKE, residing at 21 Clifford Road, Greenock

PURSUER

against

THE RIGHT HONOURABLE LORD STEWART OF DIRLETON K.C., THE ADVOCATE GENERAL FOR SCOTLAND, the Office of the Solicitor General for Scotland, Queen Elizabeth House, Edinburgh EH8 8FT as representing the Department for Transport

DEFENDER

The pursuer craves the court:

1. To reverse the decision of the Secretary of State for Transport, issued on 14 March 2023 to revoke the pursuer's driving licence.
2. To find the defender liable in expenses.

CONDESCENDENCE

1. The parties are as designed. The defender represents the Secretary of State for Transport ('the Secretary of State').

2. The pursuer resides at 63 Hartnell Road, Greenock. This address is within the Sheriffdom of North Strathclyde. This court has jurisdiction in terms of Section 100(1) of the Road Traffic Act 1988.

3. On 14 March 2023 the Secretary of State served upon the pursuer under Section 93(1) of the Act a written notice revoking the pursuer's driving licence with immediate effect. The Secretary of State purported to be satisfied that the pursuer was suffering from a condition prescribed as a relevant disability as defined by Section 92 of the Act. This purported condition was epilepsy, as more particularly defined in Regulation 73 of the Motor Vehicle (Driving Licences) Regulations 1999. The Regulation refers to a driver having suffered two epileptic seizures in five years.

4. Service of the notice was unjustified and the revocation should be reversed. Believed and averred that the pursuer's GP made a report to the DVLA following an appointment with the pursuer in February 2023.

5. The pursuer is not suffering from epilepsy or any disability likely to cause the driving of a vehicle by him to be a source of danger to the public. The pursuer is able to drive safely. Reference is made to the report by Dr Patrick Pertwee, dated 17 April 2023 produced herewith. The decision to revocation of the pursuer's licence should be reversed as craved.

PLEA IN LAW

The pursuer not suffering from any disability likely to cause the driving of a vehicle by him in pursuance of a licence to be a source of danger to the public, the revocation of his licence should be reversed.

IN RESPECT WHEREOF

Solicitor
Hubble Law
Totters Lane, Greenock
Agent for the pursuer

7. HOEY AND PEPPERDAY, APPLICANTS

Guardianship order — Adults with Incapacity (Scotland) Act 2000 — Power to sell heritage

Application

SHERIFFDOM OF SOUTH STRATHCLYDE DUMFRIES AND GALLOWAY AT DUMFRIES

SUMMARY APPLICATION UNDER THE ADULTS WITH INCAPACITY (SCOTLAND) ACT 2000

APPLICATION

by

HEIDI HOEY, residing at 18 Bonaparte Crescent, Sanquhar DG4 9TR (Assisted Person)

FIRST NAMED PURSUER

and

DOROTHY PEPPERDAY, residing at 34, Cornwallis Gardens, Dalkeith, Ontario, Canada.

SECOND NAMED PURSUER

The pursuers crave the court:

1. To grant a guardianship order in terms of Section 58(1) of the Adults with Incapacity (Scotland) Act 2000 appointing the applicants as joint guardians to DORIS BLANCHEFLEUR, born on 12 July 1944 and residing at the Pandora Care Home, 75 Thrieve Road, Ae, Dumfries and Galloway DG1 6RE, for a period of five years or such other period as to the court shall seem reasonable, with the following powers: and to find the second named pursuer entitled to the expenses of this application and procedure to follow hereon out of the estate of the said Doris Blanchefleur.

Financial Powers

(a) In terms of Section 64(1)(d) of the said Act to manage the property and financial affairs of the said Doris Blanchefleur;

(b) Without prejudice to the generality of the foregoing power, power in terms of Section 64 (1)(a) of the Act to deal with the following particular matters on behalf of Doris Blanchefleur;

i) To have access to information confidential to Doris Blanchefleur and pertaining to her financial affairs.

ii) To access, amend, re-set and maintain as confidential any passwords, usernames, security questions and answers necessary to deal with the financial affairs of Doris Blanchefleur including, but not restricted to, the operation of any accounts under the Government Gateway, His Majesty's Revenue and Customs, the Department of Work and Pensions and other government bodies and in connection with any banks, utilities, facilities or services.

iii) To obtain and pay for any goods or services which may benefit Doris Blanchefleur.

iv) To use the funds of Doris Blanchefleur to pay all proper debts and liabilities due by her and to meet her living expenses.

v) To obtain, maintain, fund, alter or surrender any insurance policy on behalf of Doris Blanchefleur.

vi) To purchase, vary, exchange or sell stock and shares and other investments belonging to Doris Blanchefleur.

vii) To open, close and operate accounts holding funds belonging to the said Doris Blanchefleur.

viii) To sign and endorse any cheques, deposits, receipts or bank drafts issued and to be issued in the name of Doris Blanchefleur or payable by her.

ix) To claim and to receive on behalf of Doris Blanchefleur all pensions, benefits, allowances, services, financial contributions, repayments, rebates and other sums to which Doris Blanchefleur may be entitled and to vary or appeal arrangements.

x) To deal with the tax affairs of the Doris Blanchefleur including submitting tax returns and settling, adjusting and compromising any claim for tax.

xi) To take all necessary legal action to conserve, protect or vindicate the rights and interest of Doris Blanchefleur or in any of her property.

xii) To maintain and to pay any expense in connection with the property of Doris Blanchfleur.

xiii) To do anything ancillary or consequent upon the foregoing powers might may reasonable be necessary or appropriate for the full and proper exercise thereof.

xiv) To make payment of any outstanding utility service charges arising from the interest of Doris Blanchefleur in 82 Lighthouse Road, Southerness, DG2 7WD and to reclaim and receive on her behalf any sums overpaid in relation to her utility services.

xv) To sell or lease or provide as security the interest of Doris Blanchefleur in the heritable subjects known as and forming 82 Lighthouse Road, Southerness, DG2 7WD and registered in the Land Register of Scotland under title number DUM3987.

xvi) To repay the indebtedness of Doris Blanchefleur to Golden Twilight Ltd, Raptor House, Leighton Buzzard LU7 5WE or any successor or assignee and to obtain and register a discharge of the secured loan held by said creditor over the heritable subjects known as and forming 82 Lighthouse Road, Southerness, DG2 7WD and registered in the Land Register of Scotland under title number DUM3987.

xvii) To do everything reasonably required for the purposes of marketing the subjects including the employment, instruction and remuneration of estate agents, solicitors, surveyors, tradespeople, specialists, experts and removal contractors.

xviii) To terminate any contracts for services pertaining to the subjects and to correspond with any local or national authority in relation to the disposal of the subjects.

xix) To execute and deliver on behalf of Doris Blanchefleur any disposition, undertakings, affidavits, declarations and other ancillary documents necessary to the disposition of the subjects and to deliver any keys, guarantees, warranties, consents, reports, permissions, warrants, certificates or moveable property in relation thereto.

xx) To have access to confidential information about the Will or any testamentary documents of Doris Blanchefleur.

xxi) To make gifts on behalf of Doris Blanchefleur in accordance with Section 66 of the Act.

xxii) To reimbursement from Doris Blanchefleur's estate of outlays reasonably incurred by the pursuers in the exercise of their functions as guardians, in terms of Section 68(1) of the Act.

xxiii) To appoint any suitable qualified person to act as solicitor or independent financial advisor of Doris Blanchefleur or as agent or advisor in any other capacity and to allow payment from the estate to such person of the usual professional remuneration for his or her services.

xxiv) To represent the financial interests of Doris Blanchefleur and to protect her rights as resident of the Pandora Care Home, 75 Thrieve Road, Ae, Dumfries and Galloway DG1 6RE.

Welfare Powers

(b) In terms of Section 64(1)(b) of the Act to deal with all aspects of the personal welfare of Doris Blanchefleur;

Without prejudice to the generality of the foregoing power, power in terms of Section 64 (1)(a) of the Act to deal with the following particular matters on behalf of Doris Blanchefleur;

A. To decide where Doris Blanchefleur is to live, whether permanently or temporarily.

B. To decide matters relating to the healthcare, dental and medical treatment of Doris Blanchefleur, to consent to any such treatment that the pursuers may consider to be in her best interests, to refuse to consent to any proposed treatment that the pursuers may consider not to be in her best interests or which does not accord with her known wishes and feelings, to arrange for Doris Blanchefleur to attend for any healthcare and treatment, including assessments, investigations and similar, and to arrange access to her for the purpose of any health assessments, investigations and similar.

C) To access, open and read and post, email or other communications addressed to Doris Blanchefleur or received by or on her behalf.

D) To decide matters relating to the dress and appearance of Doris Blanchefleur.

E) To decide the persons with whom Doris Blanchefleur may associate or keep company and the times and circumstances under which this should occur.

F) To determine the educational, travel, cultural and social activities of Doris Blanchefleur and the extent and level of her participation in these.

STATEMENT OF FACT

1. This application is made in respect of Doris Blanchefleur ('the Adult'). She was born on 12 July 1944. The first named pursuer is the

Adult's sister. She was born on 8 December 1950. The second named defender is the Adult's daughter. She was born on 7 May 1969. The Adult has a brother. He is Rupert Marston, He lives at Nirvana Glen, 16 Rhynie Gardens, Inverurie, Aberdeenshire AB45 8YD. He is 94 years old. He is incapax. No purpose would be served by the service of Form 20 upon him. The Adult has no relatives other than the pursuers and Mr Marston. Her husband died in 2015.

2. The Adult is habitually resident at Pandora Care Home, 75 Thrieve Road, Ae, Dumfries and Galloway DG1 6RE. It is a registered establishment in terms of Section 35(1) of the Adults with Incapacity (Scotland) Act 2000. That address is within the Sheriffdom of South Strathclyde, Dumfries and Galloway. The sheriff at Dumfries is the appropriate sheriff to which this application ought to be made. Reference is made to Section 85 of, and Rules 1(1)(a) and 2(1) of Schedule 3 to, the Act. The pursuers gave notice to the Chief Social Work Officer of Dumfries and Galloway Council on 31 January 2023 for the purposes of Section 57(4) of the Act.

3. The Adult has no guardian, continuing attorney or welfare attorney. No intervention order or guardianship order has previously been made in relation to the Adult. The second named pursuer is her nearest relative as defined by Section 254 of the Mental Health (Care and Treatment) (Scotland) Act 2003.

4. No Disclosure Scotland Check has been carried out in respect of the pursuers. The second named pursuer emigrated to Canada in 1997 and underwent Confidential Disclosure and Criminal Record Check procedure prior to her taking up employment in schools. A certificate from the Ontario College of Teachers is produced. Neither pursuer has any convictions, in Scotland, Canada or elsewhere. Neither has ever been barred from working with children or vulnerable adults. Neither has been sequestrated or made subject to a bankruptcy restriction order or signed a trust deed for creditors or been subject to or applied for a debt payment programme. Neither has been subject to an order under the Company Directors Disqualification Act 1986 or subject to an Inhibition. Neither has been affected by any analogous or similar procedures in Canada or elsewhere.

5. The Adult has Alzheimer's disease, As a result, she is incapable of managing her own welfare and financial affairs or giving instructions for their management. She is likely to continue to be so incapable. Reference is made to both medical reports produced herewith.

6. The Adult is the sole owner of heritable subjects known as and forming 82 Lighthouse Road, Southerness, DG2 7WD (hereinafter 'the subjects'). The subjects are currently valued at about £185,000. There is a secured loan under an equity release scheme. The loan is currently £14,000. The lender is Golden Twilight Ltd, Raptor House, Leighton Buzzard LU7 5WE.

7. Also, she is the sole owner of household contents, the value whereof is estimated to be £5,000, and two accounts. One account is with the Bank of Heligoland. It contains around £2,500. The other is with Rutland Building Society. It contains around £6,000. In addition, she holds Premium Bonds with a value of £15,000.

8. The Adult receives a State Pension of £100 per week. She also receives Winter Fuel payments.

9. For the purposes of caution the sum of £200,000 would be adequate to cover the value of the estate.

The Adult has lived in the Pandora Care Home, at the address in the instance, since April 2022. The home is owned and managed by Elephant Care Ltd, 17 Troubadour Street, Stoke on Trent. The company operates around 15 homes in the UK and in 2020 a Care Inspectorate report found Pandora Care Home to be 'Adequate' to 'Excellent'. Having regard to the Adult's state of health, it is highly improbable that she will be able to live outwith a care home. It is expedient that the secured loan be discharged and the subjects sold. This proposed course of action accords with her stated wishes and feelings.

10. In the circumstances, it is necessary that the Adult's property and financial affairs be managed, and that all aspects of her personal welfare be dealt with, on her behalf. A guardianship order, with powers as craved, is necessary for the protection of the Adult's property, financial affairs and personal welfare. An intervention order would not be sufficient to enable the pursuers to take adequate steps to protect the Adult.

11. The pursuers are best placed to act as guardians. The first named applicant is a practising chartered accountant and is aware of the functions of a guardian. She visits the Adult at least twice a week. She lives 40 minutes by car from Pandora Care Home. She already looks after the Adult's finances in practice. She is the Adult's main carer. The second named pursuer is a classroom assistant in Beaver Canyon High School, Dalkeith, Ontario, Canada. She speaks to the Adult by telephone each week. Since the end of Covid restrictions in 2022 she has visited the Adult twice. Prior to Covid she visited twice yearly, on average. The MHO report herewith is supportive of the application and identifies no undue concentration or power or any other concerns. The application ought to be granted, as being in the Adult's best interests.

12. A Guardianship Order in the terms craved represents an intervention which will benefit the Adult in a way that cannot reasonably be achieved otherwise. It is the intervention least restrictive to the freedom of the Adult whilst consistent with that benefit.

13. The following reports are produced and their terms incorporated for the sake of brevity:

1) Samantha Brooke, MHO, Dumfries and Galloway Council, report dated 17 May 2023.
2) Dr Hamish Taylor, GP, 28 May 2023.
3) Dr Humphrey Feldman, psychiatrist, 4 June 2023.

IN RESPECT WHEREOF

Drummond Piper
7 Montmorency Street
Dumfries DH1 5RW
Solicitor for the pursuers

APPENDIX; SHERIFFDOM OF NORTH STRATHCLYDE AT DUMFRIES

Act of Sederunt 1999/929 Chapter 3, Part XVI – Adults with Incapacity (Scotland) Act 2000.

List of persons for the purposes of Rule 3.16.4(1):

1) Doris Blanchefleur, Pandora Care Home, 75 Thrieve Road, Ae, Dumfries and Galloway DG1 6RE (service to by means of service on the manager of the establishment in terms of Rule 3.16.4(3).

2) Heidi Hoey, 18 Bonaparte Crescent, Sanquhar DG4 9TR.

3) Dorothy Pepperday, 34, Cornwallis Gardens, Dalkeith, Ontario, Canada.

4) The Office of the Public Guardian (Scotland), Hadrian House, Callander Business Park, Callander Road, Falkirk FK1 1XR.

5) The Mental Welfare Commission for Scotland, Thistle House, 91 Haymarket Terrace, Edinburgh EH12 5HD.

6) The Chief Social Work Officer, Dumfries and Galloway Council, English Street, Dumfries DG1 2DD.

8. MUIR v CHUNKY GIBBON LIMITED

Administration of Justice (Scotland) Act 1972

SHERIFFDOM OF SOUTH STRATHCLYDE DUMFRIES AND GALLOWAY AT HAMILTON

HAM-B28-23
SUMMARY APPLICATION

Under Section 1 of the Administration of Justice (Scotland) Act 1972

in the cause

HEATHER MUIR as representative of Shirley Knott and residing at 16 Keir Hardie Street, Bellshill ML4 7RS

PURSUER

against

CHUNKY GIBBON LIMITED, a company incorporated under the Companies Acts, number 736475 and having its registered office at 11 Slipper Road Potters Bar Hertfordshire EN6 4TD

DEFENDER

The pursuer craves the court:

1. To ordain the defender to disclose such information as it may possess as to the name and address of the person known as 'Kylie' or 'Kyrie' who witnessed or may have witnessed the incident concerning Shirley Knott's injury at the premises known as Chunky Gibbon soft play area, Zenith Centre, Motherwell ML1 6TY on or around 19 June 2033; and

2. To authorize and grant power to Dr Shane Fontana, vending industry consultant or such other person as to the court shall seem appropriate to inspect, photograph and experiment upon the 'Jackanapes' toy vending

machine, manufactured by Claw-to-Matic Inc. located at the premises known as Chunky Gibbon soft play area, Zenith Centre, Motherwell ML1 6TY, and available for the use of customers on 19 June 2023 the said experimentation to be whilst the machine is stationary and in operation provided always that there shall be no risk of damage to the machine; and

3. To find the defender liable in expenses.

CONDESCENDENCE

1. The parties are as designed in the instance. Shirley Knott ('the child') was born on 19 May 2018. Heather Muir ('HM') is her mother. HM is the child's legal representative in terms of Section 2(1)(d) of the Children (Scotland) Act 1995.

2. On 19 June 2022 HM and the child attended a soft play area named 'Chunky Gibbon' at the Zenith Centre, Motherwell ML1 6TY. The child showed an interest in a toy vending machine. It bore the name 'Jackanapes' and featured a laughing monkey. It was bright yellow in colour and was approximately 1.8m in height. Near its base was a plate bearing the name of its manufacturer. This is Claw-to-Matic Inc. The machine has a protruding 'bin' into which the operator drops soft toys grabbed by a claw on a manoeuvrable pendant. The bin can be accessed from outside the machine through a hinged metal flap.

3. At around 3.15pm on 19 June 2022 HM required to go to the toilet. Whilst she was there, the child approached the machine and put her hand through the flap. As she withdraw her arm the flap jammed downwards, trapping her wrist and causing serious injury that required treatment at the Princess Desdemona Hospital, Motherwell.

4. The incident was witnessed by others at 'Chunky Gibbon'. Staff advised that they had not seen the child insert her arm into the machine but that a customer named 'Kylie' or 'Kyrie' had done so. This customer accompanied a young boy named Tyson.

5. HM was in a state of distress. She accompanied the child in an ambulance. She did not have the opportunity to speak to the said witness. Thereafter, agents for HM contacted the defender seeking details of the witness. The defender advised that details had been taken for Covid track and trace and for fire safety purposes but that these would not be disclosed 'for GDPR reasons'.

6. Civil proceedings are likely to be brought. Counsel has advised that there are good prospects of success. This opinion is currently with the Scottish Legal Aid Board. The Board has asked for sight of a witness precognition.

7. In addition, HM reasonably seeks to obtain a report into the safety of the machine. The defender confirms that it is still upon the premises. The defender has delayed unreasonably in making arrangements to allow inspection. Access was first requested in January 2023. It has still not been allowed, with no explanation provided.

8. Dr Shane Fontana, vending industry consultant is an appropriate expert to prepare a report. He has examined many machines similar or identical in design to the 'Jackanapes' toy vending machine, including similar machines designed and made by Claw-to-Matic Inc.

PLEAS IN LAW

1) It being likely that civil proceedings will be brought, and the person condescended upon being a potential witness therein, an order should be granted as first craved, in terms of Section 1(1A) of the Administration of Justice (Scotland) Act 1972.

2) It being likely that civil proceedings will be brought, and the machine condescended upon being property in relation to which a question may relevantly arise, an order should be granted as first craved, in terms of Section 1(1) of the Administration of Justice (Scotland) Act 1972.

IN RESPECT WHEREOF

Olivia Wiggley Dyson
Solicitors
36 Crusader Street
Saltcoats KA3 7DS

IX MISCELLANEOUS PROCEEDINGS

1. CLEMINSON v HARVEY

Application for an exceptional attachment order – paper apart to Form 22, Act of Sederunt (Debt Arrangement and Attachment (Scotland) Act 2002) 2002

Paper Apart

PAPER APART TO FORM 22, SECTION D

Rule 25(1)

Cleminson v Harvey

The creditor requests that in considering whether to grant this application the sheriff consider the following issues as relevant for the purposes of Section 47(1) and (4) of the Debt Arrangement and Attachment (Scotland) Act 2002:

1. The debt arises from the provision of gardening services by the creditor at the request of the debtor.

2. The debtor is a hotelier. Both he and his wife advised the creditor that the debtor's business has been very successful in the period since Covid restrictions were lifted by the Scottish Government.

3. The debtor is self-employed. The creditor is unable to arrest his earnings.

4. The debtor is a discharged bankrupt. The debtor was sequestrated at the instance of Her Majesty's Revenue and Customs (now His Majesty's Revenue and Customs) in relation to a failure to pay income tax. Said bankruptcy occurred on 17 August 2015. A copy of the relative entry in the *Edinburgh Gazette* is produced. Believed and averred that the debtor has failed to pay a builder, Francis Mulgrew, in relation to the installation of a gazebo and a fish pond at his dwellinghouse.

5. The creditor is also self-employed. His work is seasonal. A failure to recover the debt will leave him and his family in financial hardship. Schedules of his gardening business income and outgoings during 2022 and his family income and expenditure since 1 July 2021 are produced.

6. In terms of the parties' contract the creditor agreed to pay the creditor weekly. As well as having provided labour the creditor outlaid sums on plants, fertiliser, herbicide, pesticides and other supplies. These sums are part of the debt. The creditor would never have undertaken work for the debtor had he known that he would be left with a debt of over £5500.

7. The debtor repeatedly promised payment both before and after decree was granted and after a charge was served. On or about 5 June 2022, during a telephone conversation he said that payment of £2000 would be paid that week with the balance paid a fortnight later. No payment was ever made.

8. The debtor's dwellinghouse has a market value of around £450,000. Its garden grounds extend to 0.75 hectares. On or about 5 May 2022 the debtor advised the creditor that he had had a Tanyong home cinema experience system installed in the dwellinghouse at a cost of over £11,000. He could have used part of said sum clearing his indebtedness to the creditor but chose not to do so.

2. SAUNDERS v HERIOT

Warrant to sell moveable property

Initial writ

SHERIFFDOM OF NORTH STRATHCLYDE AT DUNOON

INITIAL WRIT

in the cause

DOMINIC SAUNDERS, residing at 16 Florizel Street, Rashfield, Dunoon PA23 8RW

PURSUER

against

EILDON HERIOT residing at 91 Flavius Wynd, Edinburgh EH2 8TD.

DEFENDER

The pursuer craves the court:

1. To grant warrant: (1) to the pursuer to remove the Monterey 250 Cruiser boat named 'Hesperus' belonging to the defender and currently berthed at the pursuer's premises at Cowal Marina, Longfellow Road, Coylet, Argyle and Bute PA23 8TS from those premises to those of Dirk and Hatteraick Vessel Sales, marine auctioneers, Dunoon Harbour PA23 9YD; and (2) to the said Dirk and Hatteraick to sell the boat by public roup.
2. To appoint the free proceeds of the sale of the Monterey 250 Cruiser boat 'Hesperus' after deduction of the expenses of removal and sale and of this action, to be consigned with the sheriff clerk to await the further orders of the court.
3. To find the defender liable in expenses.

CONDESCENDENCE

1. The parties are as designed in the instance.
2. This action relates to sale under warrant of moveable property, namely the Monterey 250 Cruiser boat 'The Hesperus'. It is located at the

pursuer's premises at Cowal Marina, Longfellow Road, Coylet, Argyle and Bute PA23 8TS. These premises are situated within the Sheriffdom of North Strathclyde. Accordingly, this court has jurisdiction in terms of Section 20 of and Rule 2(i) of Schedule 8 to the Civil Jurisdiction and Judgments Act 1982.

3. On or about 16 February 2018 the parties entered into a contract whereby the defender could berth The Hesperus at the Cowal Marina. The defender was required in terms of the contract to pay berthing fees of £275 plus VAT per month. As at the 16 February 2023 there were 21 months of arrears of berthing fees totalling £6,930.

4. In addition, the pursuers had repairs undertaken to the boat, at the defender's request, in the sum of £720 including VAT. This sum has never been paid by the defender, despite numerous requests.

5. The defender has never disputed the debt. Instead, he has promised to make payment. Reference is made to the copy emails dated 18 December 2022 and 18 February 2023 produced herewith.

6. The boat has a market value of around £34,000. The pursuer has a lien over it but is losing income as a result of being unable to lease to third parties the berth currently occupied by The Hesperus. The loss is reasonably estimated at £350 per month.

7. In these circumstances, it is reasonable that warrant be granted to remove the vessel to auction sale rooms and for auctioneers to sell it by public roup, as craved.

8. Dirk and Hatteraick Vessel Sales are experienced and reputable ship auctioneers, and will achieve a fair market price for the vessels. They ought to be appointed.

PLEA IN LAW

The pursuer having a lien over the Monterey 250 Cruiser boat 'The Hesperus' the defender delaying unreasonably in making payment of the sum due to the pursuer and the pursuer incurring loss as a result of the storage of the said vessel, as condescended upon, it is reasonable that warrant be granted for its removal and sale, and decree as craved should be granted accordingly.

IN RESPECT WHEREOF

Cove and Clynder
solicitors
15 Clyde Street
Dunoon PA23 7RW
Agent for the pursuer

3. SAINT JUDE HOUSING ASSOCIATION LTD v PEPLOE

Rectification of non-testamentary document – Section 8 of the Law Reform (Miscellaneous Provisions)(Scotland) Act 1985

a. Initial writ

SHERIFFDOM OF SOUTH STRATHCLYDE, DUMFRIES AND GALLOWAY AT STRANRAER

INITIAL WRIT

in the cause

SAINT JUDE HOUSING ASSOCIATION LTD, a housing association established under the Housing Associations Act 1985 and registered under the Co-operative and Community Benefit Societies Act 2014, having a Mutuals Public Register number 3975RS and a place of business at 4 High Street Portpatrick DG3 6TR.

PURSUER

against

HUNTER PEPLOE, residing at 16 Merivale Gardens, Stranraer DG2 9GA

DEFENDER

The pursuer craves the court:

1. In terms of the powers conferred upon the court by Section 8 of the Law Reform (Miscellaneous Provisions)(Scotland) Act 1985, to order the rectification of the disposition by HUNTER PEPLOE, residing at 16 Merivale Gardens, Stranraer DG2 9GA, in favour of SAINT JUDE HOUSING ASSOCIATION LIMITED, a housing association established under the Housing Associations Act 1985 and registered under the Co-operative and Community Benefit Societies Act 2014, having a Mutuals Public Register number 3975RS and a place of business at 4 High Street

Portpatrick DG3 6TR of the heritable subjects known as and forming 5 Ryan Sands, DG2 7TD, Title Number WGN 39628, dated 2 October 2022 and registered in the Land Register for Scotland on 7 October 2022 and that by substituting for the plan annexed to the said disposition a plan in accordance with that contained in the schedule hereto.

2. To find the defender liable in expenses.

CONDESCENDENCE

1. The parties are as designed in the instance. The pursuer is a housing association established under the Housing Associations Act 1985 and registered with the Financial Conduct Authority under the Co-operative and Community Benefit Societies Act 2014. It has a Mutuals Public Register number 3975RS, and having a place of business at 4 High Street, Portpatrick DG3 6TR.

2. These proceedings have as their object rights *in rem* in heritable subjects known as and forming 5 Ryan Sands, Stranraer DG2 7TD ('the subjects'). These are situated In the Sheriffdom of South Strathclyde, Dumfries and Galloway. Accordingly, this court has exclusive jurisdiction in terms of Section 20 of and Rule 5(1)(a) of Schedule 8 to the Civil Jurisdiction and Judgments Act 1982.

3. By missives dated 30 June and 3 and 17 July 2022 the pursuer agreed to buy and the defender agreed to sell the subjects. By disposition dated 2 October 2022 and registered in the Land Register for Scotland on 7 October 2022 the defender disponed the subjects to the pursuer. A plan was annexed to the disposition purporting to show the extent of the subjects thereby disponed. The plan erroneously omitted the area of ground to the rear of the subjects on which is located the septic tank servicing the subjects. That ground formed part of the subjects at the material time agreed to be sold by the defender to the pursuers in terms of the missives. It was the common intention of the parties at the time the missives were concluded that the ground and tank should be disponed. The disposition was intended to give effect to the parties' agreement embodied in the missives aforesaid.

4. The pursuer raised its concern with the defender. He has failed to respond. Believed and averred that he may be about to sell the ground and tank to his niece Margot Peploe. The Scottish Environmental Protection Agency have stated that they continue to hold the pursuer liable for the tank.

5. In these circumstances, the disposition, being intended to give effect to an agreement between the parties, has failed to express accurately the common intention of the parties to that agreement at the date when it was made. Accordingly, the disposition should be rectified as craved.

PLEA IN LAW

The disposition, being intended to give effect to an agreement between the parties but failing to express accurately the common intention of the parties to the agreement at the date when it was made, should be rectified as craved.

IN RESPECT WHEREOF

Solicitor
Newt and Bassett
16 Smith Road, Stranraer
Agent for the pursuer

b. Motion

SHERIFFDOM OF SOUTH STRATHCLYDE, DUMFRIES AND GALLOWAY AT STRANRAER

MOTION FOR THE PURSUER

in the cause

SAINT JUDE HOUSING ASSOCIATION LTD, [*designation*]

PURSUER

against

HUNTER PEPLOE, [*designation*]

DEFENDER

The pursuer moves the court to grant warrant to the pursuer to place a caveat in the Land Register of Scotland in terms of Section 67(1)(c) of the Land Registration (Scotland) Act 2012 on the grounds that:

1) The pursuer has a *prima facie* case on the merits;

2) There is a real and substantial risk that the enforcement of any decree would be prejudiced on the basis that the defender is likely to deal with the land; and

3) It would be reasonable to grant warrant.

IN RESPECT WHEREOF

Solicitor
[*designation*]
Agent for the pursuer

4. MORRISON v BUCHANAN

Rectification of testamentary writing – Section 3 of the Succession (Scotland) Act 2016

a. Initial writ

SHERIFFDOM OF SOUTH STRATHCLYDE, DUMFRIES AND GALLOWAY AT AIRDRIE

INITIAL WRIT

in the cause

JULIE MORRISON, residing at 63 Lamont Walk, Coatbridge, North Lanarkshire ML5 6TW, executor nominate of the late Albert Buchanan in terms of the will of the deceased dated 15 May 1994.

PURSUER

against

BROOK BUCHANAN, residing at 24 Charles Street, Buxton, AK17 5AH

DEFENDER

The pursuer craves the court:

1. In terms of the powers conferred upon the court by Section 3 of the Succession (Scotland) Act 2016 to order the rectification of the codicil of Albert Buchanan dated 28 July 1997 by deletion of 'Andrew Hewitt' in Clause 4 thereof and by substitution therefor of 'Alexander Hewit'.

2. To find the defender liable in expenses in the event of his opposing the order sought.

CONDESCENDENCE

1. The pursuer is the executor nominate of the estate of the late Albert Buchanan who formerly resided at 16 Victoria Gardens, Glenmavis (hereinafter 'the testator') in terms of the will of the testator dated 15 May 1994. The defender is the residuary beneficiary of the estate

of the testator. Neither the will nor the codicil have yet been registered in the Books of Council and Session. The pursuer has not applied for confirmation.

2. The testator was domiciled in Scotland at the date of his death. Also at said date he was habitually resident at the said address. It is within the Sheriffdom of South Strathclyde, Dumfries and Galloway. The sheriff at Airdrie is a relevant sheriff as defined by and for the purposes of Section 3(6) of the Succession (Scotland) Act 2016.

3. The testator died on 4 October 2021. The codicil was discovered on around 16 June 2022. The pursuer seeks to have this application considered outwith the period of six months from the date of the death of the testator in terms of Section 4(2) of the Act.

4. On 15 May 1994 the testator granted a will. On 28 July 1997 he granted a codicil thereto. The will was prepared by Dougall and Beith, solicitors on the instructions of the testator. The codicil was prepared by a company named Wills B Us, 17 Arthur Road, Chelmsford. The company advises that there are no notes or correspondence pertaining to the codicil. Copies of the will and codicil are produced herewith and referred to for their terms which are incorporated herein *brevitatis causa.*

5. The codicil amended the will solely by the addition of the following clause;

> '4. I bequeath in favour of my grandson Andrew Hewit residing at 11 Wallaceway Street, Twechar the sum of FIVE THOUSAND POUNDS'.

6. At no time did the testator have a grandchild named Andrew Hewitt. He did have a grandchild named Alexander Hewit. As at 28 July 1997 the said grandchild resided at 11 Wallaceway Street, Twechar.

7. Believed and averred that the testator intended that his codicil would have the effect of leaving a bequest of £5,000 to the said Alexander Hewitt. In or about July 1997 the testator advised his friend Gerard Turnbull that he was delighted about the birth of his grandson Alexander Hewitt and that he wished to change his will to leave him a bequest.

8. In these circumstances, the codicil, being intended to give effect to the testator's instruction that a legacy of £5,000 be left to Alexander Hewitt has failed to express accurately that intention.

9. The Pursuer seeks an order as craved with the intention that she will lodge same with the Books of Council and Session in terms of Section 4 of the Succession (Scotland) Act 2016 and that she will lodge the will and codicil similarly.

PLEA IN LAW

The codicil of the late Albert Buchanan residing formerly at 16 Victoria Gardens, Glenmavis dated 28 July 1997 being intended to leave a bequest of £5,000 to Alexander Hewitt residing at 11 Wallaceway Street, Twechar, all as condescended upon, and the pursuer being entitled to seek rectification thereof in terms of Section 3 of the Succession (Scotland) Act 2016 an order should be granted as craved.

IN RESPECT WHEREOF

Solicitor
Weedon and Innes
17 Glenmavis Way, Airdrie
Agent for the pursuer

5. PRESTON HAILES v HADDINGTONSHIRE LICENSING BOARD

Licensing (Scotland) Act 2005 appeal — Premises licence — Licensing board acting contrary to natural justice

a. Note of Appeal

SHERIFFDOM OF LOTHIAN AND BORDERS AT EDINBURGH

NOTE OF APPEAL UNDER LICENSING (SCOTLAND) ACT 2005

APPEAL

by

PRESTON HAILES residing at 19 Duns Road, Haddington, East Lothian EH41 8TF

APPELLANT

This appeal is in respect of the decision of Haddingtonshire Licensing Board made on 20 January 2023 in terms of section 23(4)(b) and (5)(e) of the Licensing (Scotland) Act 2005 (hereinafter 'the Act') to refuse the premises licence application by the appellant under section 20 of the Act for a premises licence in respect of his public house premises known as 'The Duke of Tantallon' at 12 Cheviot Street, Haddington EH41 9TW. The principal office of the Licensing Board is at 1 Pencaitland Street, Haddington EH41 8YD.

The Board is requested to state a case.

The appellant appeals against the decision on the following grounds:

1. The appellant submitted a premises licence application under section 20 of the Act for such a licence in respect of his premises 'The Duke of Tantallon' at Cheviot Street, Haddington EH41 9TW. The Licensing Board considered the application. It did so at its quarterly meeting on 20 January 2023. It refused the application.

2. The Board did so in terms of section 23(4)(b) of the Act. In so doing, it purported to find that a ground of refusal applied, namely that set forth in section 23(5)(e) of the Act, which so far as material provides: 'The grounds of refusal are … that, having regard to the number and capacity of licensed premises of the same or similar description as the subject

premises in the locality in which the subject premises are situated, the Board considers that, if the application were granted, there would, as a result, be overprovision of … licensed premises of that description in the locality.'

3. In reaching its decision the Board acted contrary to natural justice. Prior to the said meeting, one objection to the application was made by letter. At the meeting, however, there was no appearance for the objector nor were any other objections to the application made. The application therefore proceeded unopposed. In making his submissions in support of the said application, the appellant's agent stated to the Board that there was no element of over provision in the case and that there were indeed no objections on those grounds.

4. The Board took no steps to correct that statement or to alert the appellant that that it was concerned with the issue of over provision.

5. The Board proceeded to refuse the said application on that ground. In these circumstances, the appeal falls to be allowed in terms of Section 131(3)(a)(ii) of the Act and the case remitted back to the Board for reconsideration of the decision in terms of Section 131(5)(a) of the Act.

The appellant craves the court:

1. To allow the appeal against the decision of Haddingtonshire Licensing Board made on 20 January 2023 in terms of section 23(4)(b) and (5)(e) of the Licensing (Scotland) Act 2005 to refuse the premises licence application by the appellant under section 20 of that Act for a premises licence in respect of his premises 'The Duke of Tantallon' at Cheviot Street, Haddington EH41 9TW and to remit the case back to the Licensing Board for reconsideration of the decision; or to make such other order as the court thinks fit.

2. To find the Licensing Board liable in the expenses of this appeal.

IN RESPECT WHEREOF

Solicitor
Traprainlaw Solicitors
12 Dunbar Street, Haddington
Solicitor for the appellant

6. FITZROY, PETITIONER

Sequestration of living individual — Section 2, Bankruptcy (Scotland) Act 2016 – Apparent insolvency constituted by non-compliance with statutory demand

a. Petition

SHERIFFDOM OF GRAMPIAN, HIGHLAND
AND ISLANDS AT ABERDEEN

Rule 6.1(1) PETITION

Bankruptcy (Scotland) Rules 2016,
SSI 2016/313

By

BAILEY FITZROY, residing at 16 South Utsire Avenue, Aberdeen AB3 8TD

PETITIONER

for sequestration of the estate of

SHANNON FISHER, residing at 14 Portland Avenue, Aberdeen AB1 5WE

DEBTOR

The petitioner craves the court:

1. To grant warrant to cite the debtor to appear before the court on such date as shall be specified in the warrant, being a date not less than 6 nor more than 14 days after the date of citation to show cause why sequestration of her estate should not be granted.
2. To award sequestration of the estate of the debtor.
3. To declare that the said estate belongs to the creditors of the debtor.
4. To appoint Malin Dogger, Chartered Accountant, 101 Forth Street, Aberdeen AB2 6DS, as trustee; and to appoint as interim trustee the said Malin Dogger whom failing the Accountant in Bankruptcy, 1 Pennyburn Road, Kilwinning KA13 6SA.

5. To make such other and further orders as may seem appropriate to the court.

6. To find the petitioner entitled to the expenses of this application out of the debtor's estate.

STATEMENT OF FACTS

1. (a) The petitioner is as designed in the instance. The debtor was habitually resident within the Sheriffdom of Grampian, Highland and Islands in the year immediately preceding the date of presentation of this petition, and this court accordingly has jurisdiction.

(b) As far as within the knowledge of the petitioner, the centre of main interests of the debtor has been at Aberdeen.

(c) As far as within the knowledge of the petitioner, the debtor does not possess an establishment in any member state of the EU.

(d) As far as within the knowledge of the petitioner, insolvency proceedings have not been opened in relation to the debtor elsewhere.

2. The petitioner is a qualified creditor of the debtor, as defined by Section 7 of the Bankruptcy (Scotland) Act 2016, to the extent of £17,630 as evidenced in the Form 6, Schedule 1 of the Bankruptcy (Scotland) Regulations 2016 (oath by creditor) and supporting vouchers attached. The debtor is not the subject of an approved debt payment programme within the meaning of Section 2 of the Debt Arrangement and Attachment (Scotland) Act 2002. Form 6.2 is attached.

3. The debtor is apparently insolvent in terms of Section 16(1)(i) of the Act. On 15 March 2023 there was personal service upon the respondent by an officer of court, of a demand in the prescribed form requiring her either to pay the debt or to find security for its payment. The debtor failed within 21 days thereof to comply with the demand or to intimate to the petitioner that she denied the debt or that the sum claimed was immediately payable. This all occurred within four months before the presentation of this petition.

4. In order to realise the estate of the debtor for the benefit of her creditors, the petitioner requires to apply to the court for the sequestration of the debtor's estate in terms of the Bankruptcy (Scotland) Act 2016.

5. Malin Dogger, CA, 101 Forth Street, Aberdeen AB2 6DS satisfies the conditions specified in Section 51(1)(b) of the Act and his undertaking as required by Section 51(1)(c) is attached.

6. A debt advice and information package was provided to the debtor on 18 April 2023 as required by Regulation 11 of the 2016 Regulations.

7. A copy of this petition has been sent today to the Accountant in Bankruptcy as required by Section 13 of the Act.

8. The petitioner seeks the appointment of the said Malin Dogger, whom failing the Accountant in Bankruptcy as interim trustee, in terms of Section 54(1)(b) of the Act Such an appointment is necessary to protect the interests of the debtor's creditors, including the petitioner. The debtor operates a business selling clothes and jewellery on internet auction and other sales sites. The sites indicate by the use of phrases such as '30 available' and '125 already sold' that the debtor possesses substantial stock worth many thousands of pounds. Printouts of Website pages are produced herewith and referred to for their terms. The petitioner is apprehensive that the debtor will dispose of the remaining stock in early course and that funds thereby raised would easily be alienated to the detriment of the debtor's creditors, including the petitioner. In the circumstances, it is reasonable and appropriate that an interim trustee should be appointed, as craved.

PLEAS IN LAW

1. The debtor being apparent insolvent within the meaning of the Bankruptcy (Scotland) Act 2016, her apparent insolvency having been constituted within four months of presentation of this petition and the petitioner being a qualified creditor of the debtor in terms of Section 7 of the Act decree should be granted as craved.

2. The appointment of an interim trustee being justified in the circumstances, such appointment should be made in terms of Section 54(1)(b) of the Act.

IN RESPECT WHEREOF

Tyne and Cromarty LLP
1 Finesterre Street, Aberdeen
Agent for the petitioner

7. THE BLACK COUNTRY FOUNDRY LIMITED, PETITIONER

Winding-up of deceased person's estate — Appointment of judicial factor

SHERIFFDOM OF GRAMPIAN HIGHLAND
AND ISLANDS AT ABERDEEN

ABE- B29-23
SUMMARY APPLICATION

Section 11A of the Judicial
Factors(Scotland) Act 1889

and

The Act of Sederunt (Judicial Factors
Rules) 1992
Rules 6 and 22

By

THE BLACK COUNTRY FOUNDRY LIMITED, a company incorporated under the Companies Act, number 639764 and having its registered office at 73 Holder Road, Wolverhampton WV6 9AT

APPLICANT

For the appointment of a Judicial Factor to the estate of the late NIGEL LINGEN, formerly trading as Mastrick Anvil, Lochnagar Workshop, Lord Byron Street, Aberdeen AB1 8TR and who died on 18 May 2023

The Applicant craves the court:

1) To appoint intimation of this application by display on the walls of court.

2) To appoint intimation to the Accountant of Court, Hadrian House, by first class post of this application together with copies of schedules and productions.

3) To appoint service of this application together with copies of schedules and productions on Bethia Dashwood, 19 Elgood Terrace, Bath BA1 7RD and the Athelstaneford Building Society, The Rookery, Pencaitland EH34 7GH as being persons having an interest herein.

4) To direct that notice of the application be made by Form 1 in the *Aberdeen Northern Lights* newspaper.

5) To appoint that this application be advertised once by the display of Form 3 in the *Edinburgh Gazette*; and

6) To ordain them and all other parties interested to lodge answers, if so advised, within 21 days after such intimation, advertisement and service; thereafter, upon resuming consideration hereof, with or without answers and after such inquiry if any as may be thought necessary, to appoint Roger Tweed, Chartered Accountant, 16 Bearpit Lane, Bathgate EH48 8YT, or such other person as the court thinks fit, to be judicial factor with the usual powers on the estate of the late Nigel Linden, who resided latterly at 67 Slains Castle Road, Hazelhead, Aberdeen AB1 7RD and who died on 18 May 2023; and to find the petitioner entitled to the expenses of this application and the procedure to follow hereon out of the estate of the late Nigel Linden.

CONDESCENDENCE

1) The applicant is a supplier of ironmongery and mild steel products. This application is in respect of the estate of Nigel Lingen ('the deceased'). He traded as Mastrick Anvil ('the business') having premises at Unit 4, the Lochnagar Workshop, Lord Byron Street, Aberdeen, AB1 8TR. He held himself out as being a sole trader. At the date of his death he lived at 67 Slains Castle Road, Hazelhead, Aberdeen AB1 7RD.

2) Between April 2021 and May 2023 the applicant sold goods to the business. These were supplied in the order of the deceased. The price was £173,600. Only £14,400 was paid. £159,200 remains due. The contract between the applicant and the deceased included retention of title clauses. Agents for the applicant emailed the deceased repeatedly, with no response. They had instructions to raise proceedings for payment. A writ had been prepared and was ready to be sent for warranting when the applicant learnt that the deceased had died.

3) In the year immediately prior to the making of this application the deceased residing in and carried on business in the Sheriffdom of Grampian, Highland and Islands. He owned heritable property, namely

Unit 4 within the Lochnagar Workshop, Lord Byron Street, Aberdeen, AB1 8TR and within the said Sheriffdom. Accordingly, this court has jurisdiction in terms of Section 11A of the Judicial Factors (Scotland) Act 1889.

4) Believed and averred that the deceased was intestate. No party has sought appointment as executor dative or executor-creditor. No party has obtained confirmation as executor nominate.

5) Enquiries by the applicants have disclosed that the deceased hired haulage services and rented warehouse premises in the Isabella Buchan Industrial Estate, Aberdeen. In addition, the deceased was a shareholder in a limited company named Prussian Steel Ltd. Its Articles of Association state that its objection is the manufacture and sale of metal items. The applicant is concerned that goods supplied by the applicant have or will come into the possession of third parties, to the prejudice of the applicant.

6) The estate of the deceased may be insolvent. It is necessary for the protection of the interests of the persons with an interest in the succession to the estate and the creditors of the estate that a judicial factor be appointed to administer the estate, and in particular to manage the business of Mastrick Anvil. Believed that the business is a going concern and may be sold as such.

7) The applicant, as a creditor of the deceased, has an interest in the estate of the deceased. The only other persons known to the applicant as having such interest is the daughter of the deceased, Bethia Dashwood and the Athelstaneford Building Society. They are as designed in crave 3. The latter is a heritable creditor. It holds a standard security over 67 Slains Castle Road, Hazelhead, Aberdeen AB1 7RD.

8) The estate of the deceased so far as known to the applicant, including heritable and moveable property, stock in trade, and debts owed to and by the deceased, is as set forth in the appendix to this application.

PLEAS IN LAW

1) Nigel Lingen having died leaving no settlement appointing trustees or other parties having power to manage his estate or any part thereof, or any such persons not accepting or acting, the applicant is entitled in terms of Section 11A of the Judicial Factors (Scotland) Act 1889 to seek the appointment of a judicial factor to administer the estate of the said Nigel Linden.

2) The appointment of a judicial factor being necessary to protect the interests of persons with an interest in the estate of the deceased, decree should be granted as craved.

3) Roger Tweed, Chartered Accountant, 16 Bearpit Lane, Bathgate EH48 8YT being a suitable person for appointment as judicial factor, he ought to be appointed.

IN RESPECT WHEREOF

Naesmith Todd and Co
18 Marshalsea Avenue
Aberdeen AB1 7TD
Agent for the applicant

8. BANK OF UPPER VOLTA (UK) PLC, PETITIONER

Liquidation — Company unable to pay its debts as defined by non-compliance with charge for payment — Petition by creditor

a. Petition

SHERIFFDOM OF GRAMPIAN HIGHLAND
AND ISLANDS AT FORT WILLIAM

PETITION

of

BANK OF UPPER VOLTA (UK) PLC, a company registered under the Companies Acts, number 873657 and having its registered office at Burkina Faso House, 84 Celle Street, London WC3 7TD

for

An order to wind up

BONNIE AND FRIED LIMITED, a Company incorporated under the Companies Acts, number SC2864 and having its registered office at 8 Inverlochy Way, Corpach, Fort William PH33 6RS.

The petitioner craves the court:

1) To appoint this petition to be intimated on the walls of court; and

2) To appoint this petition to be served on Bonnie and Fried Ltd, 8 Inverlochy Way, Corpach, Fort William PH33 6RS.

3) To appoint that this application be advertised once in in the *Invernessshire Intelligencer* newspaper.

4) To appoint that this application be advertised once in the *Edinburgh Gazette*; and

5) To ordain all parties interested to lodge answers, if so advised, within eight days after such intimation, advertisement and service; and thereafter, upon resuming consideration hereof, with or without answers and after such inquiry if any as may be thought necessary, to order that

Bonnie and Fried Ltd be wound up by the court under the provisions of the Insolvency Act 1986; to appoint Fawad Abbasi, Chartered Accountant, 11 Hanover Alley, Inverness IV3 5RS, or such other person as the court thinks fit to be interim liquidator of the company; and to find the expenses of this application to be expenses in the liquidation.

STATEMENT OF FACTS

1. The petitioner is as designed in the instance. It is a creditor of Bonnie and Fried Ltd, 8 Inverlochy Way, Corpach, Fort William PH33 6RS ('the company'). The company is as designed in the instance. It is a private limited company. The share capital of the company is £100, divided into 4 ordinary shares of £25 each, all of which are issued and are fully paid up. So far as is known to the petitioner: (1) the centre of main interests of the company is at 8 Inverlochy Way, Corpach, Fort William PH33 6RS; (2) the company has no establishments in a member state of the EU; and (3) there are no insolvency proceedings elsewhere in respect of the company. This court has jurisdiction.

2. The objects of the company are to carry on business cooking and selling on a takeaway or sitting in basis fried fish, chicken, pies, chipped potatoes, pizzas, kebabs and similar foods. The assets of the company are worth around £41,000.

3. The company is unable to pay its debts for the purposes of Section 123 (1)(c) of the Insolvency Act 1986. On 16 March 2023, a charge for payment proceeding upon a decree in favour of the petitioners for payment of the sum of £13,420, with interest and expenses, was duly served on the company. Extract decree and execution of charge are produced. The days of charge have expired without payment. In these circumstances, the petitioner seeks an order that the company be wound up by the court under the Act.

Fawad Abbasi, Chartered Accountant, 11 Hanover Alley, Inverness IV3 5RS is a suitable person for the office of interim liquidator. He is qualified to act as an insolvency practitioner in relation to the company.

PLEA IN LAW

The company being unable to pay its debts, should be wound up as craved.

IN RESPECT WHEREOF

Solicitor
Morison Burns and Co
17 Lally Street
Ballachulish
Agent for the petition

b. Note for leave to commence proceedings against company: Summary Application

SHERIFFDOM OF GRAMPIAN HIGHLAND
AND ISLANDS AT FORT WILLIAM

FTW- SQ-47-22

NOTE

By

WAYLAND SMITH residing at 77 Uffington Crescent, 21 Edinburgh EH12 6RA, continuing attorney of Norman Smith, residing at Grantchester Meadows Care Home, 67 Barrett Way, Cambridge CA93 7DK in terms of the power of attorney granted on 12 January and registered by the Office of the Public Guardian (Scotland) on 23 November 2019.

NOTER

In the liquidation of

BONNIE AND FRIED LIMITED, [designation] a Company incorporated under the Companies Acts, number SC2864 and having its registered office at at 8 Inverlochy Way, Corpach, Fort William PH33 6RS.

for

Leave to commence proceedings

The noter craves the court:

To appoint this note to be served on Fawad Abbasi, Chartered Accountant, 11 Hanover Alley, Inverness IV3 5RS, liquidator of Bonnie and Fried

Limited (in liquidation) and to ordain him to lodge answers, if so advised, within 21 days after service; and thereafter, upon resuming consideration hereof, with or without answers and after such inquiry if any as may be thought necessary, to grant leave to the noter to commence proceedings in the Sheriff Court against Bonnie and Fried Limited (in liquidation) and the liquidator for reparation for loss, injury and damage sustained by the noter as a result of an accident which occurred on or about 28 November 2021.

STATEMENT OF FACTS

1. The noter is as designed in the instance. He is continuing attorney for his father, Norman Smith ('Mr Smith'). Mr Smith is capax. He elected to bring the continuing attorney into effect.

2. On or about 28 November 2021 Mr Smith was returning from a holiday on Skye to Edinburgh, where he resided at that time. He stopped for lunch at the company's restaurant at 8 Inverlochy Way, Corpach, Fort William PH33 6RS.

3. Whilst going to the toilet in the premises Mr Smith slipped on cooking oil or a similar fluid present on the floor. He lost his footing, fell to the ground and fractured his left ulna. He also suffered facial bruising and a groin injury.

4. The fall occurred as a result of the fault and negligence of the company. It is liable to make reparation to Mr Smith for loss, injury and damage sustained by him as a result of the accident. The company had public liability insurance at the material time.

5. In these circumstances, the noter seeks leave of the court to commence proceedings in the sheriff court against the company and the liquidator for reparation for loss, injury and damage sustained by the noter as a result of the incident.

PLEA IN LAW

It being appropriate that the noter be given leave to commence proceedings aforesaid in terms of Section 130(2) of the Insolvency Act 1986, decree should be granted as craved.

IN RESPECT WHEREOF

Enrolled solicitor
19 Whitelaw Place, Glasgow
Solicitor for the noter

9. ADVOCATE GENERAL v FORMBY

Child Support Act 1991 – Failure to pay child support – Answers to Summary Application seeking civil imprisonment or disqualification from holding driving licence

SHERIFFDOM OF GLASGOW AND STRATHKELVIN AT GLASGOW

GLW-B197-23

ANSWERS
to

SUMMARY APPLICATION UNDER RULE 5A of the CHILD SUPPORT RULES 1993 as amended

in the cause

THE RIGHT HONOURABLE LORD STEWART OF DIRLETON KC THE ADVOCATE GENERAL FOR SCOTLAND, the Office of the Solicitor General for Scotland, Queen Elizabeth House, Edinburgh EH8 8FT

as representing

THE SECRETARY OF STATE FOR WORK AND PENSIONS, CHILD MAINTENANCE GROUP

APPLICANT

against

PRESTON FORMBY, residing at 11 Cheesemakers' Gait, Yoker, Glasgow G14 SA

RESPONDENT

ANSWERS

1. Admitted that on 14 October 2022 the applicant obtained a liability order under Section 33(2) of the Child Support Act 1991.

2. Admitted that on 1 November 2022 the applicant wrote to the respondent to advise that if he did not pay the amount referred to in the liability order further action would follow, namely an application to the court for the orders sought in this action. Sections 40B(2) and (12) preclude the court from granting orders in terms of both craves one and two. The applicant also advised that an order might be sought depriving the respondent of his passport. This would have the effect of depriving the child of a holiday. The respondent has a brother in Fuerteventura, Spain. The respondent and the child have been invited to visit. The respondent wishes to accept, and to take the child, but he cannot travel there without a passport.

3. The respondent cannot make payment of the sum referred to in the liability order because he lacks the financial means to do so. Reference is made to the Statement of the Defender's Financial Position annexed to the forms of citation Form 5A which the respondent completed and lodged. Denied that he has wilfully refused to pay. Denied that there has been culpable neglect by him.

4. The respondent is self-employed as a window cleaner. He developed a fear of heights after hearing of a colleague of his who fell from his ladder and struck a greenhouse, sustaining serious injury. Since then the respondent's fear has evolved into a phobia. His condition, acrophobia, is a medically recognised mental condition. The respondent has had to restrict his work to bungalows. This has seriously affected his income. During Covid lockdowns he incurred significant debt. He is unable to obtain a loan from a conventional lender. He borrowed money from individuals who threatened him with violence unless he repaid with considerable interest. He prioritised repayment of these debts due to fear of assault. The respondent has very poor literacy skills. He struggled to understand theapplicant's correspondence and procedures for appeal and review. The respondent acknowledges that he ought to have sought advice at an early stage. He did so only following the service of this summary application.

5. An order as first craved, to deprive the respondent of his driving licence, should not be granted. This would merely hamper him from working and therefore from earning, to the detriment of the parent with care and the child. The respondent has never been disqualified from driving before. He was fined £100 and his licence was endorsed with three penalty points in relation to a speeding offence committed on 17 June 2020.

6. An order as second craved, committing the respondent to imprisonment should not be granted. With the exception of the speeding offence already referred to the respondent has no criminal record. He

requires to hold a window cleaner's licence in terms of Section 43 of the Civic Government (Scotland) Act 1982. His application to Glasgow City Council required that he disclose convictions. An order for civil imprisonment being analogous to a custodial sentence the respondent would feel compelled to disclose it to the licensing authority. This in turn could jeopardize his licence and therefore his livelihood.

7. The orders sought are sanctions disproportionate to the gravity of the respondent's failure to make payment. The respondent has supported the child to the best of his ability despite challenging financial circumstances.

8. The respondent expects to be able to earn more soon due to his recently been granted a contract to clean windows at the Mansa Musa Industrial Estate, Tradeston, Glasgow.

PLEAS IN LAW FOR THE RESPONDENT

1) There having been no wilful refusal by the respondent to make payment in respect of the liability order granted in favour of the applicant and no culpable neglect by him a warrant for committal in terms of Section 40A(1) (a) the Child Support Act 1991 as amended should be refused.

2) In the event of the court's determining that there has been wilful refusal or culpable neglect, any period of imprisonment should be fixed and a postponement granted in terms of Section 40A(1) (b) of the Child Support Act 1991 as amended.

3) There having been no wilful refusal by the respondent to make payment in respect of the liability order granted in favour of the applicant and no culpable neglect by him disqualification in terms of Section 40B(1) (a) the Child Support Act 1991 as amended should be refused.

4) In the event of the court's determining that there has been wilful refusal or culpable neglect, any period of disqualification should be fixed and a postponement granted in terms of Section 40B(1) (b) of the Child Support Act 1991 as amended.

IN RESPECT WHEREOF

Barry Addie & Co

14 Whimbrel Circus

Glasgow G3

Agent for the Respondent

10. LIONEL BULL SHEDS AND GARAGES LTD v SHILLINGHAM

Minute for recall of sequestration – Bankruptcy (Scotland) Act 2016 section 30

SHERIFFDOM OF GRAMPIAN HIGHLAND AND ISLANDS AT TAIN

TAI-SQ1-22
MINUTE FOR RECALL OF SEQUESTRATION

Under Sections 29 and 30, Bankruptcy (Scotland) Act 2016

in the cause

LIONEL BULL SHEDS AND GARAGES LIMITED, a limited company incorporated under the Companies Acts, company number 8076254 and having its registered office at 13 Godiva Street, Coventry CV1 6DA

PETITIONER

against

PETRA SHILLINGHAM, residing at 'Fitzroy', Dunrobin Road, Golspie Sutherland KW10 8DS

DEBTOR AND RESPONDENT

ANSWERS

1. The parties' designations are admitted. Admitted that this court has jurisdiction.

2. Denied that the petitioner is or ever has been a qualified creditor of the respondent as defined by Section 7 of the Bankruptcy (Scotland) Act 2016.

3. Denied that the respondent is or ever has been apparently insolvent as defined by Section 16 of the Act. Believed to be true that sheriff officers instructed by the petitioner attended the respondent's address on 17 May 2022 with a demand in terms of Section 16(1(i) of the Act and a debt advice and information package as required by Regulation 11 of the 2016 Regulations. The respondent did not make payment or dispute the purported debt for the purposes of Section 16(3) only because she never received the demand. Neither did she receive the debt advice and information package. On the said date she was staying in St Helier, Jersey on business.

4. Believed to be true that sheriff officers instructed by the petitioner attended the respondent's address on 29 August 2022 in order to serve the petition.in terms of Section 16(1(i) of the Act. The petitioner did not receive the petition. On the said date she was staying in Kent, again on business.

5. The statutory demand and service copy petition were handed to the respondent's husband. He is Rex Barker. He and the respondent separated in August 2020 but they continued to live at the address in the instance until December 2022. During that time relations between him and the respondent were challenging. In December 2022 Mr Barker moved out. He has admitted having taken delivery of documents intended for the respondent including those which form the basis of these proceedings. The respondent has never had valid service of them. The petitioner has no valid basis on which to have brought this petition.

6. Not known and not admitted that Rupert Beresford satisfies the condition specified in Section 51(1)(b) of the 2016 Act. No trustee ought to have been appointed.

7. In any event, the respondent is not and never has been indebted to the petitioner. The purported debt referred to in the statutory demand relates to a contract between the petitioner and a limited company of which the respondent is director. The company is Golspie Biofuels Ltd. There has never been any contract between the parties.

8. The petition is unfounded and ought never to have been presented. The respondent seeks recall by the court as opposed to recall by the Accountant in Bankruptcy. The respondent seeks recall of the warrant granted on and the order for sequestration granted on and the appointment of Rupert Beresford.

PLEAS IN LAW FOR THE RESPONDENT

1. The petitioner never having been a qualified creditor of the respondent as defined by Section 7 of the Bankruptcy (Scotland) Act 2016 has no title to raise these proceedings.

2. The defender never having been apparently insolvent as defined by Section 16 of the Act is not liable to sequestration.

3. The petitioner never having been a qualified creditor, the respondent never having been apparently insolvent and the respondent never having

been indebted to the petitioner the warrant of should be recalled, the sequestration granted on should be recalled in terms of Section 30 of the Insolvency (Scotland) Act 2016, the appointment of Rupert Beresford, Chartered Accountant ought to be recalled and the petition should be dismissed.

IN RESPECT WHEREOF

Pagan Hill and Co
63 Prebble Street
Dornoch
IV25 8RA
Agent for the Minuter and Respondent

11. BABYLON SECRETARIAL SERVICES LTD v THE HARPISCHORD ASSOCIATION

Motion for expenses taxed on agent- client scale

SHERIFFDOM OF NORTH STRATHCLYDE AT PAISLEY

PAI-SQ1-22
MOTION FOR THE RESPONDENT

in the cause

BABYLON SECRETARIAL SERVICES LIMITED, a limited company incorporated under the Companies Acts, company number SC5487 and having its registered office at 27 Almond Grove, Dunbar EH42 7TR

PETITIONER

against

THE HARPISCHORD ASSOCIATION, a trade union in terms of Section 10(1)(b) of the Trade Union and Labour Relations (Consolidation) Act 1992 and having its registered office at residing at 67 McArthur Park, Paisley PA1 6EW

RESPONDENT

RAMOS for the respondent moves the court:

To find the petitioner liable in expenses taxed on an agent-client basis in respect that the whole conduct of the proceedings was an abuse of process and manifestly defective insofar; as

The petition is unfounded and proceeded on a statutory demand which ought never to have been issued as the petitioner must well have known. The demand referred to the sum of £17,500 as allegedly being due. This sum was the price of a consignment of 20,000 sheets of 'Pavilion' music manuscript paper. The respondent had already paid £11,500 and disputed £6,000 on the basis that only 13,000 sheets were delivered. This was made clear in a series of emails, which were answered. The respondent's warehouse supervisor qualified the delivery note signed by him to reflect the fact that there was partial delivery. The emails and counterfoil delivery note were produced. The respondent believes that the statutory demand was a device, improperly used, as a means to compel the respondent to make payment to avoid the publicity of insolvency proceedings. This constitutes an abuse of process and is akin to wrongful diligence.

IN RESPECT WHEREOF

Wendy Ramos
Fort Matilda Legal
16 Sugar Street
Greenock
PA16 8RD
Agent for the respondent

12. SHEILA GIGGS, PETITIONER

Restoration of company name to register of companies

a. Petition

SHERIFFDOM OF SOUTH STRATHCLYDE
DUMFRIES AND GALLOWAY AT HAMILTON

PETITION under Section 1029
Companies Act 2006

of

SHEILA GIGGS, residing at 92 Harvey Street, Blantyre G72 TRD

PETITIONER

for

An order restoring HAIRMYRES HAIR SALON LIMITED SC7461 Renee Walk, Hamilton ML4 8TD, to the Register of Companies

The petitioner craves the court:

To appoint this petition to be intimated on the walls of court and to be served on the Lord Advocate and the Registrar of Companies and to be advertised in the *Edinburgh Gazette* and the *Hamilton Piper* newspapers; to ordain any parties interested to lodge answers hereto, if so advised, within 21 days after intimation, service and advertisement; thereafter, upon resuming consideration hereof, with or without answers and after such inquiry if any as may be thought necessary, to order that the name of Hairmyres Hair Salon Limited SC7461 be restored to the register of companies and to direct the registrar of companies to advertise such order in the *Edinburgh Gazette*; and to authorise the expenses of this application and of the procedure following thereon including the expenses to be paid to the registrar to be paid out of the first and readiest funds of the company.

STATEMENT OF FACTS

1. The petitioner is a creditor and former employee of Hairmyres Hair Salon, a limited company registered under the Companies Acts, number SC3867, with its registered office at Renee Walk, Hamilton ML4 8TD ('the company'). The share capital of the company is £100, comprising 100 ordinary shares of £1 each, all of which are issued and are fully paid up.

2. The company's seat is at the address in the instance. This is within the Sheriffdom of South Strathclyde Dumfries and Galloway. This court has jurisdiction in terms of Section 20 of and Rule 5(1)(b) of Schedule 8 to the Civil Jurisdiction and Judgments Act 1982.

3. On 6 October and 1 November 2022 the registrar of companies sent communications to the company in terms of Section 1000 of the Companies Act 2006. Having received no response a notice was sent. Neither of the communications was met with a response. Neither was the notice. The company was struck off in terms of Section 1000(4) of the Act. This occurred on 20 January 2023.

4. At the date of striking off the company was carrying on business, providing hair care and styling services, manicures, pedicures and beauty treatments. It employed three full time hair stylists and manicurists and engaged the services of a holistic therapist. Copy accounts and promotional material are produced herewith.

5. The petitioner was employed as a hairdresser by the company until 16 September 2022. She is due £11,560 in respect of unpaid wages, bonus payments and re-imbursement of expenses.

6. The petitioner seeks an order that the name of the company be restored to the register of companies in terms of Section 1029 of the Companies Act 2006.

PLEA IN LAW

Hairmyres Hair Salon Limited having been carrying on business at the time of the striking off, an order should be granted as craved that its name be restored to the register of companies under Section 1029 of the Companies Acts should be granted as craved.

IN RESPECT WHEREOF

Farquhar Sanquhar and Co
71 Bismarck Street
Glasgow G2 6RD
Agent for the petitioner

13. JOHN v SAELIM

Reduction of testamentary writing

SHERIFFDOM OF NORTH STRATHCLYDE AT GREENOCK

INITIAL WRIT

in the cause

ALEXANDER JOHN residing at 14 Haakon Street, Largs KA30 6TY

PURSUER

against

KANYA SAELIM, residing at 7 Belmont Road, Port Glasgow G48 9RS

FIRST NAMED DEFENDER

and

GEORGE JOHN, residing at 16 Sexton Way, Carlisle CA5 8SB

SECOND NAMED DEFENDER

The pursuer craves the court:

1) For production and reduction of the pretended Trust Disposition and Settlement granted by the late Ethelred John on 11 May 2019.

2) To interdict the first named defender or anyone acting on her behalf from registering in the Books of Council and Session the pretended Trust Disposition and Settlement granted by the late Ethelred John on 11 May 2019; and to grant interim interdict.

3) To interdict the first named defender or anyone acting on her behalf from seeking confirmation as executor to the estate of the late Ethelred John residing formerly at 7 Belmont Road, Port Glasgow G48 9RS and who died on 27 May 2022; and to grant interim interdict.

4) To interdict the first named defender or anyone acting upon her behalf from selling, gifting, consuming, transferring ownership or otherwise disposing of any item within the collection of whisky bottles,

artifacts and accessories forming part the estate of the late Ethelred John who died on 27 May 2022; and to grant interim interdict.

5) To interdict the first named defender or anyone acting upon her behalf from removing from the Sheriffdom of North Strathclyde any item within the collection of whisky bottles, artifacts and accessories forming part of the estate of the late Ethelred John who died on 27 May 2022; and to grant interim interdict.

6) To find the first named defender liable in expenses as taxed.

7) To find the second named defender liable in expenses as taxed only in the event of his defending these proceedings.

CONDESCENDENCE

1) The parties are as designed in the instance. The pursuer is the only son of the late Ethelred John who was born on 12 May 1934 and died on 1 May 2022 (hereinafter 'the deceased). The first named defender is a former cohabitant of the deceased. The second named defender is the brother of the deceased. The second named defender is called for his interest.

2) The first named defenders domiciled in Scotland and in the Sheriffdom of North Strathclyde. Greenock sheriff court has jurisdiction in terms of Section 20 of and Rule 1(g) of Schedule 8 to the Civil Jurisdiction and Judgments Act 1982. The pursuer is not aware of any other proceedings pending before any court which are in respect of the subject matter of this writ. There is no agreement to prorogate the jurisdiction of any other court.

3) The deceased collected rare and valuable bottles of whisky. He did so over a period of over 35 years. In 2005 he had his collection valued for insurance purposes. The valuation was undertaken by Nisbett and Co, auctioneers and valuers. They estimated that the collection was worth £27,000. They have advised that at the value is currently £32,000.

4) Believed and averred that the collection is the most valuable asset in the estate of the deceased. The deceased and the first named defender lived in rented accommodation. The deceased did not have substantial savings. On many occasions he advised the pursuer that he wished him to have the collection and that he hoped that the pursuer would bequeath it to his own son.

5) Following the death of the deceased, on 27 May 2022, the first named defender advised the pursuer that she was in possession of a Trust Disposition and Settlement (hereinafter 'the pretended will'). Also, she advised that with the said document was a deed headed 'Codicil to my Will' dated 22 January 2020. The deed bears to be a codicil to the pretended will.

6) The pretended will bears to have been signed by the deceased. His signature bears to have been witnessed by a neighbour, Eric McLean.

7) The deceased had been employed as an accounts manager at the Rhodesian Bank. He retired in 2016 at the age of 76. From around 2019 he began to suffer from memory loss and a lack of awareness of danger when, for example crossing roads. He relied on signs and cards to tell him when to eat and go to bed. As well as being his cohabitant the first named defender acted as his carer. In addition, Inverclyde Council provided home help and other support. The deceased was diagnosed as having early stages of dementia. He consulted solicitors with a view to granting a power of attorney. Believed and averred that they refrained from taking instructions from him due to their concerns about his capacity.

8) At the date on which the pretended will bears to have been signed the deceased lacked the capacity to understand the nature of a will. He was unable to make decisions affecting his own welfare or finances. The document falls to be reduced. Decree should be granted as first craved.

9) The first named defender has stated that she regards the pretended will as valid. The position of the second named defender is unknown. Until the validity and status of the document is determined by this court it ought not to be registered in the Books of Council and Session and nor should it be included as a testamentary writing in any application by the defender for confirmation. Confirmation cannot properly be applied for until the validity and status of the document is determined by this court. Interdict should be granted as second and third craved.

10) The pursuer is entitled as sole beneficiary to the deceased's collection of whisky bottles, artifacts and accessories. He has a reasonable apprehension that the first named defender or someone acting on her behalf may dispose of part or all of the collection or may remove same from the jurisdiction of this court. The first named defender's family is based in Leicester. She has expressed to the pursuer a wish to return there. Decree should be granted as fourth and fifth craved.

11) Having regard to the balance of convenience interim interdict should be granted as craved. The pursuer is the only beneficiary. Neither defender is prejudiced by the first named defender's refraining from registering the pretended will or from obtaining confirmation. Believed and averred that confirmation is unnecessary in respect of the winding up of the deceased's estate given that there is no heritable property and there are no substantial assets in the control of any party other than the first named defender. Further, the obtaining of confirmation would be detrimental insofar as reduction thereof would necessitate proceedings in the Court of Session, causing further delay and expense.

PLEA IN LAW

1. The deceased having lacked the capacity to execute the pretended will dated 11 May 2019 it ought to be reduced as first craved.

2. The first named defender having evinced an intention to intromit with the estate on the basis that the pretended will is valid the pursuer is

under the necessity of seeking interdict as second, third, fourth and fifth craved and decree should be granted therefor.

3. Having regard to the balance of convenience interim interdict should be granted as craved.

IN RESPECT WHEREOF

Elder and Barnes
Solicitors
7 Gourock Road
Greenock

14. ELGAR v BALFOUR

Lawburrows

SHERIFFDOM OF NORTH STRATHCLYDE AT OBAN

SUMMARY APPLICATION

Lawburrows Acts 1429 and 1581
Civil Imprisonment (Scotland) Act 1882

in the cause

CORNELIUS ELGAR residing at Van Diemens House, Pennyfuir, PA34 7TD

PURSUER

against

MORRIS BALFOUR residing at 14 Dunstaffnage Road, Connel PA37 9BH

DEFENDER

The pursuer craves the court:

1) To ordain the defender to find sufficient caution of law burrows that the pursuer shall be harmless and skaithless and free from injury and damage in his body, land, possessions and goods and in no way molested or troubled therein by the defender or by others sent by him otherwise by order or law and justice and that under a penalty of TWO THOUSAND POUNDS (£2000) STERLING or such other sum as to the court shall seem fit and in the event of his failing to find caution as aforesaid within such period as the court shall appoint to adjudge the defender to be imprisoned for such period, not exceeding six months, as the court shall appoint, or until he finds such caution as may be ordered.

2) To grant warrant to officers of court accordingly.

3) To grant to the parties warrant to cite witnesses.

4) To find the defender liable in expenses as taxed.

CONDESCENDENCE

1) The parties are as designed in the instance. The pursuer is a retired teacher. The defender is a former pupil of the pursuer. He is a plumber and owns a plumbing business named MB Argyll.

2) This action is in relation to a delict or quasi-delict where harm occurred and where further harm may occur at the pursuer's address in the instance or in Oban or in the vicinity thereof and in the Sheriffdom of North Strathclyde. Oban sheriff court has jurisdiction in terms of Section 20 of and Rule 2(c) of Schedule 8 to the Civil Jurisdiction and Judgments Act 1982. The pursuer is not aware of any other proceedings pending before any court which are in respect of the subject matter of this writ. There is no agreement to prorogate the jurisdiction of any other court.

3) Until 2019 the pursuer taught music at McCaig Academy, Oban. The defender was a pupil there until he left school in around 2020. The defender was disruptive and unruly in the pursuer's class. He swore at the pursuer and threatened to 'do' him. Since he left school the defender has periodically been undertaking plumbing work at a house in Pennyfuir, around 200 metres from the pursuer's home. On or about 18 May 2022 a skip was left blocking the pursuer's driveway. On around 15 January 2022 a powerful construction site light was aimed at the windows on the pursuer's home. Loud music was played on the site, to the annoyance of the pursuer. On or about 2 March 2022 in the Safeway Megamarket, Oban, the defender approached the pursuer and advised that he would 'get even' and that the pursuer should not leave his car parked in his driveway. The pursuer interpreted this as a threat to damage his car.

4) The pursuer lives alone. He was born in 1946 and suffers from hypertension and depression. He takes medication therefor. The pursuer has been and continues to be subjected to nuisance, threats and annoyance by the defender and tradesmen employed by him.

5) The pursuer seeks the protection of a decree as craved. The caution sought is reasonable having regard to the likely means of the defender. The pursuer is content if the court orders that caution be satisfied by the consignation by the defender with the sheriff clerk of the sum of Two Thousand pounds.

PLEA IN LAW

The defender having molested the pursuer and having threatened to injure him and his property, as condescended upon, should be ordered to find caution as craved.

IN RESPECT WHEREOF

Boag Rollo and Co
Solicitors
14 Tobermory View
Oban
G48 5RD

15. TORVILLE v MESTON

Protection from Harassment Act 1997 – Damages – Interdict – Non-harassment order

SHERIFFDOM OF LOTHIAN AND BORDERS AT EDINBURGH

EDI-A398-23
INITIAL WRIT

in the cause

ORSON TORVILLE, residing at 16 Inchcolm View, Leith EH6 8DT

PURSUER

Against

LESTER MESTON, residing at 14 Inchcolm View, Leith EH6 8DT

RESPONDENT

The pursuer craves the court:

1) To grant decree against the defender for payment to the pursuer of the sum of TWO THOUSAND POUNDS (£2,000) STERLING with interest at eight *per centum per annum* from the date of citation; and

2) To interdict the defender from molesting the pursuer by harassing him, threatening him, abusing him verbally, or putting him into a state of fear, alarm or distress, and to grant interim interdict, in terms of Section 8(5)(b)(i) of the Protection from Harassment Act 1997; and

3) To attach a power of arrest thereto in terms of Sections 1(2) and (3) of the Protection from Abuse (Scotland) Act 2001 for a period of three years or such other period as to the court shall seem appropriate; and

4) To grant a non-harassment order in terms of Section 8(5)(b)(ii) of the Protection from Harassment Act 1997, for an indefinite or such other period as to the court shall seem appropriate; and

5) To find the defender liable in expenses as taxed.

CONDESCENDENCE

1) The parties are as designed in the instance. They are immediate neighbours.

2) The cause is in respect of harmful events which, unless prevented by the orders sought, are likely to occur at the pursuer's address in the instance and within the Sheriffdom of Lothian and Borders. This court has jurisdiction in terms of Section 20 and Rule 2(c) of Schedule 8 to the Civil Jurisdiction and Judgments Act 1982. There are no proceedings pending before any court which are in respect of the subject matter of this initial writ.

3) There exists between the parties' properties a boundary the exact location of which is disputed. The pursuer raised an action (number EDI-83-22) in this court and against the defender for declarator and for removal of an encroaching fence. The pursuer was successful. Final decree was granted on 11 February 2023.

4) During the week after the decree was issued the defender advised the pursuer that he would make his life 'a living hell'. He was laughing in a menacing manner. Since then he has repeatedly and relentlessly harassed the defender.

5) On around 20 February, 5, 16 and 22 March and on 11 and 13 April 2023 the pursuer received unsolicited deliveries of takeaway meals, causing him nuisance. He was also visited by timeshare and funeral plan salesmen who claimed that they had been invited to attend. Believed and averred that the defender was responsible. The pursuer has lived at his current address since 2015. Such deliveries and visits had never occurred before 11 February 2023.

6) The pursuer has had to curtail his favourite hobby of gardening due to the defender's conduct. On around 4 March the defender entered his garden to clear flower beds. The defender immediately entered his own garden, stood at the boundary fence and pointed his smartphone at the pursuer, apparently recording him.

7) On Friday 17 March and on several subsequent Fridays the pursuer observed the defender searching and rummaging in the pursuer's wheeled bins, removing litter and strewing it in the pursuer's driveway and front garden. This has attracted seagulls, to the pursuer's annoyance.

8) The pursuer has been caused stress, anxiety and depression as a result of the defender's harassment. The pursuer attended his GP Dr Noah Fortinbras at the King Wenceslas Hospital, Portobello and has been prescribed Paroxetine and referred for counselling. He suffers mood swings, lack of concentration and sleep disturbance. A report from Dr Fortinbras is produced herewith.

9) The pursuer has contacted the Leith police. They opined that it was 'a civil matter' and that the pursuer should obtain a power of arrest. They have refused to assist meantime. The orders sought are necessary.

PLEAS IN LAW

1) The defender having harassed the pursuer and thereby caused him the loss and damage as condescended upon is liable to make reparation

therefor in terms of Section 8(5)(a) of the Protection from Harassment Act 1997.

2) The sum sued for being a reasonable estimate of the pursuer's loss and damage decree should be granted as first craved.

3) The defender having harassed the pursuer as condescended upon and having shown an intention to persist therein interdict should be granted as second craved in terms of Section 8(5)(b)(i) of the Protection from Harassment Act 1997.

4) Having regard to the balance of convenience, interim interdict should be granted as craved.

5) The conduct of the pursuer constituting abuse in terms of Section 7 of the Protection from Abuse (Scotland) Act 2001 and the interdict craved being for the purpose of protection against abuse, a power of arrest should be attached thereto in terms of Section 1 of the said Act for three years or such other period as to the court shall seem appropriate, and;

6) The defender having harassed the pursuer as condescended upon and it being appropriate to grant a non-harassment order to protect the defender from further such harassment, decree should be granted as third craved in terms of Section 8(5)(b)(ii) of the Protection from Harassment Act 1997

IN RESPECT WHEREOF

Pericles and Co
1815 Plantagenet Street
Edinburgh EH7 5SQ
Agent for the pursuer

16. AHMAD JAFFAR v BEEF OF BAGHDAD LIMITED

Motion for defender – dismissal of action due to delay OCR 15.7.

SHERIFFDOM OF CENTRAL TAYSIDE AND FIFE AT FALKIRK

A382-12
MOTION FOR THE DEFENDER

In the cause

AHMAD JAFFAR, residing at 18 Hormuz Street, Grangemouth FK3 8TS

PURSUER

BEEF OF BAGHDAD LIMITED, a company incorporated under the Companies Acts and having its registered office at 18 Mesopotamia Avenue, Coventry CV1 7TF

DEFENDER

ELPHINSTONE for the defender moves the court:

1) To recall the sist granted on 25 April 2012; and
2) To re-enrol the cause for further procedure; and
3) To dismiss the cause in terms of OCR 15.7. in respect that:
   a) There has been inordinate and inexcusable delay by the pursuer or the pursuer's agents in proceeding with the cause. The cause was raised on 7 April 2011. It was sisted on 10 May 2011 to enable him to apply for legal aid. The sist was recalled on the defender's opposed motion on 8 February 2012. It was sisted again on 25 April 2012 for possible settlement. No proposals were made by or on behalf of the pursuer. It is believed that in around December 2012 the pursuer travelled to stay with his family in Basra, Iraq, and that the pursuer's agents were unable to contact him to obtain his instructions for around 20 months. There were sporadic settlement discussions from August 2014 until summer 2015 when the pursuer's agents were again unable to contact the pursuer. They withdrew from acting in April 2016 when new

agents immediately began to act. No peremptory diet took place. The new agents were unable to recover the file from the previous agents. They were unable to obtain instructions and in June 2017 advised the defender's agents to contact the pursuer directly. The defender's agents attempted to do so. Believed that the pursuer returned to Iraq in early 2018. The case was dormant until the defender's agents were contacted by the pursuer in March 2020. He advised that due to Covid-19 lockdown he could not return to the UK. He returned in summer 2022. Settlement could not be agreed. Discussions ceased in January 2023.

b) The delay has caused unfairness that cannot now be addressed. The defender's principal witness, Ifzal Manzoor died unexpectedly on 18 December 2020. No affidavit had been taken from him. He would have spoken to the pursuer's numerous breaches of the parties' franchise agreement. In addition, due to the passage of time other witnesses have stated that their recollection of the parties' initial discussions, in summer 2009, has deteriorated to a point where their reliability is seriously compromised. The defender would be seriously and unfairly prejudiced if the cause is not dismissed. The pursuer's conduct of the case demonstrates a lack of interest therein.

4) To find the pursuer liable to the defender in expenses as taxed.

IN RESPECT WHEREOF

Euphrates Law
17 Canal Street
Glasgow G3 7TD
Agent for the defender

Index